THE
WASHINGTON
HYPOTHESIS

THE
WASHINGTON HYPOTHESIS

A MODERN-DAY INVESTIGATOR EXPLORES
THE POSSIBLE CONNECTION BETWEEN
THE AMERICAN COVENANT, LATTER-DAY
TEMPLES, AND GEORGE WASHINGTON

TIMOTHY BALLARD

DESERET
BOOK

Salt Lake City, Utah

To my great-grandfather Nephi Anderson,
and to all those who have gone before us,
whose angelic presences go before us still

First printing in hardbound 2016
First printing in paperbound 2018

Library of Congress Cataloging-in-Publication Data

Names: Ballard, Timothy, author.
Title: The Washington hypothesis : a modern investigator explores the possible connection between the American covenant, latter-day temples, and George Washington / Timothy Ballard.
Description: Salt Lake City, Utah : Deseret Book, [2016] | ?2016 | Includes bibliographical references and index.
Identifiers: LCCN 2016003792 (print) | LCCN 2016006092 (ebook) | ISBN 9781629721781 (hardbound : alk. paper) | ISBN 9781629724522 (paperbound) | ISBN 9781629734491 (ebook)
Subjects: LCSH: Washington, George, 1732–1799. | United States—History—Religious aspects—The Church of Jesus Christ of Latter-day Saints. | United States—History—Religious aspects—Mormon Church. | Mormon temples.
Classification: LCC E312.17 .B17 2016 (print) | LCC E312.17 (ebook) | DDC 973.4/1092—dc23
LC record available at http://lccn.loc.gov/2016003792

Printed in the United States of America
Edwards Brothers Malloy, Ann Arbor, MI

10   9   8   7   6   5   4   3   2   1

Contents

Publisher's Note

A hypothesis is not a statement of fact, though it often reads like one. It is, rather, a jumping-off point, a tentative assumption made that provides a framework for examining and organizing facts. Most scientific or historical queries begin with a hypothesis, which is calculated based on the facts already known and then either supported or rejected by additional research.

The Washington Hypothesis is a bold conjecture based on extensive historical research. The miraculous events of the Revolution and the remarkable strength of character embodied in George Washington are demonstrable facts. In this gripping book, Timothy Ballard has shared many of those facts and drawn some fascinating conclusions from them. Whether or not you come to the same conclusions—whether you support his "hypothesis" or not—we believe you will gain a new appreciation for the events that shaped America as a nation and for the greatness of its first president, George Washington.

PROLOGUE

The Window

A few years ago I got a call one day from Todd, my best friend from childhood. Some had predicted the end of our friendship when he started dating my little sister in high school. We proved them all wrong. He even married her after serving an LDS mission, and we stayed as close as ever. So when I saw his name on my caller ID that day, I thought little of it; he called a lot. But this conversation was different than any we had ever had before.

"I think I know what the window has been trying to tell us!" His usually calm and steady voice was more amped up and excited than I had ever heard it before.

I knew exactly what window he was talking about, and I was thrilled at the prospect that he had perhaps deciphered its rather cryptic meaning. Through the years, Todd and I had talked about the strange window, with its signs and symbols. The reason it had always been forefront in our minds was because we had each looked upon it hundreds of times. It stretched across the wall behind the pulpit in the LDS chapel we attended together as children and teenagers in La Cañada, California. I had since moved away from La Cañada, but Todd was still there, serving in the ward bishopric, still gazing at the window multiple times a week.

"George Washington!" he said. "All the things you have been telling me about George Washington. They are in the window!"

For years, I had been studying and discussing with Todd some interesting connections I had been proposing—connections that linked George Washington with the Book of Mormon and LDS temples in a fascinating way. Needless to say, Todd's declaration to me was more than intriguing.

As I listened to Todd, my mind shot back to a childhood memory that marked my first serious experience with the window. I was only eleven years old on the night that it happened. Somehow this memory was consistent with what Todd was saying. Looking back, I felt as if this window had set my eleven-year-old self on a journey. A journey that has lasted until the present day. A journey I will call the *Washington Hypothesis* quest.

It all started at a Boy Scout meeting. It began like any other. On that Tuesday night, my dad dropped me off at the La Cañada church building as usual. And, as usual, he returned an hour later to pick me up. When I looked up and saw that he had entered the building to retrieve me, my young heart was disappointed. I was hoping he would have arrived later than he did because I was involved in a very fun after-meeting game with my fellow Scouts.

To understand this game (which I had invented and organized for the first time that particular night), and to understand why it proved to be such a pivotal event in my life, you must understand a little bit about the La Cañada chapel. At the time, I had not been to many other LDS chapels, so I had no idea what a unique place it was. It had been built in the days when local congregations were charged to get their buildings built with minimal financial assistance from Church headquarters. So local congregations naturally had the opportunity to build more or less what they wanted. This, at times, resulted in the creation of unique buildings—unique in their ability to push the limits of what today many would recognize as more uniform LDS architectural standards. In fact, the La Cañada building is so unusual that it has been named as a historic property by the LDS Church History Department.

The building was completed in 1952, just in time for my mother to be the first baby blessed there. My great-grandfather Nephi Anderson had donated the multiacre plot of land for the project. He was the stake patriarch. He was also the general contractor for the building project. These facts are precious to me. They seem to tie me to the building on a deeply emotional level. But it wasn't until the strange discovery I made that night while playing with my fellow Scouts that the building became truly significant to me and set me on a historical journey that has yet to end.

"Dad!" I yelled out with a tennis ball in my hand, while standing on the far side of the basketball court (or what the adults strangely called "the cultural hall") of the church building. "How much will you give me if I make this shot?"

That was the game I had invented. I admit, it seems too simple to be worthy of the title *invention*, until you learn what the shot was. And this is where the unique architectural taste of Nephi Anderson comes into play.

You see, the cultural hall in the La Cañada building boasts of great beams—very thick beams—that rise up and support the high-pitched roof. This was all part of the English Tudor structure that characterized the building. I had been challenging my fellow Scouts to stand near the half-court line, then throw their tennis balls high up against the wall that sat behind the basket. The idea was to make the tennis ball hit on the wall high above and behind the backboard and basket in such a way that it would cause the ball to bounce off and up and hit the tall beam hovering over the court. From there, so my theory went, if the ball hit what I was calling "the beam's sweet spot," it would then be sent earthbound, bank off the backboard, and shoot right through the iron hoop.

"That's an impossible shot, Timmy!" my dad said with a smile. "But I'll give you a hundred bucks if you can make it."

The thought that I had triumphed in getting my dad to gamble—inside the church, no less!—was trumped only by the thought that I had a chance to triumph in a way that would make any eleven-year-old's head spin. One hundred dollars! This amount, I need not remind you, is nothing short of a fortune to an eleven-year-old.

None of us had even come close so far. Dozens and dozens of attempts had resulted in nothing. We immediately gained bragging rights if we got our tennis ball to hit the backboard on its downward trajectory—that is, if we could even get the ball to hit the beam in the first place.

I stepped up to the line. Glancing back to my dad to make sure he was watching, I began to wind up.

I launched!

Seconds later the tennis ball flew rapidly through the center of the hoop, after having hit each preplanned point, first on the wall and then on the beam, with exact precision.

The room fell silent. But the silence did not remain.

I screamed with joy and shouted obnoxiously. I looked at the stunned expression on my dad's face as it broke into a smile, then a chuckle, then a full laugh. He hooted, cheered, and clapped his hands along with me and the other Scouts. He was proud.

But this was not the climax of the story. My achievement had increased the confidence level in my fellow Scouts that they too could make the shot. My dad even stepped up to try as well. Because of this, I was given the chance to stay at the church far later than usual, launching tennis balls up into the air. And one of those balls I launched landed in *no-man's-land.*

The cultural hall sits exactly perpendicular to the chapel. A large green partition/curtain separates the two large rooms. On Sundays, the cultural hall served as the overflow seating area, and the curtain was opened up. On Tuesday nights, it was closed to keep basketballs (or in this case tennis balls) from flying into the chapel.

Nobody had noticed—at least I had not noticed—that on that particular Tuesday night, the curtain was cracked open slightly, right in the middle, precisely where the backboard sat against the wall. We usually played with basketballs, so the crack would not have been a problem. But this night was different, and my rogue tennis ball, far from hitting the intended target, moved swiftly through the partition and landed somewhere in that very dark chapel.

"Don't leave that ball in there, Timmy."

Darn. My dad had seen my great miss. I had hoped he had not seen it because the last thing I wanted to do was go into that big, dark room. I didn't think anybody even knew where the light switch was, so I would be forced to go searching in the dark. After my heroic feat that night, I wasn't about to lose face by telling anyone I was too scared to go alone. So I walked through the corridor that led around to the foyer of the chapel. I looked at the double doors made of wood and glass. I entered.

As I walked into the blackness, my eleven-year-old mind began filling up with the scariest thoughts I could put into it. Every funeral I had attended in that chapel excited my memory, and I was suddenly filled with the conviction that the ghosts of the deceased I had mourned at those funerals were all sitting in the pews waiting to haunt me.

Just get to the middle pews and drop to the ground. I knew the tennis ball was somewhere in the middle. I would run down the aisle, flop on my stomach, find the ball on the ground, grab it, and get out of there. I dropped to my belly halfway down the aisle. My plan failed. No tennis ball. I was petrified to get back up. One of the ghosts might see me.

It was at that moment that I allowed myself to sense a light coming from the direction of the pulpit. I looked up and saw it. I had, of course, seen it there many times before, but I had always taken it for granted. I suppose I had never seen it against the backdrop of pitch black. Nor had I been in a situation before that required the calming light it provided. And so I soaked it in. I stood up peacefully as my eyes fully analyzed this curious creation that stretched across the wall behind the pulpit and choir loft.

It was a stained-glass window: the original one Nephi Anderson had installed. The one Todd would call me about some thirty years later. It was beautifully lit up by the bright lights shining through from the backside of the window. Apparently somebody had accidentally left those backlights on. I had never realized before how very curious the window was. Years later, after visiting dozens of other LDS chapels, I would understand that better.

The center of the window is filled with a full-length depiction of Christ standing at a large wooden door. With His right hand He is knocking. With His left hand He is holding a lantern.

But it was the series of images surrounding Christ that caught the attention of my eleven-year-old self. In fact, it still catches my attention, just as it catches the attention of many adult spectators who have sat in the congregation asking, *What does all that mean?*

Directly to the left of the Christ depiction is an image of a scroll with the words, *Stick of Judah.* Directly to the right of the

Stained-glass window in the La Cañada chapel.

Christ image is an identical scroll with the words, *Stick of Joseph.* Below the Judah scroll starts a series of smaller depictions that together form an inverted arch—my young boy's mind thought it looked like a smile—that spread out under the depiction of the Savior. The series of images in this arch seem to tell a story in sequential order.

There is a dove with a branch in its beak, a set of old-fashioned keys, two hands facing each other (one of a man and one of a woman) whose arms are draped with what appear to be white robes. The hands are forming a tight handclasp. And finally, there is a pyramid. The pyramid is emanating what appear to be rays of glory, and inside the pyramid is an opened human eye.

The whole thing seemed so strange to me. And not only because I was a small boy ignorant of anything to do with symbology. No, it was strange simply because *it was strange.* Through the years I would hear intelligent adults ask aloud why these images are presented in an LDS chapel. I have even heard adult critics balk at it. But no matter the questions or criticisms I heard, I always knew the window was special. It was special because my great-grandfather had something to do with it. It was special because it bridged the gap between him and me, a gap created by the fact that he had died before I was born. It was special because it calmed me on that Tuesday night. It was special because I knew it meant something. Something profound.

Perhaps my mind on that night was playing tricks on me. But it seemed that this imagery was echoing something uniquely American. In all fairness, I had recently returned with my fifth-grade class from a week-long field trip to Philadelphia to study the American Revolution up close and personal. Perhaps I had seen some of these symbols in the old American architecture of the area. Or perhaps it was the fact that the prominent colors on the stained glass were red, white, and blue. Or perhaps it was the lantern that Christ was holding in the window's central image. The lantern seemed to be wrapped in an American flag—the stars and stripes throwing off the light that Christ seemed to be offering to whoever stood behind the closed door.

As I listened to Todd interpret the images almost three decades later, it all made perfect sense. There *was* something truly American about the window. I had always known it—or at least felt it. Even as Todd spoke, my mind was making new connections between American history and the symbols in the window—connections I had not yet revealed to Todd. There was something about the window that tied the restored gospel to the United States in a profound way. Something that placed George Washington at the center of it all. Each piece of the window told a part of the story. Nephi Anderson was, after all, a lover of American history. My mother told me of the framed picture he had hung over his fireplace mantle at his La Cañada home. It depicted Betsy Ross sitting in her living room presenting the

Benjamin Franklin on the $100 bill.

first American flag to George Washington. Nephi had even found the same type of tile from Betsy Ross's home depicted in the image and used it to build the mantle over which the picture hung. Today, though Nephi has over four hundred direct descendants, somehow, through a series of events I cannot explain, I inherited that picture, which now hangs in my office.

That night in the chapel was fittingly memorialized a few days later when my dad presented me with a framed one-hundred-dollar bill.

"What!?" I exclaimed. "I can't even spend my reward?"

"No, Son, you can't. I want this to be a lesson to you about why you should never gamble."

I decided I would get nowhere reminding him that for me, at least on that night, gambling had actually paid off quite nicely. He was the one who had lost. *He* needed the lesson, *not* me. Wisely, I kept my mouth shut and decided that one hundred dollars, even stuck in a glass frame, was better than soap in my mouth. (Full disclosure: A few years later, I came across a color printer. You know what I had to do. I swiped the bill from the frame, copied it, cut out the copy, and returned the fake bill to the frame. And then I bought a hundred dollars' worth of junk.

My dad will be learning about this for the first time as he reads this book. I chuckle.)

But as it turns out, I did learn much from that framed bill, though not necessarily the lesson that was intended. I learned something that in many ways culminated in the conversation with Todd, though the learning took place during the many years leading up to that phone call. For years, even decades, that bill (the real one or the fake one) hung on my bedroom wall, then on my office wall, always reminding me of that Tuesday night. Always reminding me of that stained-glass window. I would often study that bill and focus intently on the face depicted thereon: Benjamin Franklin, with his Mona-Lisa–like expression, looking back at me. Challenging me. Taunting me. I was compelled to investigate the history of the American founding. I read every book I could find. I visited every historical site and every battlefield I could get to.

Figure out what the window means! I could almost hear Franklin demanding. *Figure out what it's trying to teach!*

I think I finally have. . . .

The Bulletproof Soldier

George Washington was a farmer. That was all he ever wanted to be. But he knew there was more to life. He felt called to serve his God and his fellow men. So he did.

In addition to rendering service as a vestryman and warden of his church, he was also active in local politics. As a gentleman of the state of Virginia, he served his country well, and not just from the comforts of his private office or from the cozy quarters inside the legislative house. He was willing to do *whatever* was asked of him.

For example, in 1770, at the request of the governor of Virginia, Washington led a small party into the Ohio wilderness in order to survey lands. (In his youth, Washington had made a name for himself as a professional land surveyor, which was one reason he was chosen for the job.) The lands he sought to survey had been promised by the British to the brave American soldiers who had fought fifteen years earlier for the Crown in the French and Indian War. Frustrated by the fact that many of these American veterans had yet to receive their deserved reward from Britain, Washington was more than happy to do his part to serve them. He had, after all, led these men in battle during that war. He would do right by them. He loved them.

Fittingly, the wilderness he sought to explore was near to the very place he had fought with these soldiers. While Washington

Washington in the French and Indian War.

and his small party camped in the woods near the Kanawha River, a small party of peaceful Indians entered their camp. Though surprised, Washington stood and greeted them politely. It became clear to Washington that the leader of this band of Indians was an elderly man—the Grand Sachem, as he was called. And it soon became clear that the Grand Sachem, after hearing that Washington was in the territory, had traveled quite a distance to catch up with him and lay eyes on him.[1]

Why this Indian chief would sacrifice so much just to meet the thirty-eight-year-old Washington was, on the surface, a strange thing. For, at this time in history, Washington was not the man of fame he would one day become. Indeed, the Revolution and his role in it were still years away. But as the chief began to speak, Washington realized why he had come for him.

"I am a Chief and ruler of many tribes. My influence extends to the waters of the Great Lakes, and to the far Blue Mountains.

I have traveled a long and weary path that I might see the young warrior of the great battle."[2]

He signaled to Washington. Washington understood instantly.

Scenes of that great battle flashed through Washington's mind. Though it had occurred close to a decade and a half earlier, he remembered it well. He could still see the long, thin lines of British troops snaking their way through the untamed American wilderness, their bright red coats practically shining against the backdrop of lush green trees and bushes. It was a scene that marked the beginning of the French and Indian War—a fierce contest between the French and British over who would control the American continent.

Though only twenty-three years old at the time of that war, Washington had been commissioned to be a colonel under the command of British General Edward Braddock. Washington was of course respectful to the British command, but had grown increasingly frustrated with Braddock's maneuverings. *Sir,* Washington would plead continuously, *I fear we are walking into a French trap. Please reconsider my suggestion!*

For some time, Washington had been making his case to Braddock that the style of fighting in the American wilderness was unlike anything seen in Europe. The French had employed Native Americans, who were not going to line up in the open field of battle and face off with the enemy as gentlemen soldiers in Europe were accustomed to doing. Instead they would hide in the brush, perch in the trees, and ambush the British and American troops—blindside them from every angle. Washington told Braddock that he needed to employ the help of Indian warriors to form a scouting party in advance of the British troops. Braddock became enraged at Washington. "The Indians may frighten [American] continental troops, but they can make no

General Edward Braddock.

impression on the King's regulars."[3] The British general was not about to let himself be lectured to on warfare by the upstart, buckskin American colonel who was barely more than a teenaged boy.

As the now-older Washington thought back on the scene, he wondered if things might have turned out differently had he made one last attempt to change Braddock's stubborn mind. As Washington was playing out the rest of the battle scene in his mind's eye, he was jolted back to the present by the words of the Grand Sachem. There was no need for Washington to replay the scene on his own, as the old chief would instead narrate it for the entire camp. For he himself had been there with Washington.

By the waters of the Monongahela, we met the soldiers of the King beyond the Seas, who came to drive from the land my French Brothers. They came into the forest with much beating of drums and many flags flying in the breeze. Like a blind wolf they walked into our trap, and the faces of these red-clad warriors turned pale at the sound of our war-whoop. It was a day when the white man's blood mixed with the streams of our for-ests, and 'twas then I first beheld this Chief. [Points to Washington.] I called my young men and said: "Mark you tall and daring warrior! He is not of the red-coat tribe, he is of the Long-knives. He has an Indian's wisdom. His

> One Indian chief at the battle named Red Hawk often told his account of the story. According to Red Hawk, he shot at least eleven rounds at Washington and missed each time. Convinced that the Great Spirit was protecting the American soldier, he put down his weapon and submitted to the will of heaven.[4]

warriors fight as we do—himself alone is exposed to our fire. Quick! Let your aim be certain and he dies.

Our muskets were leveled—muskets that, for all but him, knew not how to miss. I, who can bring the leaping squirrel from the top of the highest tree with a single shot, fired at this warrior more times than I have fingers. Our bullets killed his horse, knocked the war bonnet from his head, pierced his clothes, but 'twas in vain; a Power mightier far than we shielded him from harm. He cannot be killed in battle.[5]

Washington's travel companions listened in amazement. Washington knew that what the old man recounted—though most bizarre—was in fact the truth. It had been a hellish nightmare. For two hours, the enemy had butchered the British-led forces. Of the 1,300 American and British soldiers in the battle, more than 700 were killed or wounded. (Conversely, of the roughly 850 French and Indian warriors, only 23 were reported killed and only 16 wounded.)[6] The casualties were even worse among the British officers: of the 86 in the battle, 62 were killed or wounded.[7]

The Indians had been instructed to wipe out all soldiers riding on horses. And so they did, with one exception. Washington was the only mounted officer not slain. After Braddock himself fell (he died of his wounds a few days later), Washington remained mounted, bravely leading his troops. One eyewitness recorded, "I expected every moment to see him fall. Nothing but the superintending care of Providence could have saved him!"[9]

> Upon her deathbed, Washington's mother told her son, "Go, George, fulfill the high destinies which Heaven appears to have intended for you."[8]

Shortly after the battle, Washington put his thoughts on paper. "By the miraculous care of Providence," he wrote, "I have been protected beyond all human probability or expectation; for I had four bullets through my coat and two horses shot under me and yet escaped unhurt, although death was leveling my companions on every side of me."[10]

As the Grand Sachem recounted to the group what he had come to tell them, vivid and sobering thoughts of the bloody scene raced through their minds. After a brief pause, the old Indian opened his mouth again to make his concluding remarks, or, better said, his concluding prophecy:

> I am old and soon shall be gathering to the great council fire of my fathers, in the land of the shades, but ere I go, there is a something, bids me speak, in the voice of prophecy. Listen! The Great Spirit protects that man, and guides his destinies—he will become the chief of many nations, and a people yet unborn will hail him as the founder of a mighty empire. I am come to

pay homage to the man who is the particular favorite of heaven, and who can never die in battle.[11]

After a moment of silence, the camp looked to Washington, who up until that time had remained silent, his eyes politely fixed on his elderly visitor. Finally, he responded:

"Our destinies are shaped by a mighty Power, and we can but strive to be worthy of what the Great Spirit holds in store for us. If I must needs have such lot in life as our Red Brother presages, then I pray that the Great Spirit give unto me those qualities of fortitude, courage, and wisdom possessed by our Red Brother. I, the friend of the Indian, have spoken."[12]

CHAPTER 1

The Dove and the Covenant

As Latter-day Saints, our perception of the history of our country is colored by our understanding of fundamental truths about mortality. One of those truths has direct bearing on our discussion of George Washington. It is this: The war in heaven never ended. It simply changed venues. It came to earth. Whether we want to recognize it or not, we find ourselves presently in the middle of it. The sooner we recognize this, the sooner we can get on with victory.

Those who have loved the Lord throughout history have often understood this principle. And so they girded up their loins, grabbed their weapons, rose up, and fought this war. George Washington was one of them.

One can hardly mention the name *Washington* without invoking the idea of liberty. That is one reason we know Washington was on the frontlines of this war against the adversary, for this war—beginning in heaven and landing on earth—was *always* about liberty.

One of the most famous war strategists of all time was an ancient Chinese general named Sun Tzu. He wrote what would become one of the world's most read books on war. It is called *The Art of War,* and perhaps its most important lesson to warriors today is this: To defeat the enemy, you must know the enemy. Like most, I don't like talking or thinking much about the adversary,

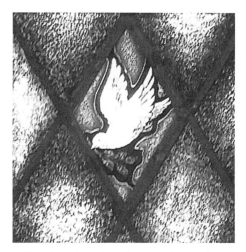

Detail of dove from La Cañada window.

but having fought some of the evilest men on earth for most of my professional life, I know that what Sun Tzu wrote is the truth. We have to understand the enemies of God in order to beat them, triumph over evil, and win the war. Indeed, we must understand Satan. So, here we go.

"And there was war in heaven: Michael and his angels fought against the dragon; and the dragon fought and his angels, and prevailed not" (Revelation 12:7–8). "Wherefore," stated the Lord, "because that Satan rebelled against me, and sought to *destroy the agency of man* . . . I caused that he should be cast down" (Moses 4:3–4; emphasis added).

Why? Why is Satan so concerned with agency and liberty? Why was this the trigger that set him off and compelled him to fight a war against the Father of all creation?

First off, Satan is arrogant. I think we can all agree on that point. Arrogant people want the glory. They want to set themselves above and apart from the rest. And so, in the premortal existence, when the Father gathered His children around and explained to them that all He had could be theirs, this must have rubbed Satan wrong. Imagine this arrogant "son of the morning" grappling with the idea that all God's children could grow in glory and exaltation, even becoming like the Father. Perhaps this challenged his self-perceived grandeur relative to all of us "little people" gathered around. We simply could not be allowed to progress so far. So he came up with a clever plan.

On the surface, his plan seemed great. Yes, he packaged it quite well, as he often does when promoting his products. *Salvation for all!* That's how he sold it. *We will take away their agency,* he proposed, *so none can fail.* He promised: "I will redeem all mankind, that one soul shall not be lost, and surely I will do it; wherefore give me thine honor" (Moses 4:1). I can just see his sly smile as he declares to the council in heaven: *We will force them into salvation.*

And there is the deception. One cannot be forced into salvation. How is that even possible? If I'm forced to make a covenant, am I really making a covenant? If I'm forced to go to church, am I really going to church? If I'm not permitted to make bad choices, to then feel the consequence of those choices, to then change inside, seek light, repent, apply the Atonement, and covenant with God because I *want* to, then am I really changing or progressing at all? If I don't have the liberty to choose, can I ever really become like the Father?

The answer is no! Satan knew it. Take away agency, and you take away exaltation and eternal life. Sure, he will tell us we are "saved," but exaltation and eternal life as defined by scripture would not be part of this "plan of salvation." And Satan, of course, would remain above us forevermore, as he sat on his throne of lies as the only "exalted one." As he himself envisioned, "I will exalt my throne above the stars of God: . . . I will ascend above the heights of the clouds; I will be like the most High" (Isaiah 14:13–14).

Clever. Sick, but clever. And one-third of the hosts of heaven bought off on it.

Here is the application in the here and now: the evil one has not given up. He is after us still. Sure, he lost the battle in heaven, but, having since been "cast out into the earth, and his angels were cast out with him" (Revelation 12:9), he and his minions walk amongst us today. I know, none of us wants to think about that dark application, but we must. Why? Because he hunts us. And his modus operandi has not varied in the least. He knows now, like he knew then, that taking away our liberty will greatly hurt our chances of attaining eternal life. So he attacks liberty any way he can. He has made good on his promise to take over nations, to raise up dictators and tyrants, and to use their military might for his own evil designs. Commenting on such adversarial ploys, Brigham Young University religion professor Andrew Skinner points out that "temple teachings expose Satan's tactics: rebellion, ignorance, violence, tyranny, and the destruction of agency in this world."[1] It's all part of his plan from the beginning to destroy liberty and halt our progression.

And he has been successful. It is estimated that, since the beginning of history, fewer than five percent of God's children have lived under the banner of freedom.[2] That is fewer than five percent who have lived during a time when there was enough freedom to support the limitless expansion of ideas, churches, prophets, temples—to support Christ's Church and the fulness of His gospel on earth. Tragic.

We need only look back a hundred years or so to see how successful Satan has been. Think Communist China. The Soviet Union. Nazi Germany. Saddam's Iraq. And on and on. We can even see him creeping into countries founded upon freedom and democracy—indeed he has hit and is hitting free republics all throughout the world; he seeks to take their liberty away.

Yes, he has compromised armies and navies, and he has raised up tyrants to do his bidding. Through them, he has taken away precious liberty from God's children. Maybe he could not control every aspect of their lives, but his overall goal of limiting freedom, and thus limiting opportunity for progression, has been met. For example, by attacking religious freedom through the years, he has done a splendid job keeping priesthood, covenants, and temples of God out of so many places. Indeed, he has kept the fulness of salvation from the reach of millions upon millions of precious souls.

This is Satan fighting the war that began in heaven. We have followed Sun Tzu's advice. We are figuring him out.

So, now what? What is our response going to be? Or, better phrased, what is God's response going to be? Of course He is not going to just sit back and let this happen without some sort of response. But what is His move in this situation? We should know this so we can help Him.

God has made it clear that His ultimate purpose is to bring to pass the "eternal life of man" (Moses 1:39). This requires a place where His gospel and temples might flourish. As His temples are that portal into eternity where covenants are made that allow for eternal life, there is very little He won't do to protect their existence. But remember, we are now dealing with an enemy who has purchased nations and uses those nations, along with their armies and navies, to assert wicked politics. He uses them to attack freedom and liberty—to attack temples. It may not be as easy as just dropping a prophet into these infected nations and expecting that God's truths and gospel will take hold. That would be akin to throwing perfect seeds into a pot of cement. No, first the Lord will provide the fertile soil. At times, He even goes so far as to remove the righteous from the wicked lands run by Satan and plant them in that soil. As the Lord teaches us so eloquently in Jacob, chapter 5, He will start over again and again.

Indeed, if necessary He will take His righteous followers to a new land of promise. He will then make a nation of them. A nation! Indeed, it won't just be a solitary band of righteous disciples traveling to and living in a distant land—at least not in the long run. We are talking about an enemy that wields great power—armies and navies. So God will take that band of disciples and mold them into a powerful nation. A nation blessed with powerful tools—even tools of war—to stand up and push back against the constant threat of evil and tyranny that will inevitably strike, whether from the outside or from within. Indeed, He will not leave His prophets and priesthood unprotected and exposed. He will give them the liberty, protection, and prosperity they require to do their job.

For example, the Old Testament prophet Samuel had been chosen by God to teach His gospel, but this prophet also sought national protection for the promised land in God-fearing leaders like David. The prophets Alma and Helaman (his son) had the same priesthood authority to bring the gospel, but were protected by the likes of the national leader, Captain Moroni. Joseph Smith and Brigham Young possessed the fulness of the gospel but recognized the need for the United States of America to protect it by way of righteous leaders, like Abraham Lincoln.[3] This is the pattern.

Perhaps the most important part of this pattern, as applied to us, is the fact that it is connected to a covenant. A national covenant. We are familiar with covenants we make as individuals, such as those we make at baptism. This is similar, but it's a covenant made, not between God and one of His children, but between God and an entire nation. He will grant His nations the liberty, protection, and prosperity necessary for temples and priesthood to do their job, but He expects something in return. He expects general obedience from His people in these special lands. He makes a covenant with these people. The leaders of these special lands need to understand this covenant so they can lead the people to righteousness and thus to the blessings of heaven. "If my people . . . shall humble themselves, and pray, and seek my face, and turn from their wicked ways; then will I hear from heaven, and will forgive their sin, and will heal their land" (2 Chronicles 7:14). Before every great restoration of the gospel— and there have been many since the beginning of time—there is a national covenant element that God provides first. The foundation. The land of promise.

> Said God to Noah: "But with thee will I establish my covenant . . . that of thy posterity shall come all nations."
>
> —*Genesis 6:18; JST, Genesis 8:23*

My mind immediately takes me to the La Cañada church building I wrote about in the prologue of this book. First, a disclaimer: I don't know what precise meaning the artist intended with the images. After some effort, I have not been able to find out who or where the artist is. As is often the case with symbols, the meaning of the window as expressed in this book is derived from my own and from others' interpretations. For me, the window has served as a kind of abstract reminder and guide.

So, I see the first image in the string of images that underline the depiction of Christ: a dove with a branch in its beak. Admittedly, without the artist with me to interpret meanings,

I'm left to my own devices to figure this out. But in the dove, I instantly see God's plan with righteous nation building and national covenant making. For in that image I see the story of one of the first times God employed this strategic response to the adversary's war here on earth. I see Noah. I see the ark.

God had removed his righteous disciples from the evil works of darkness in a most drastic and stunning act. He placed them on a large boat and allowed them to start over. Part of His promise was that He would bring them back to land. He would take them to a place where they would be free to practice true religion and seek out their salvation. As Noah and his family stood on the deck of the ark, they saw the dove, a symbol of this promise. The branch in its beak meant their land of promise was near. This was followed by the rainbow, another symbol of that covenant God made with Noah and the new nation.

This pattern of God providing special lands for chosen groups, then marrying these groups to the land through covenant, has recurred through history. And this pattern is part of the gospel, albeit a generally underrated part. For example, after Noah, we see the pattern repeated with Abraham.

Much has been written and discussed about Abraham and the great covenants associated with him: the *Abrahamic covenant.* These covenants, as outlined in the LDS Bible Dictionary, are promised to "all of his mortal posterity," and include "baptism (which is the covenant of salvation)," "the higher priesthood," and "celestial marriage (which is the covenant of exaltation)." But remember, that is not all. There must be national protection to fight against an adversary that will seek to tear down the temple. I again quote from the Bible Dictionary: "Included in the divine promises to Abraham were the assurances that . . . Abraham's posterity would receive certain lands."[4]

But what lands? Certainly, the land of Israel. The Old Testament, after all, is dedicated to telling the story of the building of the Israelite nation and the fight for preserving this nation under God. But the scriptures speak of *lands* and *nations*—plural. Abraham was set apart to be the "father of many nations" (Genesis 14:4–6). Said God to Abraham: "I will make thee exceeding fruitful, and I will make *nations* of thee (Genesis 17:6; emphasis added). So again I ask, what other nations? The Bible itself answers that question.

The Abrahamic covenant, including its promise of national covenants connected to promised lands, was clearly passed down to Abraham's son Isaac and to his grandson Jacob (see Genesis 26:4). And Jacob would ensure it continued further down Abraham's great line. So, before his death Jacob did something—something astonishing that still affects us all today. He took his son Joseph (yes, the one with the coat of many colors) and pronounced the Abrahamic covenant upon him. In so doing, he emphasized the part of the covenant that we do not emphasize enough today. The land. The nation. I now take you to my favorite Old Testament chapter: *Genesis 49.*

With his hands placed upon Joseph's head, Jacob declared: "Joseph is a fruitful bough, even a fruitful bough by a well; whose branches run over the wall" (Genesis 49:22).

Latter-day Saint doctrine is clear on the point that Jacob was telling Joseph that his descendants would be a fruitful people who would make their home "over the wall"—that is, over the great ocean dividing the Old World from the New. Joseph would inherit America. America was one of the lands associated with Abraham's covenant. It was one of *those* lands; one of *those* nations.[5]

Jacob prophesies more about these chosen people who would

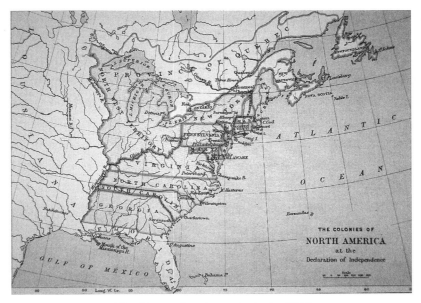

The thirteen American colonies in 1776.

inhabit this new land. He tells of how they will face an enemy there, who will hate him and who will "sho[o]t at him." But the Lord will bless this new nation; specifically, He will bless their arms of war—what Jacob refers to as their "bow"—and they would "ab[i]de in strength, and the arms of [the people of Joseph's] hands were made strong by the hands of the mighty God of Jacob" (Genesis 49:23–24).

The American story told through this prophecy continues. Jacob proclaims this land to be a land of prosperity, with blessings that "have prevailed above the blessings of [Jacob's] progenitors." (Now, that is saying a lot, considering how prosperous Jacob's forebears were.) They will have "blessings of heaven above, blessings of the deep that lieth under, blessings of the breasts, and of the womb" (Genesis 49:25–26). And finally, as an extension to this blessing, it is recorded that Jacob also blessed Joseph's posterity to be "a light unto my people, to deliver them in the days of their captivity, from bondage; and to bring salvation unto them" (JST, Genesis 48:11).

Altogether, this is no small prophecy regarding this promised land and the people God would send there. This land was to be something grand, overflowing with God's liberty, protection, and prosperity. Place prophets and priesthood in a land such as this, and the Lord will certainly have His temples. He will certainly be able to carry out His purpose to bring to pass the eternal life of men and women.

And one more hint regarding this new land. Jacob describes these people of the promised land to be "separate from [their] brethren" of the Old World, in a place of "everlasting hills" (Genesis 49:26). I don't know for certain what Jacob meant about everlasting hills. But I do know this. The longest mountain range in the world—the Andes—stretches 4,300 miles and resides in the Americas. The second longest mountain range in the world—the Rockies—stretches more than 3,000 miles through North America, boasting widths of up to 300 miles and ages of up to 3.3 billion years. As seen from space, using satellite imagery, these majestic mountain ranges appear to the eye to be extensions of one another. "Everlasting hills" certainly comes to mind. In fact, there is no other place on earth that more accurately fits the description of "everlasting hills." Did Jacob see a geographically based, satellite-like image or vision of the New World as he blessed his son Joseph?

Whatever Jacob meant, one thing is certain. Joseph's people were to inherit a great and prosperous land; a covenant land under God. So, where does the biblical account fulfill this great prophecy? When do we see Joseph's people make the great migration to the great land? At the same time Jacob blessed Joseph, he blessed another son, Judah, indicating to him that the Messiah would be born of his royal line. Certainly the biblical account tells the story of Judah and Christ and the fulfillment of that great prophecy. But, again I ask, what of Joseph's people? Where is their blessing fulfilled? The Bible is silent.

Well, almost silent. There is a clue. As a young and rather naive missionary at the Missionary Training Center in Provo, Utah, I remember studying the Old Testament prophecies regarding Joseph and being troubled over the apparent lack of fulfillment. Someone wisely referred me to the prophet Ezekiel, who seemed troubled over the same question. Apparently, the Lord blessed him with an amazing answer. And Ezekiel shared it: "Moreover, thou son of man, take thee one stick, and write upon it, For Judah . . . then take another stick, and write upon it, For Joseph . . . and join them one to another into one stick; and they shall become one in thine hand" (Ezekiel 37:16–17). Many biblical scholars believe the word *stick* in this passage refers to wax-filled tablets utilized in the Near East during the days of Ezekiel to keep records. In 1953, such ancient wax-filled tablets were discovered in the Near East. After the discovery, the New English Bible changed the word *stick* in this passage to *wooden tablet.*[6] Indeed, we have every reason to believe that when Ezekiel spoke of writing on "sticks" he was referring to what we might today call *books.*[7]

My mind flashes back to the La Cañada church window. Flanking the depiction of Christ holding an Americana-looking lantern are two scrolls/books labeled *Stick of Judah* and *Stick of Joseph.* The symbols are coming together.

The fulfillment of Joseph's promise would be recorded in another record—it would be recorded in the *Stick of Joseph,* just as the fulfillment of Judah's promise was recorded in the *Stick of Judah* (the Bible). Indeed, another book must surface that will tell the story of Joseph's people crossing over the wall of water and inheriting the promised land of everlasting hills. The Restoration of the gospel produced that second record; it produced the Book of Mormon. And this new book of scripture leaves little room for speculation as to whether it claims to be Joseph's story and his Old Testament prophecy fulfilled. When Christ appeared to the Nephites, He declared to them: "Ye are my disciples; and ye are a light unto this people, who are a remnant of the house of Joseph" (3 Nephi 15:12).

I love picturing Father Lehi as he fulfilled the promises and prophecies pertaining to Joseph. I picture him crossing the ocean with the brass plates (similar to our Old Testament record) in his hands. He certainly read in those plates about how Joseph's people—even his "fruitful bough"—would cross "over the wall" of water and into the promised land. He must have been thrilled to know that, in that very moment, he and his family were those people. He was fulfilling the prophecy. Think about it: when he sent his boys back to Jerusalem to get the brass plates from the wicked Laban, it wasn't just so he could formulate family home evening lessons while in the New World. "The Lord hath commanded me," declared Lehi, "that thou and thy brethren shall return to Jerusalem. For behold, Laban hath the record of the Jews and also a *genealogy of my forefathers*" (1 Nephi 3:2–3, emphasis added). He needed his posterity to know who they were. He needed them to know that they were the people of Joseph, even that nation God would establish in the promised land for His purposes.

Declared Lehi: "I am a descendant of Joseph who was carried captive into Egypt. And great were the covenants of the Lord which he made unto Joseph. Wherefore, Joseph truly saw our day. And he obtained a promise of the Lord, that out of the fruit of his

THE DOVE AND THE COVENANT • 21

loins the Lord God would raise up a righteous branch unto the house of Israel" (2 Nephi 3:4–5).[8]

The pattern was repeated. As He did with Noah, Abraham, Moses, and others before, the Lord took Joseph's Lehites out of lands that had been compromised by the devil and started anew. The Lord tapped once again into the Abrahamic covenant and built a new nation empowered to fight the adversary in his ongoing efforts to destroy agency, salvation, and, ultimately, temples.

This national covenant component was not lost on Lehi, who tried to ingrain the concept into his people. Before he fully rolled out the more important spiritual elements of the Abrahamic covenant in the new land, such as the building of temples, Lehi first established the thing that would protect those temples. He established the national covenant: "Yea, the Lord hath covenanted this land unto me, and to my children forever. . . . It shall be a land of liberty unto them; wherefore, they shall never be brought down into captivity; if so, it shall be because of iniquity" (2 Nephi 1:5, 7). As with all covenants, the land would remain blessed only through the people's righteousness. Lehi needed his people to understand this, or his entire mission to America would be lost. "Inasmuch as ye shall keep my commandments," declared the Lord through Lehi, "ye shall prosper in the land" (2 Nephi 1:20).

At this point you may be thinking: *Great, but what on earth does this have to do with George Washington? This book is about George Washington, right?* The exciting answer to that question is the central hypothesis of this book: one can't fully understand George Washington's mortal mission without first understanding these principles. In other words, to understand Washington in the fullest, you must understand the Book of Mormon! Why? Because of where Lehi's story goes next. You see, the righteous people of the Book of Mormon knew the national covenant pattern. They understood that they were neither the first nor the last group that would fulfill the promise. God would call another group, a future group, to the promised land; and, like them, this group would have a leader to teach and preach and live and act out the covenant on this land for the same purposes of God. This leader would be George Washington.

A vision was opened to Lehi's son Nephi. He learned a tragic truth—his people would eventually break the covenant and lose everything. Nephi described what he had seen in the vision. "Because of the pride of my seed, and the temptations of the devil," explained Nephi, the enemy "did overpower the people of my seed." And the whole of his father's posterity would "dwindle in unbelief" (1 Nephi 12:19, 22). The gospel would be taken from the earth. The Great Apostasy would dig in hard in America and throughout the whole world.

> "The United States is the promised land foretold in the Book of Mormon—a place where divine guidance directed inspired men to create the conditions necessary for the Restoration of the gospel of Jesus Christ. It was the birth of the United States of America that ushered out the Great Apostasy, when the earth was darkened by the absence of prophets and revealed light. It was no coincidence that the lovely morning of the First Vision occurred just a few decades after the establishment of the United States."[9]
>
> —Elder L. Tom Perry, January 24, 2012

But as Heavenly Father is a God of light and hope, He always provides the solution. And He gives it to us—or, more accurately, He gave it to Nephi—in the very next chapter after describing the end of the Nephites. At the conclusion of 1 Nephi, chapter 13, the Lord showed Nephi another vision. He showed him latter-day America. He showed him "other books, which came forth by the power of the Lamb," which books "shall make known the plain and precious things which have been taken away from them" (1 Nephi 13:39–40). What Nephi saw was the Restoration of the gospel of Jesus Christ in the latter days.

But let's not forget the established pattern that must be adhered to. Before that Restoration comes to light, we should see the formation of a national covenant like unto the covenant proclaimed by Father Lehi upon the land. We should see the establishment of a sociopolitical foundation under God that will protect that Restoration. In Nephi's vision, the Lord also showed him this component of the plan. Just before opening Nephi's eyes to the latter-day Restoration, the Lord explained the following:

> And it came to pass that I, Nephi, beheld that the Gentiles who had gone forth out of captivity did humble themselves before the Lord; and the power of the Lord was with them.
>
> And I beheld that their mother Gentiles were gathered together upon the waters, and upon the land also, to battle against them. And I beheld that the power of God was with them, and also that the wrath of God was upon all those that were gathered together against them to battle. And I, Nephi, beheld that the Gentiles that had gone out of captivity were delivered by the power of God out of the hands of all other nations. (1 Nephi 13:16–19)

He saw the American Revolution. He saw American independence delivered by God Almighty. He saw the Lord entering the battlefields of America, just as He had done with the Nephites, and just as He had prophesied in Genesis 49. He saw the creation of a covenant nation, unlike any on earth, soon to be equipped with the tools to host the Restoration.

So important was this future event that the Savior Himself,

EXCERPTS FROM
WASHINGTON'S EULOGIES

"[Washington] has been the same to us, as Moses was to the Children of Israel."

"Moses led the Israelites through the Red Sea; has not Washington conducted the Americans thro' seas of blood."

"He who had commanded Moses at the Red Sea, also inspired Washington on the banks of the Delaware."

Of the nearly 350 surviving eulogies given at the time of Washington's death, as many as two-thirds of them directly compare him to Moses.[10]

while visiting the Nephites, prophesied about it. "For it is wisdom in the Father," declared the Christ, "that [latter-day Americans] should be established in this land, and be set up as a free people by the power of the Father . . . that the covenant of the Father may be fulfilled which he hath covenanted with his people, O house of Israel" (3 Nephi 21:4).

Mormon, one of the last remaining Nephites in the land, appeared to take some comfort in these prophecies. Though his people had broken the national covenant and lost the blessings, he knew that one day the good would all return to his promised land. "The Lord," declared Mormon, "hath reserved their [the Nephites'] blessings, which they might have received in the land, for the Gentiles [latter-day Americans] who shall possess the land" (Mormon 5:19). The Lord had revealed earlier that "none come into this land save they shall be brought by the hand of the Lord" (2 Nephi 1:6). Certainly these Gentiles—America's Pilgrims and other early settlers—fit the bill. In fact, before his vision of the American Revolution, Nephi saw God bringing these settlers to the land: "And it came to pass that I beheld the Spirit of God, that it wrought upon other Gentiles; and they went forth out of captivity, upon the many waters. And it came to pass that I beheld many multitudes of the Gentiles upon the land of promise" (1 Nephi 13:13–14).

So, what is the Lord's next step with these settlers who are arriving on His land? I take you back to the inspirational window in the La Cañada chapel. Next to Noah's dove, in chronological order, is a set of keys. Somebody must be given the keys to unlock this power, to open the national covenant and welcome the Lord's covenant blessings into the promised land of latter-day America. The covenants of the Father to the house of Israel, particularly that American covenant promised to Joseph, were longing to resurface in the latter days to kick off the Restoration of the gospel, which would at long last remedy the darkness caused by universal apostasy. But someone had to unlock it. That someone was called. He led the efforts of those Gentiles seen in Nephi's vision. He worked tirelessly to bring forth one nation under God—to bring forth liberty, protection, and prosperity under the American covenant. His name was George Washington.

But what does this mean? Is it too bold to place the likes of George Washington in the same national-covenant-maker role as Noah, Moses, Abraham, Lehi, or Captain Moroni? Certainly Washington, though a good man and a great leader, did not have the knowledge or spirituality of these other national covenant leaders. Certainly he did not understand God's covenants with nations as set forth in the Book of Mormon. Certainly he did not really comprehend that America was counted as one of these covenant nations associated with the promises of Joseph and the house of Israel. Certainly he did not have any idea of the importance of temples, which have been the ultimate fruit of promised lands.

Or maybe he did. . . .

CHAPTER 2

Miracle at Boston

Years ago, I was assigned to be the home teacher to a good and very active LDS family. During one of my visits to this family, the wife posed a perplexing question: "Why are we not prospering, even though we are righteous?" She was referring to the fact that her small family struggled so much financially, even though they were keeping all the commandments to the best of their ability. She continued, "Doesn't the Book of Mormon promise us that as we keep the commandments we will prosper in the land?"

I immediately gave her the answer that many in my place, I imagine, would give. "Prospering in the land," I explained, "doesn't refer to financial reward, but to spiritual growth and spiritual progression." She nodded, somewhat satisfied, and I quickly changed the subject. I was not comfortable with my response.

In fact, when I returned to my home I could not get the brief conversation I had had with her out of my head. How I responded was not necessarily incorrect, but I knew I had dodged the issue at the heart of her concern. For, reading the Book of Mormon, the facts are the facts, whether we like them or not. When the Nephites were righteous, the Lord prospered them financially and economically in the land. How else do we explain the famed "Nephite Pride Cycle"? The Lord clearly recognizes general righteousness by showering the ancient American nation with riches (see 4 Nephi 1:2, 7–8); when they turn prideful and wicked, prosperity declines unless and until repentance brings them back. Yes, financial reward is part of the covenant relationship. It's a constant pattern in the Book of Mormon.

My struggling friend had indeed been on to something. But she was missing the central point of it all. It is a point we must not fail to understand if we are to help the Lord wage His war against the adversary. Our baptismal and temple covenants are certainly the most important covenants, bar none. However, in receiving those priesthood covenants, among the many blessings we are promised (the Holy Ghost, the priesthood, eternal life), where are we promised a land of liberty, physical protection from wicked armies and navies, or economic prosperity? Though the Lord can bless us through our priesthood covenants any way He chooses (including personal wealth), these more temporal blessings are *not* guaranteed to us at baptism or in the temple, even if we live righteously. These temporal blessings, though they serve to protect the ability to make the more important priesthood covenants, are directly associated only with the *national* covenant.

After that home teaching visit, I decided to sit down and read the Book of Mormon over again with a pen and notepad. I decided to read it this time with different eyes. I began to identify and note when the Lord and His prophets were referring to priesthood covenants (those more spiritual and eternal promises made to individuals) and when they were referring to the national covenant—those temporal promises made to the nation, such as the Old Testament promises Jacob made to Joseph's people, to include protection in war and economic prosperity. It was as if I were reading a whole new book. I saw nations covenant with God so that He could bless them with all the resources they needed, including great riches in the aggregate (not necessarily to each individual), so the righteous nation could stand strong against physical attacks by the armies of the wicked. I then saw protected individuals and families free to enter houses of worship and covenant with the Father to fill the measure of their creation. There appear to be two types of covenants working together and all wrapped up and packaged under the Abrahamic covenant.

Then I thought of my country. I thought of America. As we discussed in the previous chapter, this same covenant theology applies to America today. Same land. Same covenant. So we'd better figure it out. We'd better understand our responsibilities, not only as individuals under priesthood covenants but as a nation under the American covenant. The Nephites eventually abandoned their national covenant, which allowed the enemies of God to enter and destroy liberty and eventually push the fulness of the gospel from the earth. It was the end of priesthood power in the land, the end of true temple worship. Let this be a warning to all who live in a covenant land. So much hangs in the balance.

After my national covenant study of the Book of Mormon, I decided the next best thing to do would be to study American history. I figured that if latter-day America truly was the place Nephi saw in vision, even the place the Lord Himself referred to in the Book of Mormon as the place where His children would "be set up as a free people by the power of the Father" (3 Nephi 21:4), then I would see the fulfillment and application in American history. Perhaps there would be lessons there about how to build, live in, and manage a covenant land. Perhaps these would be lessons our America desperately needs today, especially as we face decisions about which direction to take the nation, which policies to adopt, and which leaders to elect.

I also realized that through studying American history, I would be able to more easily delineate between priesthood and national covenants. As America was founded before the restoration of the priesthood, it is easy to narrow in on the national covenant component without confusing it with the priesthood covenant component. (It may be more difficult to get that clarity and delineation in the Book of Mormon story.) That priesthood part, of course, comes later in American history, and is built upon the national covenant. All together, we are provided with a clear depiction of how it is designed to function.

My first order of business in this study was to identify the American Moses. Who would bring the national covenant? Who would try it out in the land to see if it would actually work? One of the reasons we acknowledge Noah, Abraham, Moses, Joshua, Lehi, and Captain Moroni as great national-covenant makers is because miracles followed them. And therefore, people followed them. We have scriptural proof that the Lord worked His miracles through them to build promised lands, which laid the foundations for temples.

Let us see if George Washington fits this model. Let us see if he really is the American Moses. My hypothesis states that he is. But to prove this hypothesis, we must prove that he understood the national covenant, as other national leaders of God did. Through the balance of this book, we will explore the battles he led to see if he fought them, under God's covenant, like Joshua or Captain Moroni fought their battles. We will also see if his fellow countrymen followed his example. Then we will explore the more difficult question of what Washington knew of the restored gospel. More particularly, toward the end of this book we will investigate his understanding of temples in this latter-day American land of promise. As we shall see by the end of this study, if the hypothesis holds true, there are terrific consequences for good or ill that apply to us in the here and now.

◆ ◆ ◆

"Fly to the Woods." That was the instruction John Adams gave to his wife, Abigail, should the British attack their home outside of Boston. It was a real possibility. Just a week earlier, the first shots of the Revolution at Lexington and Concord had shaken the foundation of America. And Adams, an important delegate to the Continental Congress, was most certainly on the British hit list. Unfortunately, Adams had been called back to Philadelphia to make war preparations. His country needed him badly. He was horrified at having to leave his wife and small children home alone, with the battle lines between British and American forces a mere thirty minutes' ride away.[1]

It was the summer of 1775. The British had come to Boston, the American hotbed of rebellion. The American cries and demands for liberty—the kind of liberty required for the upcoming Restoration of the gospel—had become intolerable to the monarchical British system. They would hear no more of it. They would silence the Americans by force.

As John Adams was heading back to Philadelphia, the British had complete control of Boston. The Americans had staged their relatively few arms and militias across the river from Boston at Cambridge and upon Bunker and Breed's Hills. Several weeks after Adams had returned to Congress, it happened. The British would wait no longer. They attacked their American foes, who were building a small redoubt on the hills overlooking Boston and its harbor. The Battle of Bunker Hill would commence, leaving behind forever any possibility of peaceful resolution between the once friendly nations.

Abigail Adams was not of a mindset to "fly to the Woods." In fact, such a notion was contrary to her very makeup. She was a fighter. "I glory in calling myself a daughter of America," she would say. She would not back down from what she called

The Battle of Bunker Hill.

"tyranny, oppression, and Murder" by the hand of the British. And she encouraged her husband to take these sentiments and convert the American Congress and public to the cause of independence and liberty. "Is it not better to die the last of British freemen," she would ask rhetorically, "than live the first of British Slaves?" She feared the American Congress would purchase peace "at the price of liberty."[2]

As cannon fire rocked Boston and its surrounding areas, Abigail took the hand of her seven-year-old son, John Quincy. She calmly walked to the top of Penn's Hill near her home to show him what tyranny attacking righteousness looked like. They wept as they watched hundreds of bodies fall to the ground, including that of their dear friend Dr. Joseph Warren, who had only days earlier placed splints on John Quincy's hand, saving his broken finger. The Americans fought bravely but ultimately lost the battle and with it the strategic high ground of Bunker and Breed's Hills.[3]

Abigail Adams.

Why would Abigail take her seven-year-old through such a traumatic experience—one that would, in John Quincy's words, leave "an impression in my mind" that would haunt him forevermore? She understood the principles of the war in heaven. She understood the fight America was in, and she knew the Lord needed more recruits then and in the future. She was trying to prepare her son to be a future recruit. More important, she understood the national covenant and knew it was that covenant which would bring victory and liberty. She needed John Quincy to know that as well.

Wiping tears from her eyes as she descended Penn's Hill, Abigail entered her home with her son, and they immediately knelt in prayer. "Thy kingdom come. Thy will be done." She spoke these words to the Father, and young John Quincy soaked it in. She then had her son help her unwrap each piece of her prized pewter spoons and melt them into molds to make musket balls for her American patriots.[4]

SON OF A PATRIOT

John Quincy Adams eventually became American minister to six countries, secretary of state, a senator, a congressman, and sixth president of the United States. He fought passionately until the end of his life for the abolishment of slavery. The memory of Bunker Hill, he once said, "riveted my abhorrence of war to my soul . . . with abhorrence of tyrants and oppressors . . . [who] wage war against the rights of human nature and the liberties and rightful interests of my country."[5] His mother's plan had worked.

Yes, John and Abigail Adams seemed to clearly understand that there was a covenant relationship between God and America. In other words, they believed that turning to the Lord in their righteous cause would produce the desired results. It would produce the miracles. There was only one way a nation of citizen-soldiers could beat the world's superpower at war. It was through God and the national covenant He had given to America. A few days after the Battle of Bunker Hill, Abigail wrote to her husband, "Scarcely a day that does not produce some [hostilities], but like good Nehemiah . . . we will say unto them 'Be not afraid. Remember the Lord who is great and terrible, and fight for your brethren, your sons, and your daughters, your wives, and your houses.'"[6] As if commenting on Jacob's promises to Joseph and the land, she declared, "The race is not to the swift, nor the battle to the strong, but the God of Israel is he that giveth strength and power unto his people."[7]

John Adams agreed. Also understanding the covenant, which required faith and action on America's part, he proposed that American victory would be supported when "millions will be upon their knees at once before their Great Creator, imploring His forgiveness and blessing; His smiles on American Councils and Arms." When asked how he thought citizen-soldiers could possibly best the powerhouse that was the British military, he confidently answered like a good Nephite might. The formula was quite simple; we will win "if we fear God and repent our sins."[8]

John and Abigail are two of my very favorite characters in history. Why? Because they were just normal people—father and mother, housewife and lawyer, farmers and neighbors. Nothing was particularly noteworthy about either of them until crisis hit America. Instead of running and hiding, like more than two-thirds of the American populace wanted to do, they stood up in the power of God to fight the good fight no matter the consequences.

As Abigail was melting down pewter for the American cause, John was in Philadelphia trying to convert a very timid American Congress to the same cause. Who was on his side? It was difficult to know. Blood was being spilled in Boston, and, in the minds of the delegates, Philadelphia was next. The fear was real. John knew it. He also knew that as the most vocal, passionate, and persuasive delegate, he had people listening to him. He needed to leverage that influence sooner rather than later.

He looked across the room and noticed the tall, quiet, forty-three-year-old gentleman from Virginia. His demeanor was quite the opposite of John's. Though a passionate patriot, this gentleman was, at his core, a quiet farmer. A great listener more than a great speaker. He had been serving in Virginia's House of Burgesses, but had made few speeches there and had introduced no legislation. When he was elected to represent Virginia at the First Continental Congress, where John Adams first met him, he maintained the same low profile, declining to make any speeches on the floor and failing to earn any appointment to a congressional committee. His name was George Washington.[9]

Notwithstanding his quiet demeanor, there was something about Washington. Adams knew that while his Abigail was making weapons of war, he needed to get someone to Boston to direct the use of such weapons. America needed a commander-in-chief. There were several willing to fill the position, many of whom possessed much greater experience than Washington. Charles Lee, for example, had traveled the world as a British officer and military adviser to the king of Poland. Other professionals included Horatio Gates, Thomas Conway, and Thomas Mifflin. Even the prominent John Hancock, who presided over Congress, desired the position. Indeed, there were several available soldiers—professional soldiers—with "greater professional experience than Washington."[10]

Washington, on the other hand, had very limited formal education (he withdrew from schooling in his teens) compared to the other delegates. Though he had fought bravely in the French and Indian War, he had been retired from any military activity for *fifteen* years. As the Pulitzer Prize-winning historian David McCullough points out, "He was by no means an experienced commander. He had never led an army in battle, never commanded anything larger than a regiment. And never had he directed a siege."[11]

But Adams, whose Christian passion kept him from even traveling on the Sabbath, would use more than mere scientific analysis to choose the American savior.[12] He would use the Spirit of God, whose fight he knew this was. He stood before Congress and boldly nominated the man from Virginia as commander-in-chief of the Continental Army. After securing the appointment with a vote from Congress, Adams predicted that the "Appointment will have great Effect in cementing and securing the Union of these Colonies." Washington, he prophesied, would become "one of the most important Characters in the World."[13]

Washington did not see the appointment in this light. Stunned by Adams's actions, he stood humbled before Congress and declared: "I am truly sensible of the high Honour done to me in this Appointment, yet I feel great distress, from a consciousness that my abilities & Military experience may not be equal to the extensive & important Trust. . . . I beg it may be remembered by every Gentn [gentleman] in the room, that I this day declare with utmost sincerity, I do not think myself equal to the Command I [am] honored with."[14]

After the meeting Washington was still numb, his head spinning over what had just taken place. He wrote to his wife. He had to tell her the sad news that he would not be coming home anytime soon. In fact, he would prepare immediately to leave for Boston and begin his military campaign. The Washington family's world was instantly turned upside down. "Far from seeking this appointment," he explained to his wife, "I have used every endeavor in my power to avoid it, not only from my unwillingness to part with you and the Family, but from a consciousness of its being a trust too great for my Capacity. . . . It has been a kind of destiny that has thrown me upon this Service."[15]

Before George left for the battlefield, his mother declared to him: "My prayers are all that I can give to my country, and these it shall have. That God may protect you through all the dangers and hardships of war, and return you in safety, will be my constant prayer. With His blessing you can be a useful man in war, as in peace, and without it you can expect nothing."[16]

Destiny. That spiritual path laid out by the Lord, a path that, for Washington, was illuminated by a mother and father who strictly taught him the Bible and regularly admonished him to pray and to obey God's commands.[17] A path further made known on the wilderness battlefield near the Monongahela

River, as discussed in the introduction of this book. A path that led him to this point in history.

Surely, millions in heaven looked down. They craved a temple. They yearned for that fulness of salvation. But they knew that having a promised land in which to lay the foundation was the first step. And Washington was now the leader of that land. Joseph Smith's maternal grandfather, Solomon Mack, was the same age as Washington and served two tours of duty in the Revolutionary War.[18] And so you see, in not many years behind Washington, Joseph was coming. The Restoration was coming. Temples were coming. But before Joseph held the torch, it was Washington's to protect and to utilize. He held it now as he made his way to Boston.

My mind's eye flashes again to the keys depicted on the La Cañada window. Certainly they remind us of that priesthood authority that American independence, and the accompanying freedom of religion, would eventually usher in. But they also remind me of the doors the Lord will unlock for His servants, of the callings and assignments He will give to them. The keys of the American covenant. At last, they had been given to Washington.

Before he left, Washington stopped off at a bookstore to purchase textbooks on military strategy.[19] Hopefully nobody but the clerk witnessed this. I can just imagine a somewhat humorous scene with Continental soldiers standing near the checkout counter, watching their newly appointed commander buy books with titles that in today's language would be something like *Battlefield Strategy for Dummies*. They would be thinking, *What on earth have we signed up for?* But, you see, this is what God needed. He needed a leader who, like Joseph Smith, would rely upon *Him*—not upon his own self-perceived greatness and knowledge, and not upon the arm of the flesh. He needed a

Congressional clergyman prays for divine aid.

man willing to learn and work and sacrifice all. But more important, He needed a humble servant who would ask and listen. Washington was that man.

As evidence, I turn your attention to one final scene that took place in Philadelphia before Washington left for war-torn Boston. It was the very first official act of the American Congress. It was a prayer. "Plead my cause, O Lord, with them that strive with me," declared the congressional clergyman assigned to offer the plea to heaven, "fight against them that fight against me." John Adams would later comment that the prayer was one that "heaven had ordained" and that it brought tears to the eyes of the delegates. "It was," he said, "enough to melt a heart of stone."[20]

The Book of Mormon is clear on one matter. As Nephi saw in vision, the American revolutionaries had "the power of the Lord . . . with them" only as they "did humble themselves before the Lord" (1 Nephi 13:16). The Americans were striving to live this covenant relationship.

Most of the delegates stood during this remarkable prayer. "Washington was on his knees."[21]

◆　◆　◆

Shortly after arriving to meet his troops on the outskirts of Boston, Washington met Abigail Adams. She was grateful for the opportunity to meet the man her husband had chosen to lead the charge. "Mark his majestic fabric," she would say of the general, borrowing the words of John Dryden. "He's a temple sacred from his birth and built by hands divine."[22] Apparently she approved.

But Washington had his work cut out for him. When he arrived in July 1775, he immediately called for his war council to apprise him of the situation. The situation was bad. Almost hopeless. The troops were in disarray, the weapons and ammunition in short supply, and colonial soldiers were abandoning the dismal scene by the hundreds. Washington commented on his difficult situation, stating that, rather than commanding the army, he would have "retir'd to the back Country & livd in a Wig-wam."[23] But his faith was strong. "God in his great goodness will direct [the outcome]," he wrote during this time, "I am thankful for his protection."[24]

Washington's headquarters was at Cambridge, which was located to the west of the British-controlled Boston. The Charles River was the only thing that separated the two forces. The Americans' advantage had been the strategic high ground they held at Bunker and Breed's Hills, which hung over the harbor and looked directly into the British stronghold—perfect for launching an attack. But this ground had obviously been taken before Washington arrived. He needed to think up a plan of attack, and think it up quick. The British, after all, were in position to launch out and end the cause of American independence. Washington felt a need to strike first.

Dorchester Heights. That was the place. Since Bunker and Breed's Hills were lost already, Washington knew there was only one other location that provided sufficient high ground over Boston and its harbor. Dorchester Heights was this high ground, and it was located just south of Boston and its harbor. Would he get there? Would he launch the attack he dreamed of?

◆　◆　◆

I wanted to try to feel what Washington must have felt during these crazy months in the Boston area between 1775 and 1776. So, not long ago, I climbed Breed's Hill to learn more. At the top of the hill is the stunning Bunker Hill Monument, a 221-foot granite obelisk that looks like a smaller version of the Washington Monument. The monument sits atop the hill overlooking Boston and commemorates the great battle. I had my eleven-year-old son, Jimmy, with me. When we got to the top, Jimmy disappeared into the obelisk and ran up the almost 300 stairs to the top. I noticed that a national parks tour guide was just gathering a group on the grassy area near the obelisk. I went to listen.

The guide told the story of the battle and spoke of the bravery of those who stood their ground and lost their lives on the sacred hill we now stood upon. She spoke of the severe disadvantages the American patriots worked under. Of course, no mention of the patriots' great faith or trust in God was ever made. But even worse than that was the way the guide ended the lecture. She pointed south over the city and stated quickly and almost apathetically, "The war scene here in Boston actually ended on the high grounds of Dorchester Heights, where Washington eventually took his troops and pushed the British out of Boston. Thank you for coming to the Bunker Hill Monument. You can find bathrooms at the museum located at the base of the hill."

That was it? I thought. *One sentence on Dorchester Heights?* By that time Jimmy had made his way back down and was standing just outside the group. He was listening intently to the guide. I thought of the thousands of children who would come every year to this place and would likely never know what *really* happened. Tragic. Why? Because the true story is the story of how One Nation under God was born. More important, the true story provides the *only* real solution to maintaining this promised land today and utilizing it for the purposes of the Almighty.

I grabbed Jimmy's hand, and we walked down to the museum. I went into the map room, where there was a three-dimensional layout of the battle scene. "Jimmy, did you hear the tour guide explain how desperate the Americans were—how they had little ammunition, especially compared to the British?" Jimmy nodded, and we recounted how American General Israel Putnam stood atop Breed's Hill as the British attacked. "Don't fire till you see the whites of their eyes!" he reportedly declared to his troops, in an effort to conserve as much powder and ball as possible. I continued my questioning, "Did you hear what she said at the end, about Dorchester Heights?" I knew he had.

I pulled out a map. "Jimmy, after losing Bunker (Breed's) Hill, how on earth did Washington move that many troops from Cambridge, where his base camp was [I pointed on the map to where Cambridge was located, southwest of Bunker Hill, across the water from Boston] all the way to Dorchester Heights, just south of Boston?" He analyzed the map like few eleven-year-olds would care to. I drew an imaginary line from Cambridge to Dorchester. "Don't you see, the British would have easily seen these movements and destroyed Washington. Do you not think the British knew about Dorchester Heights? Do you not think they would have been very aware of Washington's desire to take it?" Jimmy nodded. I pulled out a book and quoted from the British General William Howe, who commented on his position in the aftermath of Bunker Hill. "We are not under the least apprehension of an attack on this place from the rebels."[25]

"You see, Son," I explained, "The British were ready. General Howe even commented that if Washington tried something so foolish as attempting to gain Dorchester Heights, he would command his powerful army to 'go at [Washington] with our whole force.'"[26]

"So Washington didn't make it to Dorchester?" asked Jimmy.

"No, he absolutely did! It is *how* he did it that is the moral of this story."

But before I told him the rest of the story, I needed to set it up further, so I continued my line of questioning. "So, Jimmy, if Washington really pushed the British out of Boston from his new position at Dorchester, with what weapons was he able to do this? Remember, with soldiers abandoning the fight by the thousands, Americans were *losing* weapons, not *gaining* them." I knew I had his attention.

Jimmy and I left the museum and hopped into a vehicle. "I need to show you something," I told him.

"Where are we going?

"Dorchester Heights!" I responded. "Or at least what's left of it."

As we drove southward from Bunker Hill through the thick downtown Boston traffic, Jimmy was anxious. "How did he get there? What guns did he use?" I just smiled and told him to be patient. I told him he needed to prepare himself for this story by

Dorchester Heights monument.

trying to block out all the cars and buildings. "Imagine it how it was back then. Clear views everywhere. Nowhere to run or hide. The Americans and British could stare each other down, each wondering who would blink first."

As we drove south around Boston, on the "American side" of the conflict, we at last started the incline. We were moving up, and Jimmy sensed correctly that we were entering Dorchester Heights. Nothing but buildings and townhomes appeared on the high ground until we got to the very top. And there it was: a small park with a rounded-out grassy area and a church-like monument sitting quietly and alone at its peak. It was the exact location where Washington and his army had been.

Jimmy scampered ahead and was making great time to the top of the mound where the monument sat. I had been to this place several times, and I knew it was sacred ground. I could feel it. I knew what had happened here. As always, I scanned the entire park, hoping to find someone there who was also seeking the truth—someone who was asking the same questions Jimmy had just asked, the *who, what, when, where* of this place. Nobody. Unfortunately, the story had been reduced to a footnote in history. Unlike Bunker Hill, which was bustling with curious tourists and government docents, Dorchester Heights hosted not a soul besides Jimmy and me. On my several visits to this place, I had only ever come across one person at the park—a man walking his dog. I had approached him and asked if he knew about the miracle that had occurred here. Though he had lived just across the street from the park for most of his life, he admitted he had no idea.

As I followed behind a very energetic Jimmy, I noticed he was about to get to the top of the hill, where the church-like monument stood. I immediately predicted his next move; and I was right. He abruptly did an about-face to the north and looked directly into Boston.

"So this is the view Washington had as the British sailed away?" he yelled down to me. "This is where he was standing?"

"Pretty much," I responded, as I caught up to him and put my arm around him. "But the more interesting view he had was that from the very streets of Boston after the British left." I explained, "He marched triumphantly into the abandoned town, then stopped. His eyes became intense as he soaked in what he saw: a battle-ready city. British fortifications that would have withstood any American attack. Though Washington had taken Dorchester Heights with a mind to do battle, he quickly realized his plan would have failed. If there had been a battle, America would have lost. The Revolution would have ended."

Standing on top of the hill, I quoted the words Washington

himself had used to assess the scene. The British position, he wrote, was "the strongest by nature on this Continent, and strengthened and fortified in the best manner and at an enormous Expence."[27] He continued. The British would have been "amazingly strong. 20,000 Men could not have carried it against one thousd [thousand]. . . . The Town of Boston was almost impregnable every avenue fortified."[28] David McCullough added that the British evacuation had saved Washington "from his headlong determination to attack, and thus from almost certain catastrophe."[29] What would have made matters even worse, unbeknownst to anyone at the time, an overwhelming British naval fleet was already on its way to support the British war effort.

"So, the question is," I declared to my son, "*Why* did the British leave all of a sudden? If their position was so superior, *why* give up this opportunity to end the Revolution right then and there? The answer, Jimmy, is the story the tour guide *should* have told the visitors of Bunker Hill. You see, the Lord, knowing any fight would have ended in British victory, scared the British right out of town. I call it the 'Quadruple Miracle at Boston.'"

As we stood alone at Dorchester Heights, I prepared to tell Jimmy the whole story. "The story begins," I said, "with a really big, fat dude."

"What?" Jimmy responded with an enormous grin.

I meant no disrespect to the heroic figure. Just trying to keep my son on his toes. I explained from there that his name was Henry Knox. The twenty-five-year-old was described as being large, gregarious, and very active and having a booming voice. A bookseller by trade, he had no military experience to speak of (though he had read every book he could find on military science). And weighing in at over 250 pounds, he did not look like a solider. But a soldier he was. One of the best there ever was.[30]

Henry Knox.

I explained to Jimmy that Henry Knox performed the first of the four miracles that led to the British evacuation. A few months after Washington arrived at the scene, Knox approached him and asked for permission to attempt the impossible. He wanted to take a team and retrieve the cannon rumored to have been abandoned by the British hundreds of miles away at Fort Ticonderoga. Though many regarded this as a fool's errand, and even though it was a mere bookseller asking to lead the effort, Washington did not hesitate. Washington sent him off immediately. Within two months, after having traveled over three hundred miles of "rough forest roads, freezing lakes, blizzards, thaws, mountain wilderness, and repeated mishaps that would have broken lesser spirits several times over,"[31] Henry Knox did it. He transported, by horse and sled, more than 120,000 pounds of mortars and cannons from Fort Ticonderoga to an anxious Washington outside of Boston.

The climactic part of the Knox story happened shortly after

he arrived at Fort Ticonderoga and began wondering how exactly he was going to get all this weaponry back to Washington. Fortunately he was a man of faith. He once wrote to his wife that he would daily "rise with or a little before the sun, and immediately with part of the regiment attend prayers, sing a psalm or read a chapter in [the Bible]."[32] And so, he employed faith. His plan was to build large sleds, even though there was little or no snow on the ground. He would do his part; then God would deliver that which he could not. He followed a Book of Mormon pattern: "it is by grace that we are saved, after all we can do" (2 Nephi 25:23).

With the sleds built, Knox and his men waited. For several days they waited. Then, on Christmas Day—the very day that commemorates the birth of Him who by scriptural decree is "the God of the [American] land" (Ether 2:12) upon which Knox stood—the blizzard hit. Not only did the sleds begin their 300-mile trek over three feet of blessed snow, but the Hudson River froze over, allowing the sleds to cross when required. From the lowest valleys to the highest peaks, a heavenly path had been laid. "It appear'd to me almost a miracle that people with heavy loads should be able to get up & down such hills,"[33] wrote Knox in his diary. By January 1776, Washington had his cannon.

"That was miracle number one," I told Jimmy as we stood upon Dorchester. "Can you guess what the next miracle would be?"

Jimmy, looking down upon the Boston scene from where we stood, and seeing how close the American and British lines were to each other, knew the great predicament. "There is no way Washington is getting all those cannon and troops up to this hill without the British noticing."

"Unless . . ." I chimed in.

Washington with cannon on Dorchester Heights.

"Unless there was another miracle," he replied excitedly.

Washington moved forward with his daring plan. He would take Dorchester Heights and he would place Knox's cannon upon those heights.

At midnight on March 2, 1776, Washington commanded his troops to launch a barrage of cannon and mortar fire from their position outside of Boston upon the British inside of Boston. The British immediately returned the gesture. The exchange continued on and off through March 4, but did little damage. Washington's intention, after all, was not to destroy, but to cause a loud distraction while his men, armed with Knox's cannon, advanced on the unoccupied heights of Dorchester. This they attempted on the night of March 4. With some four thousand troops and hundreds of wagons carrying thousands of pounds of weaponry, taking this high ground in secret, and directly in front of the British position, seemed an impossible feat. Even with the distraction of cannon fire and the scattered hay bales stretching across the landscape, which had been placed there earlier for concealment, it seemed doubtful.

Then, out of nowhere, a heavenly cover dropped down to provide concealment for the Americans. As one witness to the event, Reverend William Gordon, observed: "A finer [night] for working could not have been taken out of the whole 365. It was hazy below [the Heights] so that our people could not be seen, tho' it was a bright moon light night above on the hills."[34] Even David McCullough had to admit that it was "as if the hand of the Almighty were directing things."[35]

By the next morning at least twenty cannon and thousands of troops were in position to make a move. When daylight appeared, the shock was overwhelming to the British. "My God," exclaimed General Howe, "these fellows have done more work in one night than I could make my army do in three nights." One British officer reported back to London: "This morning at day break we discovered two redoubts on the hills of Dorchester Point. . . . They were all raised during the night, with an expedition equal to that of the genie belonging to Aladdin's wonderful lamp."[36] Another British officer looked upon the guns pointed down at Boston and simply declared that they had appeared "like magic" before his eyes.[37]

"Miracle number two," I declared to an excited Jimmy as I finished this part of the story.

"Yeah, but the British still had the advantage," Jimmy replied, "because Boston was like a fortress that could not be attacked. You told me Washington said it himself."

"That's right. But remember, I told you that this story is called the 'Quadruple Miracle at Boston,' not the 'Double Miracle.'" I smiled at my son. "We still have two more miracles to go."

Though shocked and less confident, Howe knew that his

soldiers and his Boston stronghold were still enough to defeat Washington. On March 5, Howe commanded his troops to jump into war boats, cross the harbor, and attack Washington, who stood bravely upon Dorchester. As the British troops pushed off into Boston Harbor in their advance toward the Americans, God launched miracle number three, which one of Washington's officers called the "hurrycane."[38] McCullough explains:

> What had been an abnormally warm, pleasant day had changed dramatically. . . . By nightfall, a storm raged, with hail mixed with snow and sleet. . . . Windows were smashed, fences blew over. Two of the [British transports] . . . were blown ashore. The American lieutenant Isaac Bangs, who was among those freezing at their posts on the high ground of Dorchester, called it the worst storm "that ever I was exposed to." Clearly there would be no British assault that night.[39]

Upon witnessing the storm, a Boston town official named Timothy Newell simply declared it to be "a manifest interposition of Divine Providence."[40] He knew, as everyone else knew, that hurricanes rarely hit New England, and if they do, they come during hurricane season—the fall months. For one to crash down suddenly in early spring on an otherwise pleasant day, and for it to hit right at *the* moment of military necessity, was inexplicable. There is no other word but *miracle*.

As Howe was considering his options, frightening reports were coming in. Smallpox had hit Boston—and hit it hard. Miracle number four! His men were falling physically, mentally, and emotionally. The British were losing their will to fight. "I could promise myself little success," wrote Howe, "by attacking them under all the disadvantages I had to encounter; wherefore

I judged it most advisable to prepare for the evacuation of the town."[41] And so the British left.

"The cannon, the fog, the hurricane, the smallpox," I recounted to Jimmy. "It was simply a quadruple dose of heaven too hot for the British to handle. The Lord drove them out!" My words echoed over the otherwise quiet hilltop.

In the wisdom of God, and through His power, the British withdrew, and Washington's well-intended but ill-conceived (even suicidal) plan to move on Boston would not be carried out. The Americans had been preserved that they might further prepare and fight another day. McCullough called it "the 'miracle' of Dorchester Heights."[42]

Washington would agree with McCullough. He confessed as much to his secretary, Joseph Reed, declaring that he did not ultimately "lament or repine at any Act of Providence," for, "whatever is, is right."[43] Additionally, in a letter to his brother, Washington explained that he now realized that "much blood was Saved, and a very important blow . . . prevented." Washington called it a "remarkable Interposition of Providence" and admitted that it was carried out by Heaven for a "wise purpose."[44]

As I finished recounting this story to my son, I explained how sad it was to me that the story had been hidden by most of our historians. I further explained that even when we find the precious few willing to tell the whole truth, rarely, if ever, is the vital point of it all emphasized. You see, Washington believed in the covenant on this land, which we understand from the Book of Mormon: "Inasmuch as ye shall keep my commandments ye shall prosper in the land" (2 Nephi 1:20). He was the modern-day version of Lehi. He was a Captain Moroni.

After Washington left that powerful prayer scene with Congress in Philadelphia and headed to Boston, consider his actions toward God and covenant—actions that led to the miracles. One of his very first instructions he gave to his soldiers at the Boston scene was to ban all "profane cursing, swearing and drunkenness" and to encourage "a punctual attendance on divine Service, to implore the blessings of heaven upon the means used for our safety and defense."[45] Mark these words well, for you will see them again and again streaming from the heart and mind of General Washington. This was the Washingtonian pattern. He did not just ask for prayers, and his ask certainly was not just some formality. He asked for righteous living. He asked for repentance. He recognized that America was under a covenant obligation—the blessings would be activated by righteousness. "And when we obtain any blessing from God, it is by obedience to that law upon which it is predicated" (D&C 130:21). And so Washington pled with his soldiers to "shew their Gratitude to providence, for thus favouring the Cause of Freedom and America" that they might "dese[r]ve his future blessings."[46]

And he was relentless on the point. Several times during his first months as commander-in-chief he forbade immoral behavior, to include gambling and religious intolerance.[47] Congress backed Washington by issuing, shortly after Washington took his command, the Declaration of the Causes and Necessity of Taking Up Arms. The document stated: "With a humble confidence in the mercies of the Supreme and impartial God and ruler of the universe, we most devoutly implore His divine goodness to protect us happily through this great conflict."[48] Days later, Congress backed this covenant with the announcement of a national day of prayer, which again called on Americans to "unfeignedly confess and deplore our many sins."[49] It was at this time that John Adams declared, during this month of national covenant awareness, that "millions will be upon their Knees at once before their great Creator, imploring his Forgiveness and Blessing; his Smiles on American Councils and Arms."[50]

But of all the covenant invocations that surrounded the events at Boston, the one that touches me the deepest was sent up by General Washington from the very ground Jimmy and I were standing upon. On March 6, 1776, almost immediately after having secured Dorchester Heights, and days before the British evacuation—indeed, right when the miraculous intervention would be needed—Washington issued the following General Order. It was a direct call to the American covenant.

> Thursday . . . being set apart by . . . this province as a day of fasting, prayer and humiliation, "to implore the Lord, and Giver of all victory, to pardon our manifold sins and wickedness's, and that it would please him to bless the Continental Arms with his divine favour and protection,"—All Officers, and Soldiers, are strictly enjoined to pay all due reverence, and attention on that day, to the sacred duties due to the Lord of hosts, for his mercies already received, and for those blessings, which our Holiness and Uprightness of life can alone encourage us to hope through his mercy to obtain.[51]

The quadruple miracle at Boston had not just "happened." It was by heavenly decree. It was God responding to the covenant on this land and recognizing that His American children were seeking to keep their end of the promise. "For if there be no faith among the children of men God can do no miracle among them; wherefore, he showed not himself until after their faith" (Ether 12:12). Washington and his people showed their faith. And God showed Himself.

Before Washington left New England, he would perpetuate

that covenant relationship by worshipping with the people and giving thanks to God. Washington listened to one clergyman preach a fitting sermon based on Exodus 14:25: "The Egyptians said, Let us flee from the face of Israel; for the Lord fighteth for them."[52] Another clergyman taught from Isaiah 36:20, a passage that has special implications for Latter-day Saints who know through revelation that America was to lay the foundation for the building of Zion and the New Jerusalem.[53] Declared the preacher: "Look upon Zion, the city of our solemnities; thine eyes shall see Jerusalem a quiet habitation, a tabernacle that shall not be taken down." As part of the sermon, Washington was congratulated for the service rendered to his fellow men and "before the altar of God bowed with them in gratitude to heaven."[54]

◆　◆　◆

Jimmy and I stood upon the hill of Dorchester in silence for a moment pondering this whole overwhelming scene. Suddenly, my mind flashed to another hill, south of where we were standing, which afforded a similar view into the Boston area—at least in 1775 it did. I saw a parallel scene. Another parent and another child standing on that nearby hill and pondering these same events. Abigail and John Quincy. I wanted to be like her. I wanted to teach my child about the covenant.

As Washington made his presence known upon Dorchester, Abigail—even she who would not "fly to the Woods"—climbed Penn's Hill once again, this time to witness the end of the story. She watched the final events. She watched the British sail away from her precious homeland. She knew what God had done. "Shurely it is the Lords doings," she declared, "and it is Marvelous in our Eyes."[55]

CHAPTER 3

Miracle at New York

When the British left Boston, it was no sign of their surrender. They just needed to regroup. They planned to come back stronger than ever. And they did.

Washington guessed correctly that the British would attack at the commercial and social hub of the continent—New York City. So he left with his troops and headed that way, arriving in April 1776. If he had been at all disadvantaged in Boston, Washington was next to hopeless in New York. In addition to the large population of Loyalists in New York, and the many bays, rivers, and waterways conducive to a British naval attack there, a fresh and enormous British fleet had recently arrived and joined with Howe's already powerful forces. By the end of June, this reinforced British fleet began its impressive advent into New York Harbor. With some four hundred ships, at least seventy of which were state-of-the-art warships with fifty guns or more, it was—at that time—the largest force ever sent forth by any one nation to another. One of Washington's men recorded, "I declare that I thought all London was afloat."[1] Furthermore, upon the decks of these ships were close to thirty thousand armed troops— more soldiers than the entire civilian population of New York or Philadelphia. With New York completely surrounded by water, the British could advance on land with these troops wherever and whenever they desired.

Washington, on the other hand—never having commanded a large-scale battle—led only a ragtag group of civilian soldiers numbering well under half the count of British troops; and most of these American volunteers had never even seen a battle, let alone fought in one.[2] Worse yet, Washington did not have even a single warship at his disposal.

But what he did have was a promise from the Lord on which he would rely. He had written to his close confidant in Philadelphia, John Adams, saying, "We have nothing my Dear Sir to depend upon, but the protection of a kind Providence."[3] To his other closest ally, his brother John, he wrote, "However, it is to be hoped that if our cause is just, as I do most religiously believe it to be, the same Providence, which has in many instances appeared for us, will go on to afford it aid."[4]

Washington's headquarters was at New York City on Manhattan Island, near to where the World Trade Center once stood. To the east was Long Island, separated from Manhattan by the mile-wide East River. Knowing the British would be disembarking upon Staten and Long Islands, Washington sent his troops over the river to Long Island and there met the redcoats. The first major battle of the war commenced there.

The superior British army struck hard and fast on August 27. The Americans were devastatingly defeated. Almost immediately, Washington lost between seven hundred and a thousand men, while Howe lost fewer than one hundred.[5] All the Americans could do was run back toward the western shores of Brooklyn, Long Island, in hopes of escaping over the East River back into New York City before the advancing enemy could catch up to them. The British responded by sending its fastest ships up the East River to cut off Washington's escape route, with the intention of surrounding the rebels on all sides. Howe knew that such

The Battle of Long Island.

action would compel an American surrender, as Washington's entire Continental army would be trapped. This would be the end of America's hope for independence. As one prominent historian stated, "If Washington and his army had been trapped in Brooklyn Heights . . . the war would have ended quickly."[6] After giving their all, the Americans were now in a devastatingly hopeless state, which is often when the Lord enters the scene.

As Washington and his army sat trapped at Brooklyn Heights, all they could do was think and hope upon their promise with heaven. They would hark back to a call to the national covenant Washington had made in conjunction with Congress a few months earlier, shortly after his soldiers arrived at New York. Certainly the wise general could have predicted this scenario, which was why that call had been so necessary.

GENERAL ORDERS, HEADQUARTERS, NEW YORK, MAY 15, 1776:

Friday [May] 17th, Instant to be observed as a day of fasting, humiliation and prayer, humbly to supplicate the mercy of Almighty God, that it would please him to pardon all our manifold sins and transgressions, and to prosper the Arms of the United Colonies, and finally establish the peace and freedom of America, upon a solid and lasting foundation.[7]

Again, let us not take for granted these words, which reflect the same sentiments Washington issued in his orders at Dorchester Heights. This was not a simple or formal prayer. It was the recognition of a covenant relationship. It was a call to repentance and righteousness, even those things that would bring the blessings of heaven. It was as if the American leadership were following Book of Mormon principles. Washington followed up the call shortly thereafter with another, which declared that "the fate of unborn Millions will now depend, under God, on the courage and conduct of this army. . . . Let us therefore rely upon the goodness of the Cause, and the aid of the Supreme Being, in whose hands Victory is."[8]

Within two months of Washington making these statements, his sentiments were backed by another scriptural event: the birth of the Declaration of Independence. Concerning latter-day America, the Lord declared, "I raised up [wise men] unto this very purpose, and redeemed the land by the shedding of blood" (D&C 101:80). The Declaration kicked off this redemptive movement, which led to the Constitution—a document the Lord also claimed as His own in this very verse of scripture. In the concluding paragraph of the Declaration of Independence, the founders wanted it known whose cause this was. "And for

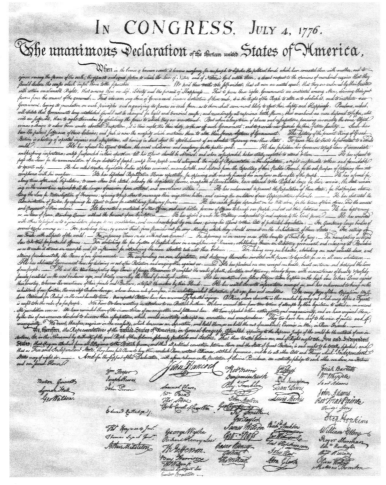

The Declaration of Independence.

the support of this Declaration," so the sacred document states, "with a firm reliance on the protection of Divine Providence, we mutually pledge to each other our Lives, our Fortunes, and our sacred Honor."

Washington was with his men in New York when word of the Declaration's issuance arrived. He instantly understood the powerful implications. He needed his men to understand too. And so he ordered that the Declaration be read to the army. In his General Order for the reading, dated July 9, 1776, he picked up where he had left off with his earlier invocations to God and covenant. He called for chaplains in each regiment to ensure that the soldiers "attend carefully upon religious exercises." The order also included the following: "The blessing and protection of Heaven are at all times necessary but especially so in times of public distress and danger—The General hopes and trusts, that every officer and man, will endeavour so to live, and act, as becomes a Christian soldier defending the dearest Rights and Liberties of his country."[9]

And again, just days before the battle at Long Island, Washington issued yet another General Order in which he recommended the keeping of the Sabbath and pleaded with his men to shun the immoral temptations that abounded in the city, exhorting them to "endeavor to check [such behavior] and . . . reflect, that we can have little hopes of the blessing of Heaven on our Arms, if we insult it by our impiety, and folly."[10] Such orders and encouragements from Washington are reminiscent of the actions of Captain Moroni, who fought in a different time but under the same national covenant. He declared to his own soldiers, "Surely God shall not suffer that we, who . . . take upon us the name of Christ, shall be trodden down and destroyed, until we bring it upon us by our own transgressions" (Alma 46:18).

One observant New Yorker, unaccustomed to seeing a pious group of soldiers, wrote of his surprise to see how Washington's men attended prayers "evening and morning regularly." "On the Lord's day," commented the observer, "they attend public worship twice, and their deportment in the house of God is such as becomes the place."[11] Washington's officers documented how they strived to live the covenant by holding prayer services and Bible studies.

The faith and influence of Washington was extended through other revolutionary leaders who caught his vision and acted upon it. One such leader, Connecticut Governor Jonathon Trumbull, upon learning of Washington's impending battle at New York, called for nine fresh regiments to march in support of Washington. In line with Washington's vision, Trumbull's call to arms sounded much like a call to the covenant: "Be roused and alarmed," declared Trumbull, "to stand forth in our just and glorious cause. Join . . . march on; this shall be your warrant: play the man for God, and for the cities of our God! May the Lord of Hosts, the God of the armies of Israel, be your leader."[12]

From a higher view, it seems the hosts of heaven would have been praying, cheering, supporting, and helping the American cause. Can we not suppose that the angels of God looked down upon Washington in his predicament at Long Island? Certainly those billions of deceased souls understood what hung in the balance, because it affected them on a very personal level. They had been waiting for priesthood and temples for hundreds, even thousands, of years. Millions upon millions were waiting for their work to be done, waiting for salvation. No government in the world had afforded the liberty necessary for the restoration of priesthood and temples to the earth. This was their chance. But that chance seemed to be fading quickly. Should Washington and his army be captured or destroyed, hope for freedom—the kind required for the Restoration—would disappear.

As Benjamin Franklin declared, "Tyranny is so generally established in the rest of the world that the prospect of an asylum in America for those who love liberty gives general joy. . . . It is a common observation here that our cause is the cause of all

A GLORIOUS CAUSE

"Never was a cause more important or glorious than that which you are engaged in; not only your wives, your children, and distant posterity, but humanity at large, the world of mankind, are interested in it; for if tyranny should prevail in this great country, we may expect Liberty will expire throughout the world. Therefore, more human *glory and happiness* may depend upon your exertions than ever yet depended upon any of the sons of men. . . . We expect soon to break off all kind of connection with Britain, and form into a Grand Republic of the American United Colonies, which will, *by the blessing of heaven, soon work out our salvation*."

—*From a 1776 letter published in the* New England Chronicle, *signed simply by "A Freeman"*[13]

mankind, and that we are fighting for their liberty in defending our own."[14] American revolutionary Thomas Paine also understood the universal possibilities of a new nation born of liberty: "We have it in our power to begin *the world* over again," wrote Paine in his renowned work *Common Sense*. He continued, "A situation, similar to the present, hath not happened since the days of Noah until now."[15]

This overwhelming burden on the shoulders of the American revolutionaries was not lost on the soldiers pinned down at Long Island. They knew what was at stake. As one of their leaders, Chaplain Samuel West, declared just weeks before the events at Long Island, "I cannot help hoping, and even believing, that Providence has designed this continent for to be the asylum of liberty and true religion."[16] It was as if these revolutionaries were reading out of the Book of Mormon: "and that after the waters had receded from off the face of this land [America] it became a choice land above all other lands, a chosen land of the Lord" (Ether 13:2).

Chaplain West continued his message from New York: "But do we not find that both religion and liberty seem to be expiring and gasping for life in the other continent?—where, then, can they find a harbor or place of refuge but in this?"[17] We see the Book of Mormon echoed once again amongst these brave American soldiers. "And it came to pass that I saw among the nations of the Gentiles the formation of a great church . . . which is most abominable above all other churches, which slayeth the saints of God, yea, and tortureth them and bindeth them down, and yoketh them with a yoke of iron, and bringeth them down into captivity" (1 Nephi 13:4–5).

Reflecting the light his commander–in–chief had been shining since he took control of the armies, Chaplain West provided the solution: "[God] will not forsake us if we do not forsake him. Our cause is so just and good that nothing can prevent our success, but only our sins."[18]

In that moment of despair at Long Island, the thought on most everyone's mind—mostly Washington's—was quite possibly something like this: "Have we done enough? Have we sufficiently forsaken our sins? So much is at stake right now in this very moment. Have we lived our covenant so as to expect the miracle? Because we need it now. Millions upon millions—at home and abroad, born and unborn—need it now!"

◆　◆　◆

The British continued to close in on Washington's army at Brooklyn, Long Island—British land troops threatening from the east and the British navy pushing up the river threatening from the west. The redcoats were already preparing dispatches back to London declaring the war over.

Washington finally spoke. He told his men that they would cross the river by cover of night, landing safely back in Manhattan. Then they would get out of New York altogether.

The obvious reply from Washington's war council was, *How?* Indeed, this was a tall order. With the British swarming about the land and water, it would seem impossible to secretly ferry more than nine thousand troops, along with their baggage, guns, horses, and equipment, across the mile-wide river, and all before the light of day exposed the scheme. If the British were to discover what was happening, it would be over for the Americans.

After laying out his plan, Washington pulled back and waited three days to execute it.[19] What was he waiting for? In the end, it seems he had received word from the Lord. It seems he was instructed from on high to wait. Apparently the timing had to be just right. The Lord was preparing something.

As the sun dropped on the third night, Washington turned to General Israel Putnam and declared: "God is propitious tonight."[20] The Lord was ready. Washington acted. He ordered his men to continue firing long-range guns through the darkness at the British land troops. He then ordered a few soldiers to maintain the noise and campfires indicative of a busy campsite, thus making the British believe the Americans were anything but on the move. The other men were ordered to the river's edge. It was August 29. The British were falling for the ruse.

Washington began loading his men on as many boats as he could find, borrow, or commandeer. The miracle began. The British navy, which should have otherwise already been in the waters Washington was crossing, was having a little problem. A ferocious wind from the north had been pushing the British back down. A total of five ships carrying more than seventy-two guns attempted but failed to advance up the river to cut off the Americans.[21] Washington would have the window of opportunity he had prayed for.

As the evacuation began, the Americans again fell into despair, as the same wind that kept the British from advancing up the river was also making it impossible for them to manage their overcrowded rowboats and transport their army westward to safety. Then, a little after nine, the wind miraculously shifted and blew in a westerly direction, facilitating the exodus with most favorable conditions.[22]

But even with the favorable wind, the night was dying fast. The rising sun would soon expose Washington's scheme. Another miracle was needed. David McCullough explains:

Troops in substantial number had still to be evacuated and at the rate things were going, it appeared day would dawn before everyone was safely removed. But again the "elements" interceded, this time in the form of pea-soup fog. It was called "a peculiar providential occurrence," "manifestly providential," "very favorable to the design," "an unusual fog," "a friendly fog," "an American fog." "So very dense was the atmosphere," remembers Benjamin Tallmadge, "that I could scarcely discern a man at six yards' distance." And as daylight came, the fog held, covering the entire operation no less than had the night . . . while over on the New York side of the river there was no fog at all.[23]

Washington waited until the last man evacuated Long Island, then he himself boarded a ferryboat. The escape was a success, and without a single casualty. Washington and his men would, yet again, live to fight another day.

Alexander Graydon, an eyewitness to the event, commented that "in less than an hour after [the complete evacuation], the fog having dispersed, the enemy was visible on the shore we had left."[24] The British were as bewildered as they had been when they awoke to see the American guns pointing down at them from Dorchester Heights. "That the rebel army had silently vanished in the night right under their very noses," according to McCullough, "was almost inconceivable." British Major Stephen Kemble wrote in his diary, "In the morning, to our great astonishment, [we] found they had evacuated . . . and the whole escaped to . . . New York." British General James Grant wrote, "We cannot yet account for their precipitate retreat."[25]

Once on the Manhattan side of the river, Washington recognized he was not yet out of the woods. The British were pursuing.

Washington directing the retreat from Long Island.

They had overtaken New York City and were hot on Washington's trail. Then, another miracle. As Washington watched for British movements, wondering what his best escape from Manhattan would be, he noticed a blazing fire in the city. The wind picked up and within twenty-four hours destroyed much of the (only recently) British-held city. British troops were highly distracted putting out the fire, allowing Washington another fortuitous window to get out of town. Commenting on the fire, General Washington concluded that "Providence, or some good honest fellow, has done more for us than we were disposed to do for our selves."[26]

McCullough summed up the entire miraculous event at New York:

> But what a close call it had been. How readily it could have gone all wrong—had there been no northeast wind to hold the British fleet in check through the day the Battle of Long Island was fought, not to say

Reverend John Witherspoon presided over the College of New Jersey (now Princeton University) and is known by many today as the most influential academic in American history. He was the personal mentor to one U.S. president, one vice president, more than fifteen delegates to the Continental Congress and Constitutional Convention, forty-nine members of the House of Representatives, twenty-eight senators, three Supreme Court Justices, eight U.S. district judges, three attorneys general, one secretary of state, and scores of other government officers and patriots.

the days immediately afterward. Or had the wind not turned southwest the night of August 29. Or had there been no fortuitous fog as a final safeguard when day broke. . . . Incredibly, yet again—fate, luck, Providence, the hand of God, as would be said so often—intervened.[27]

◆ ◆ ◆

I have spent dozens of hours standing beside the East River, peering at it from the shore. I remember once looking down at it from the Brooklyn Bridge, thinking how Washington surely could have used that bridge on the night of August 29, 1776.

Shortly thereafter, I found myself at the observation deck of the Empire State Building. I moved swiftly to the southern side of it and, once again, looked down upon the East River. I simply could not get enough of that river. I tried to imagine the thousands of soldiers being blown across it. In my mind's eye, I saw the stalled British ships, stuck in the background. I closed my eyes. I saw *the fog*.

Suddenly, I was ashamed for thinking Washington needed the Brooklyn Bridge. He had something so much better. Standing on that deck, eighty-six floors above the river, I remembered one of the signers of the Declaration of Independence—John Witherspoon. He knew what Washington had known in New York. And he revealed it to the world on that national day of fasting and prayer we discussed earlier, which Washington had called for shortly after arriving with his troops in New York. It was the national fast held on May 17, 1776. A deeply religious man, Witherspoon was certainly fasting with the rest of America on that day, per the request of the general. During the fast, he gave a sermon: "Nature affords countless chinks in its regular workings through which the Divine Artist . . . can govern events." He then got astonishingly specific. Indeed, on May 17 he prophesied the very miracle that the national fast would ultimately produce for Washington's forces several weeks later. "The armies of the enemy . . . are rendered irresolute," declared Witherspoon, "when . . . rains make the terrain of the final charge impassable; [and] an unforeseen fog brings operations to a halt."[28]

CHAPTER 4

Miracle at New Jersey

In the Book of Mormon account, Laman and Lemuel saw miracles. They saw an angel. And yet, they would not endure. So it was with many of Washington's one-time followers. Even for those who witnessed the miracles at Boston and New York, often those experiences were not enough. And many who were not there would simply describe what happened at New York as an absolute disaster for America. After all, Washington did lose the city. After the Colonial army left New York, more than sixteen thousand of the approximately twenty thousand American troops who began with Washington quit immediately, mostly by way of blatant desertion.[1]

And there stood the humiliated Washington in the middle of it all, leading the retreat out of New York southward through New Jersey. All Washington had was his remaining band of three thousand men—scarcely fifteen percent of the force he had commanded just weeks prior. And most of those remaining were due to be honorably discharged in a few months. With well over thirty thousand British troops possibly on his trail, it was no wonder he blurted out, while stroking his throat, "My neck does not feel as though it was made for a halter."[2] Washington commented about his feelings at this time, saying that "if I were to wish the bitterest curse to an enemy on this side of the grave, I should put him in my stead with my feelings. . . . In confidence I tell you that I never was in such an unhappy, divided state since I was born."[3]

Just when things could not possibly get worse, they did. During the retreat southward, Washington received word that the colonial governments, after learning of the New York "debacle," had lost interest in pursuing war and were refusing to send backup troops. According to the dispatch, his would-be new recruits were "divided & Lethargic . . . slumbering under the Shade of Peace and in the full Enjoyment of the Sweets of Commerce."[4]

The truth is, even before New York, the American cause for independence was not the popular movement we might have imagined. According to John Adams, over fifty percent of Americans—perhaps as much as sixty-five percent—believed at various times during the Revolution that the American sacrifice for independence was *not* worth it.[5] Why? For starters, by 1776 America possessed the *highest per capita wealth in the world.*[6] This record-breaking wealth was a product of British policies and benevolence. David McCullough reminds us that "the Americans of 1776 enjoyed a higher standard of living than any people in the world. . . . How people with so much, living on their own land, would ever choose to rebel against the ruler God had put over them and thereby bring down such devastation on themselves was . . . incomprehensible."[7] Another Pulitzer Prize-winning historian, Joseph Ellis, expressed a similar sense of bewilderment when, upon explaining how he understood why the faithful began the war (they indeed were justified), he concluded, "I'll be darned if I know why [they] stayed."[8] The justification simply seemed unworthy of the sacrifice.

After the loss of New York, support for the war was at its lowest point. The British knew this and wisely took advantage of it. They offered a "free and general pardon" to all American rebels, including a guarantee of the "preservation of their property, the restoration of their commerce, and the security of their most valuable rights," if they would but denounce the rebellion and swear a simple oath of "peaceable obedience" to the king, as they had done so often before the conflict.[9] Furthermore, if Washington and the leaders in the Congress would swear to the same, the British even promised to capitulate and concede to give them what they had asked for before the conflict, even to be "treated as a separate country within the framework of the empire" with "control over their own legislation and taxes."[10]

In response to this offer, thousands more would immediately betray the American cause, lining up to take their oaths.[11] With so much to lose in a land that had historically been good to its people, and with the British capitulating on some important points, it is easy to see why so many believed another round of peaceful discussions with the British would be worth it. Especially after the lessons the Battle of Long Island taught America about their severe military disadvantages against the world's superpower.

King George felt the same way as these peace-seeking Americans. He wondered out loud to his parliament how the American rebels could forget that "to be a subject of Great Britain, with all its consequences, is to be the freest member of any civil society in the known world." And though the king claimed to be "anxious to prevent . . . the effusion of blood" and would "receive the misled [revolutionaries] with tenderness and mercy," he expressed his duty not to let America go: "The object is too important, the spirit of the British nation too high, the resources with which God hath blessed her too numerous, to give up so many colonies which she has planted with great industry, nursed with great tenderness, encouraged with many commercial advantages, and protected and defended at much expense and treasure."[12]

His rationale made sense to most Americans, especially at the crucial moment of Washington's retreat. Even members of the Continental Congress, in whom Washington had trusted and upon whom he had depended for direction, had themselves blamed Washington during this time. Many of these congressmen fled Philadelphia for fear of being captured.[13] A few congressmen even betrayed the cause, offering their services to the enemy.[14] As one-time patriots began switching over to the British side by the thousands, the enemy was well aware of America's hopeless state. "The fact is," reported one British captain in the field, "their army is broken all to pieces, and the spirit of their leaders and their abettors is all broken. . . . I think one may venture to pronounce that it is well nigh over with them."[15] He was correct. By all reasonable accounts, the war was over. America had lost.

The voice of reason spoke loud and clear to Washington: "George! Enlisted men! Stop the madness! Accept the pardon! Go back to your plantations and farms. Go back to your families. Go back to the comforts of being the wealthiest nation per capita in the world. Go back to the pleasure of being counted amongst the freest societies on earth. The king's generous offer provides you with what you have asked for. Give his proposal a chance. Everyone else seems to see this and has surrendered. Nobody will blame you. It is over! Give it up!"

And yet George Washington would not listen to reason. He rejected the peace terms and the pardon and continued his sad and lonely retreat southward, his small army intact and willing to fight.

By turning down the royal pardon and continuing the fight, Washington was sealing his fate if captured. And by all estimations at the time, he would be captured. He had been given his chance, and Britain would not forgive him for rejecting it. As best-selling author and historian Stephen Ambrose pointed out, had Washington been captured, "He would have been brought to London, tried, found guilty of treason, ordered executed, and then drawn and quartered."

> Do you know what that means? He would have had one arm tied to one horse, the other arm to another horse, one leg to yet another, and the other leg to a fourth. Then the four horses would have been simultaneously whipped and started off at a gallop, one going north, another south, another east and the fourth to the west. That is what Washington was risking to establish your freedom and mine.[16]

And so the question remains unanswered by almost all trained historians. *Why? Why would Washington pursue this course of action?*

But no historian, even searching high and low for historical evidences, could ever tell us why, as only God can fully explain it. The Lord did, after all, reveal that He "raised [him] up unto this very purpose, and redeemed the land by the shedding of blood" (D&C 101:80). It is this spiritual foundation, not secular knowledge alone, that allows us to understand the actions of Washington and the few who stayed with him. No secular-based historian can explain why Washington did what he did any more than they can explain why Moses put everything on the line and did what he did, challenging the Pharaoh; or why Joseph Smith sacrificed all in doing what he did, challenging the religious establishment of the world. In each of these cases, God's chosen ones were acting on inspiration, having been "raised up unto this very purpose." And though admittedly Washington was not a prophet in the mold of Moses or Joseph, he was the closest thing God had to a prophet in that time. For his inspired actions, though not fully understood by the world in which he lived, laid the groundwork for the Restoration. Brigham Young understood this, which is why he declared that "It was the voice of the Lord inspiring

Washington was never really alone. By war's end, out of the fifty-six signers of the Declaration of Independence, nine had been killed, five had been captured and suffered great pains at hands of the British, twelve had seen their homes burned, looted, or otherwise destroyed, and others literally went bankrupt investing all they possessed into the cause.[17]

[Washington and] all those worthy men who bore influence in those trying times, not only to go forth in battle but to exercise wisdom in council, fortitude, courage, and endurance in the tented field."[18]

It was not only during this crucial moment on his retreat that Washington would show such unimaginable dedication, even at the great risk of losing everything he held dear. To be sure, Washington would push every human limit, both physical and emotional, throughout the entirety of the conflict. He would, for example, regularly rally his men by dangerously, even insanely, riding out beyond the front lines, coming within one hundred yards of the enemy, while aides would rush out to grab the bridle of his horse, forcing him to safety.[19] At one point, while British ships made plans to extort the plantations lining the Potomac River for supplies, including Washington's dear Mount Vernon, Washington expressed to his estate's caretaker that it would be "less painful . . . that . . . they burnt my House and laid the Plantation in ruins" than to comply with their demands for supplies.[20] What's more, Washington would make all these sacrifices while refusing any and all payment due to him for his service, even though his long absence was forcing him to neglect his business, thus diminishing his overall wealth.[21]

Furthermore, there is no convincing evidence to explain any alternative intention for his sacrifices, other than his love of God, country, and covenant. By all accounts, what Washington desired more than anything else was a private life at his beloved Mount Vernon. "By God," Washington would say, "I had rather be on my farm."[22] As commander of the Continental army, as chairman of the Constitutional Convention, and as president of the United States, Washington openly and repeatedly expressed his great reluctance to accept, and temptation to abandon, such callings due to his overwhelming desire to return to his neglected family, work, and peace at home.[23] Mount Vernon was *always* his to return to, from the time before his appointments (he could have declined), to the British offer of general pardon (he could have accepted), and on through his entire service to his country after the war (he could have retired). Yet he denied himself, just as his faithful contemporaries denied themselves of their own "Mount Vernons" and instead risked death for the sake of God and country.

◆　◆　◆

By December 1776, Washington's trek southward ended in Pennsylvania. He was camped with his men along the Delaware River. And he was thinking of doing something utterly insane. He desired to cross the river and attack the British at Trenton, New Jersey. That was especially crazy because it wasn't just any British force in control of Trenton. It was a mercenary group of German combatants hired by the British. The most professional and feared soldiers in the world. The Hessians. Washington was

JAMES MADISON'S FIRST IMPRESSION

Many years after the Revolutionary War, James Madison would work closely with Washington to create the United States Constitution—a document that the Lord claimed contains "just and holy principles" (D&C 101:77). But Madison first laid eyes on Washington during the retreat from New York. Madison described what he saw:

"I saw him in my earliest youth, in the retreat through Jersey, at the head of a small band, or rather in its rear, for he was always next [to] the enemy, and his countenance and manner made an impression on me which time can never efface. . . . I counted the force under his immediate command by platoons as it passed me, which amounted to less than 3,000 men. A deportment so firm, so dignified, so exalted, but yet so modest and composed, I have never seen in any other person."[24]

taking his motley group of citizen-soldiers up against the equivalent of our modern Navy SEALS.

He needed another miracle or two. He needed the Lord.

The righteous members of Congress knew his need and implored heaven once again. On December 11, 1776, the covenant was invoked once more, as the nation was officially asked to "implore of Almighty God the forgiveness of the many sins prevailing among all ranks, and to beg the countenance as assistance of his Providence in the prosecution of the present just and necessary war."[25]

The fact that Washington's army was meager, hungry, weary, and ill-equipped was just one of the great disadvantages forced upon him. Worse, perhaps, was the fact that he could not possibly keep his movements or whereabouts a secret, especially among a population that was becoming more and more afraid of the British and less and less supportive of Washington. Traitors and spies watched the American troops, only too happy to report to the enemy.

Notwithstanding, Washington decided he would cross the river on Christmas night and launch a surprise attack on the Hessians. British spies had learned of the American scheme. On December 23, a Dr. William Bryant, who lived near Trenton, called upon Colonel Johann Rall, who commanded the Hessians at Trenton. Bryant had come to pass along reports of American movements on the other side of the river. Colonel Rall readied the Hessians. Washington would walk right into their trap. The Hessians became convinced that the reports had been accurate when they spotted American gunmen approaching Trenton on the afternoon of December 25. A small battle ensued, leaving eight Hessians wounded. The Americans were driven back.

Satisfied that the predicted attack had taken place, and that the Americans had failed completely, Colonel Rall told his men to continue manning their posts while he enjoyed the rest of his Christmas playing a game of cards in the home of a friend in downtown Trenton.

In the meantime, Washington was gathering his men for their preplanned nighttime crossing of the Delaware. A Pennsylvania farmer spotted the Americans preparing for the crossing and immediately sent a note to inform Colonel Rall, who was still deep in his card game. When his servant brought him the note, Rall placed it in his pocket without reading it. He had no reason to expect another attack, after the first one revealed to him how small and weak the American effort had been. He knew his advantage. In the end, no action was made to respond to this very valuable intelligence.

But here is the funny thing. The miraculous thing. Washington had not sent anybody that afternoon to attack or probe at the Hessians. In fact, he knew nothing of the event. Some historians believe it may have been a patrol from a Virginia regiment. Others surmise that a group of angry local farmers, unaware of Washington's plans, had coincidentally come on a rampage to insult and harass the unpopular Hessians over some local grievance.[26] Nobody knows for sure. I, for one, believe in angels.

But whatever happened, this mysterious attack had the fortuitous effect of psychologically disarming the Hessians. Later on, when Washington first learned of it, he was furious, as he initially believed the mysterious action might have tipped off the British. He later realized it was a blessing. As one of his officers, Joseph Reed, concluded, this "truly casual or rather providential" event "baffled [the enemy's] vigilance."[27] The failed "phantom attack," coupled with the general perception that Washington's army was running scared, with its morale in a tailspin, led Rall and his men to feel they had little to fear. Many of them decided to go ahead and enjoy their holiday.

And so, unaware of this fortuitous gift, on Christmas night Washington divided his men into three parties. They crossed at separate locations over the Delaware River. Washington had ordered the attack to commence at the dawn of the next day. The operation got off to a bad start when large ice chunks in the river delayed the crossing. Washington's main concern at the time was to land without alerting the enemy. He knew a surprise attack was his only real advantage against the professional warriors awaiting him in Trenton. As his troops were landing on the New Jersey shore, Washington was faced with a frightful reality: the delays had now made it impossible to use the darkness of night as cover, as was the plan. The earliest the Americans could get to Trenton would be well after sunrise. Some of Washington's men surmised that he would have to call off the attack, as daylight would certainly expose the secret scheme.

One man knew better. His name was Benjamin Rush. He was the army's physician and a signer of the Declaration of Independence. Dr. Rush had been with General Washington the day before. As Rush was relaying information to Washington, he noted that the general was distracted, "play[ing] with his pen and ink upon several small pieces of paper. . . . One of them by accident fell upon the floor near my feet," remembered Rush. "I was struck with the inscription upon it. It was 'Victory or Death.'"[28] Washington had been writing out on paper the secret call sign to be used by his commanders in the field to sound the attack on Trenton. Rush knew Washington would not let something as common as sunlight get in his way. Washington knew, after all, whose errand he was on.

Though the weather had been sunny and calm leading up to

Washington crossing the Delaware.

the night of Washington's crossing, making one believe it would continue that way until the hour of attack, all of that changed, as things so often do when the Lord is running the show.[29] The Lord makes up for our delays. He can hide His foot soldiers when He needs to. The Lord began His preparation by sending a powerful storm over the Delaware right at the time of the crossing. Even as the sun began to rise, the enemy could not see or hear them coming.

After disembarking, Washington led his men on the nine-mile, covert march into Trenton. "Soldiers keep by your officers. For God's sake, keep by your officers." These were the words constantly being uttered to the footsore soldiers by a calm and serene Washington. He traveled on horseback up and down the line of parading soldiers, making sure they stayed together and battle-ready along the road. The soldiers remembered Washington encouraging them on "in a deep and solemn voice."[30] The Lord's storm would remain healthy, thus covering the Americans (both the sound and sight of them) along their trek until the early morning attack.

At just after eight o'clock on the morning of December 26, 1776, Nathanael Greene, one of Washington's most trusted officers, led the charge into Trenton. The Lord's cover had worked, and He literally *had their backs.* "The storm continued with great violence," wrote Henry Knox, "but was in our backs & consequently in the faces of our Enemy."[31] The Hessians were completely caught off guard. Knox noted that "the hurry, fright and confusion of the enemy was not unlike that which will be when the last trump will sound."[32]

After a violent display of house-to-house fighting, which lasted about forty-five minutes, the Hessians laid down their weapons and surrendered. With more than one hundred Hessians killed or wounded, and another nine hundred of them captured, Washington stood victorious with just a handful of casualties of his own.[33] Knox concluded that "Providence seemed to have smiled upon every part of this enterprise."[34] Among the brave American soldiers standing proud at battle's end were several future greats: Alexander Hamilton (first U.S. secretary of the treasury), John Marshall (second U.S. chief justice of the Supreme Court), and James Monroe (fifth U.S. president).[35]

Lying dead at the end of that bloody day of battle was Hessian Colonel Johann Rall. He was buried in the western graveyard of the First Presbyterian Church in downtown Trenton. Forgotten.

◆　◆　◆

In studying this great battle at Trenton, I had always felt drawn to Colonel Rall. I don't know why. He just intrigued me. He had traveled so far to fight a war that was not his, working for a country he was unconnected to, fighting against a country he was even less connected to. He was just doing the job he was paid to do. On the night Washington was crossing the Delaware,

Surrender of Colonel Rall.

he sat calmly and happily playing cards with his friends. He had every reason to believe he was doing his job, even as he slipped that valuable note—that life-saving piece of intelligence—into his pocket without reading it. In his defense, he did not speak English, so he would have needed to call for a translator, who was no doubt also trying to enjoy what was left of Christmas Day. He would eventually get to it.

I wanted to visit Rall. So I recently made a trip to Trenton. I drove all around the battlefield—a most interesting "battlefield." It is actually the city itself. As I spotted the Revolutionary-era buildings dotting the now modernized city, I imagined the chaos, gun smoke, yelling, and fear that filled the streets on the morning of December 26, 1776. I pictured Washington's men fighting bayonet-to-bayonet, fist-to-face, hand-to-hand, against the feared Hessians. I saw them in my mind's eye knocking down doors. I imagined them crashing through windows. Taking the town.

I drove up the hill to the junction of Warren and Broad Streets, which offers a splendid view into the city. No wonder Washington directed the attack from this location, now marked by a monument to the general. I pictured him watching the action below and I chuckled to myself when recalling his (always) humble and respectful description of the confused and defeated enemy. The surprise, he declared, made the Hessians bewildered, "undetermined how to act"[36] (hardly the stinging trash talk many would have inappropriately hurled down the hill).

Descending the hill, I turned onto State Street. As I passed the location of the house Rall played cards in that fateful night, I looked ahead down the same street and saw the church graveyard his body would lie in shortly afterward. As I entered the churchyard and gravesite of the First Presbyterian Church, I could not believe church services still took place there. It had the appearance of a condemned building (or at least one that should have been), and the graveyard was even worse. Unable to read any of the inscriptions on the tombstones, I tracked down a local historian nearby.

"Colonel Rall?" she asked, replying to my inquiry. "Yes, he is buried in that old churchyard, but you will never find the exact location. His grave was covered by that parking lot that has invaded much of the cemetery. There was a decent placard upon the church wall memorializing the fact that he is buried somewhere in the churchyard, but someone stole it a few months ago. Presumably to sell it as scrap metal."

Back in the graveyard, I saw the screw holes in the church wall where the placard once hung. Thus ended my attempt to pay my respects to the colonel.

As I stood there in the cemetery, lost in thought, I grew sad. Not for Colonel Rall (I'm sure he's just fine), but for the story he represents. Though he did not know it in the moment, he was the unassuming actor in a play inundated by miracles, unnatural courage, unprecedented faithfulness, angels, and a cause so important that countless millions would eventually be blessed by it. I was sad because just as the memory of Rall had been forgotten and sold for scrap metal, so had the story he represents. We have forgotten this story—a story brought to us by God Almighty. Forgotten. The tragedy of that forgetting lies in the fact that God brought it to us for a purpose: to teach us how to build and maintain one nation under God, even that foundation required for the restored gospel. This is a covenant land. The Lord, through Washington, has tried to teach us through history (as He always does by way of His holy scriptures) how to live this covenant. But *we the people* don't want to listen, even as we watch America (the gospel's sociopolitical foundation) deteriorate like the graveyard at Trenton's First Presbyterian Church.

I stood in the middle of the graveyard all alone. The city noise faded into silence as I replayed the death scene of Colonel Rall. Reportedly, as he lay there after being shot from his horse by a colonial sharpshooter, he began to whisper his dying refrain. As witnesses got closer, they heard these words: "If I had read this, I would not be here now."[37] He had finally taken that note, with its life-saving intelligence, out of his pocket and figured out what it said. But it was too late. I found myself hoping that America soon takes out of its pocket the life-saving note that God has placed there. American history. The scriptures. The national covenant. For it is getting late.

◆　◆　◆

In the wake of Trenton, hope for America had returned. However, within the week a new year would begin. On

January 1, 1777, all enlistments would expire. Almost the entire Continental army, at least what was left of it, would be free to go home. Washington knew this would cripple the Revolution, if not end it. As he had written to Congress a few days before the attack, "ten days more will put an end to the existence of our army."[38] With Congress helpless to respond, Washington did the only thing he could do. He gathered his troops. The drum roll began, and the general asked all those willing to extend their tours to step forward. Not a soul budged. A depressed Washington turned his horse and began riding away. Then suddenly he stopped, returned to his men, and said:

> My brave fellows, you have done all I asked you to do, and more than could be reasonably expected, but your country is at stake, your wives, your houses, and all that you hold dear. You have worn yourselves out with fatigues and hardships, but we know not how to spare you. If you will continue to stay one month longer, you will render that service to the cause of liberty, and to your country, which you can probably never do under any other circumstance.[39]

If ever there was a Captain Moroni / Title of Liberty moment during the American war for independence, this was it. Washington's message was remarkably similar to that given by Moroni, who had pled with his soldiers to take up arms and fight for God and freedom, for wives and for children (see Alma 46:12–13).

As the drums began to sound again, the men this time stepped forward. According to Nathanael Greene, "God Almighty inclined their hearts to listen to the proposal and they engaged anew."[41] Washington would capitalize on the spirit accompanying

THE AMERICAN CRISIS
BY THOMAS PAINE

Shortly before he ordered the attack on Trenton, Washington asked his men to read the newly published work by Thomas Paine called *The American Crisis*. That book contains the following words:

"These are the times that try men's souls. The summer soldier and the sunshine patriot will, in this crisis, shrink from the service of their country; but he that stands by it now, deserves the love and thanks of man and woman. Tyranny, like hell, is not easily conquered; yet we have this consolation with us, that the harder the conflict, the more glorious the triumph. . . . Heaven knows how to set a proper price upon its goods; and it would be strange indeed, if so celestial an article as freedom should not be highly rated."[40]

this renewal of covenant and attack the enemy forthwith, this time up the road from Trenton at another British stronghold—the town of Princeton, New Jersey.

The British, aware of such a possibility, employed one of their brightest field commanders, Lord Charles Cornwallis, to protect Princeton. Upon arriving at Princeton on January 1, 1777, an anxious Cornwallis left a portion of his troops to guard the town, and then led over five thousand troops down the ten-mile road to Trenton to squash the rebellion once and for all. With the temperature above freezing, the muddy roads made it very difficult for the British to mobilize troops and cannon. Washington, nestled in at Trenton, knew Cornwallis was coming, as American forces guarding Trenton had clashed briefly with Cornwallis's front guard. Not wanting to push his fatigued soldiers into battle right away, Cornwallis pulled back and camped his men just outside of view from Washington. We will "bag the fox" in the morning, he told his men.[42]

But when the British arose and launched their attack at dawn, not an American was to be found. Like at Long Island, Washington had managed to fool the British by keeping a few soldiers behind to stoke the fires, giving the perception that they had camped down for the night, when in reality the Americans had mobilized.

But this time they were not on retreat. In an almost insanely risky move, Washington, in the dead of night, led thousands of troops with horses, baggage, and cannon through obscure back roads that twisted right around Cornwallis's position. Though the Americans were traveling over the same muddy roads that had slowed Cornwallis only hours earlier, a providential drop in the temperature had frozen the roads, making it possible for the Americans to move their carriages and cannon rapidly.[43]

The Battle of Princeton.

By morning, when Cornwallis realized he had been duped, Washington was already hitting the British stronghold at Princeton. "I believe," declared Knox, "they [the British at Princeton] were as astonished as if an army had dropped perpendicularly upon them."[44] And why wouldn't they be astonished? With Cornwallis having just left in the direction of the American rebels, the prospect of Washington getting through him to Princeton would have been nothing short of miraculous. Yet it had happened.

The battle of Princeton was more violent and furious than that at Trenton. Sensing his troops' need of spirit and courage, Washington would lead the charge himself on horseback. "Parade with me, my brave fellows," one soldier recalled Washington yelling as he pulled out in front of the enemy. When Washington got within thirty yards of the enemy line, he gave the command to fire. The British returned the gesture. Colonel John Fitzgerald, one of Washington's staff officers, immediately covered his eyes with his hat. Knowing the mounted Washington had made himself a sitting duck for the British, he could not bring himself to witness the fall of such a great leader. When he pulled his hat away, the gun smoke was just subsiding. There sat Washington on his horse, exactly where Fitzgerald had seen him last. The British line broke, and the redcoats were on the run. "It's a fine day for a fox chase, my boys," declared Washington as he and his men gave chase.[45]

"I shall never forget," wrote one young officer who was present, "what I felt . . . when I saw him brave all the dangers of the field and his important life hanging as it were by a single hair with a thousand deaths flying around him. Believe me, I thought not of myself."[46] As other American troops entered in from strategic points around the town, the British surrendered.

The campaigns at Trenton and Princeton, though minor battles in and of themselves, had an enormous effect throughout the colonies. Author Mercy Warren, who personally witnessed the Revolution, wrote that "there are no people on earth, in whom a spirit of enthusiastic zeal is so readily enkindled, and burns so remarkably conspicuous, as among the Americans" and that Washington's victories created a "change instantaneously wrought in the minds of men."[47]

McCullough concluded that even though it had been only weeks earlier that America was bogged down in "as dark a time as any in the history of the country . . . suddenly, miraculously it seemed, that had changed because of a small band of determined men and their leader."[48] Though McCullough was most likely, and rightly, referring to Washington as this leader, the true leader of the victories was One who sat in a higher realm. Washington himself understood and believed this. Days after his victory at Princeton, he declared: "Providence has heretofore saved us in remarkable manner, and on this we must principally rely."[49] Convinced more than ever that his success on the battlefield was fully contingent on the binding power of America's national covenant with the Almighty, Washington would "principally rely" on it again and again.

CHAPTER 5

Miracles of 1777 and 1778

After Washington's great successes at Trenton and Princeton, he had become a hero, a legend, a superstar. Congress had given him immense powers now, and thousands of new recruits would fall in line to work under him. This is usually when good men begin to go bad. "We have learned by sad experience that it is the nature and disposition of *almost all men,* as soon as they get a little authority, as they suppose, they will immediately begin to exercise unrighteous dominion" (D&C 121:39; emphasis added).

The question for America was, What would Washington do in his moment of triumph? Would Washington gamble away the moment the way "almost all men" would have done in deference to personal pride and selfish power? Or would he hold his calling as sacred and use it only in humility and righteousness?

Washington's mother, Mary Ball Washington, was in Virginia when news of her son's great victory arrived. Neighbors dashed to her side to praise her son. She listened as they told her how George was the most illustrious general in the world, how the soldiers idolized him, how he was the savior of his country.

The wise mother, bothered, looked at them without expression. She only replied, "We must not forget the great Giver in our joy over the success in arms." She continued, "George will not forget the lessons I have taught him." She most certainly pondered over her parting words to her son as he marched off to battle for the first time: "Remember that God is our sure trust. To him I commend you. . . . My son, neglect not the duty of secret prayer."[1]

◆　◆　◆

When I was only eleven years old, not long before I had my experience at the church window, I was planning what was, at that time, the greatest adventure of my life. My fifth-grade class was taking a week-long field trip to Pennsylvania to study the American Revolution. I was excited and scared—I had never been away from my family for so long a period. "Remember who you are, Timmy!" my mom told me before I left for the airport. "And say a prayer when you get scared." Not *if*, but *when*. She knew me too well. By day's end, I was standing near Valley Forge—the very place Washington resided with his army the winter after his victories at Trenton and Princeton. Our class was staying at a small school campus designed for the education of youth: Freedoms Foundation at Valley Forge. When we got there, we had an hour or so to unpack and settle into our dorm rooms. I immediately felt lonely and scared, and the dark dorm room was not helping. I thought about my mom and how she had told me to pray. I went outside where there was still sunlight to do just that.

As I walked around the campus looking for a private location, I stumbled upon something that immediately warmed my heart and mesmerized my young mind. I didn't recognize at the time that what I was feeling was the Spirit of God testifying to me of the truthfulness of what I was seeing. I only knew that I no longer felt alone or nervous. And it was magical. What I was looking at was a large statue of George Washington kneeling in prayer. It would be years before I fully understood exactly what truth was being depicted in the large piece of sculpted art. But eventually

Washington statue at Freedoms Foundation, Valley Forge.

I found out. Just as I had gone to Valley Forge and heeded the call of my mother in 1987, so had Washington done the same in 1777.

Washington's mother had been correct about her son. Even on the heels of success, he knew to Whom the credit belonged. He did not forget the national covenant. Shortly after Trenton and Princeton, Washington made it clear that the number-one resource his country had was God Almighty. It was upon Him, the general declared, that the army would "principally rely."[2] To ensure this heavenly partnership, throughout 1777 and 1778, Washington and Congress released a flood of calls to the nation to remember God and live righteously.

And the calls to God paid off in the fall of 1777.

It all began when the British, under General John Burgoyne, were on the move from Canada. Marching southward through New York, Burgoyne intended to cut off the New England

AN ORDER FROM THE GENERAL

All the troops . . . except the guards, are to attend Divine worship tomorrow morning at the second bell; the officers commanding corps, are to take especial care, that their men appear clean, and decent, and that they are to march in proper order to the place of worship. . . . The honorable Congress having recommended it to the United States to set apart the 6th of May next to be observed as a day of fasting, humiliation, and prayer, to acknowledge the gracious interpositions of Providence; to deprecate deserved punishment for our sins and ingratitude, to unitedly implore the protection of Heaven . . . the Commander-in-Chief enjoins a religious observance of said day and directs the Chaplains to prepare discourses proper for the occasion.

—George Washington, Headquarters, April 12, 1777[3]

colonies from those in the South. While en route through up-state New York, the British were met by American forces near Saratoga. Two battles were fought within weeks of each other. In the end, the British were forced to surrender.

But it's in the details where we see God's hand. Indeed, it's in the details where we see a sharp contrast between the two opposing armies—one working under God and covenant, the other not. Two pivotal decisions shaped the course of events at the battles at Saratoga.

American General Arthur St. Clair commanded the defense of Fort Ticonderoga, the American base in upstate New York, north of Saratoga. As reports of Burgoyne's movement reached St. Clair in the summer of 1777, he knew he had to make a decision.[4] In those days, retreat of any kind was met with general scorn from the public. However, St. Clair knew that if he stayed and fought, he would needlessly watch many of his men fall and would eventually lose the fort anyway. He humbly made the decision to abandon the fort to Burgoyne and head southward toward Saratoga—a decision that would see him court-martialed. He was eventually exonerated, but he was stripped of his command, never to lead Revolutionary forces again. But the decision was the correct one. It allowed St. Clair's men to fall back, regroup, and join with other American forces. Horatio Gates ended up with command of the now stronger and more prepared American troops, who began laying the trap at Saratoga.[5]

Burgoyne would be faced with a similar decision in the months and weeks ahead. Proud and arrogant, the British general was not cut from the same cloth as St. Clair or the other God-fearing Americans. As he gave chase to the retreating American soldiers, he paused, waited, then moved sluggishly. Had he advanced rapidly, he likely would have ended the conflict and been victorious. But doing so would have required him to abandon the large stores of material goods he had selfishly seized for his personal gain, including the fine china he and his men loved and refused to part with. Furthermore, while the British meandered, they entertained themselves with alcohol and the large entourage of prostitutes (hundreds of them) that Burgoyne permitted to follow along. With his own mistress in tow, he could hardly deny his men the sinful pleasure.[6] As the award-winning Washington biographer Stephen Brumwell commented, "When not fighting the enemy or one another, [British soldiers] preferred to amuse themselves with gambling, drinking, and whoring."[7] In the meantime, Washington repeatedly rebuked such behavior in his own men. He was issuing official pleas to the Almighty and demanding strict moral behavior of his soldiers. That the Americans were fighting under a covenant with the Lord, and that the British were not, is quite clear.

> General George Washington, Headquarters, May 31, 1777:
>
> "It is much to be lamented that the foolish and scandalous practice of profane swearing is exceedingly prevalent in the American Army. Officers of every rank are bound to discourage it, first by their example, and then by punishing offenders. As a mean to abolish this and every other species of immorality, Brigadiers are enjoined to take effectual care to have Divine Service duly performed in their respective brigades."[8]

While Burgoyne's unenthusiastic advance only weakened the British, the Americans grew stronger and strategized their new position smartly. As Burgoyne inched his way toward Saratoga and the awaiting American forces, he was counseled by his officers to reconsider his options. The Americans had been given too much time and were now well prepared. It was time for Burgoyne to admit his error and return to nearby British Fort Edward to await reinforcements. But turning back would look like retreat. This was something Burgoyne—unlike St. Clair—was unwilling to consider.[9] Public perception and personal vanity meant too much. Instead he walked into battle. The British were astonished at the bravery of the Americans. Though the British had always assumed the Americans were cowards and would fight only from behind redoubts or strongholds, they witnessed something very different at Saratoga. The Continental army stood face-to-face in the open countryside with the famed and feared British and Hessian frontlines. One British officer on the scene commented that "the courage and obstinacy with which the Americans fought were the astonishment of everyone."[10] The British were defeated.

Washington understood that it was America's covenant that provided the victory. Upon learning of the triumph, he promptly ordered services of thanksgiving and stated, "Let every face brighten, and every heart expand with grateful Joy and praise to the supreme disposer of all events, who has granted us this signal success."[11]

This American victory was significant not only in that it demonstrated the power of adhering to the national covenant, but also in that it provided the proof required by would-be American allies that the American cause was winnable. As a direct result of Saratoga, France began its full and indispensable support of the American Revolution.[12]

Though St. Clair suffered a damaged reputation for giving up Fort Ticonderoga, Washington knew better. He loved St. Clair. Washington would remember that on the night before he attacked Princeton, most of his officers had opted for a retreat, knowing Cornwallis would attack their position at Trenton in the morning. It was St. Clair who put faith in Washington and suggested the risky sneak attack on Princeton, which ultimately turned the tide of the war in favor of America. No, Washington would not turn his back on Arthur St. Clair, though the rest of the world seemed to want that. Instead, Washington assigned St. Clair to serve out the remainder of the war at his side—a trusted aide and friend to the great general.[13]

While the American forces under Gates were busy taking care of the British at Saratoga, George Washington was battling the enemy outside of Philadelphia. British General William Howe had left New York to take the American capital, and Washington was prepared to do what he could to stop him. The battles of Germantown and Brandywine Creek were the result. Ultimately, the British broke through Washington's lines and took Philadelphia. But this does not mean God was not there for the Americans. In fact, upon exploring the details, it appears He *was* there and His will *was* done. But why would God want the British to take Philadelphia? I will get to that in a moment. First, let's briefly discuss the battles, that we might see the hand of God once again.

On September 11, 1777, Washington's line stood bravely near Brandywine Creek, between the enemy and the Revolution's capital, Philadelphia. But the British powerhouse overwhelmed them, sending them on the run. By all accounts, Howe was in a perfect position to pursue Washington and capture his army, per-haps ending the Revolution. For some unknown reason, however, Howe waited several days before making his advance. He caught up to the Americans on September 16. Washington's men bravely did an about-face and looked squarely at their inevitable destruc-tion. Just as the two sides made their move toward each other, a crash of thunder sounded from above. A torrential downpour of rain followed. One soldier on the field recounted: "It came down

THE BIBLES OF THE REVOLUTION

In 1777, the Continental Congress approved an order for 20,000 Bibles to be printed and distributed to patriots in every colony. Congress justified its order by declaring that "the use of the Bible is so universal, and its importance so great." By 1781 the Bibles arrived. They were known as the Bibles of the Revolution.[14]

so hard that in a few moments we were drenched and sank in mud up to our calves."[15]

The dark rain clouds dropped unnaturally low so as to hide the combatants from each other. Gunpowder became soaked and useless.[16] Even if the British could have seen the Americans through the fog, the wind and mud made a bayonet charge nearly impossible. Both sides packed it up and left the would-be scene of battle. Once again, the Americans were spared. The cause would live on. The event would go down in history as "The Battle of the Clouds." Historian Edward Gifford Jr. simply called it "the peace of God."[17]

Howe had taken Philadelphia. But Washington was not done. He took a breath and regrouped. Then, on October 4, after learning that Howe had spread his army thin to maintain more territory around Philadelphia, Washington attacked a British stronghold at Germantown, some five miles north of the city. Again, the weather interceded. Again, a fog dropped down. Though Washington was at first annoyed by the drastic change in weather, it later became clear that the fog was working to his advantage, as it prevented the British from seeing their American attackers. The Americans, after all, "usually fought at their best from cover, and the fog afforded cover of sorts."[18]

Although Washington's forces did not drive the British out of Philadelphia, they did fight bravely. Even the British noticed this and admitted their surprise at how "spirited" the American advance was.[19] And though the British could claim the victory, Washington had intimidated them to the point that Howe withdrew all his forces into Philadelphia. Washington then gained some control of the surrounding areas, to include control of the Delaware River, which frustrated the British supply chain.[20] The French liked what they saw, and they viewed America's strong showing at Germantown as another reason to join the American cause.[21]

Washington did not lament much over his defeat at Germantown. He later wrote that "the day was rather unfortunate, than injurious" and that his soldiers "were not in the least dispirited." They all appreciated the valuable, and much needed, combat experience gained.[22] All things considered—from Saratoga to Brandywine and Germantown—Washington commented that "a superintending Providence is ordering every thing for the best, and that, in due time, all will end well."[23]

But the question still lingers: *Why would the Lord be fighting on Washington's side, then allow for Philadelphia to be taken?*

I recently gave a talk to a youth group in my home ward. I had my audience listen to a song by Garth Brooks called "Unanswered Prayers." The lyrics speak of a man's gratitude to God for not answering certain prayers and granting desires that, as he later learned, would have proven disastrous if actually answered. A great lesson to us all. Such was the case here in 1777. No, the Americans couldn't keep the British from overtaking their capital. Yes, the American prayers to defend Philadelphia seemed to go completely unanswered. But the unanswered prayers turned out to be the true blessings.

Admittedly, the blessings were not immediately apparent, especially as we see where Washington and his men found themselves in the aftermath of these 1777 battles. It was a dark and dreary place outside of Philadelphia called Valley Forge.

Without proper supplies (some went without shoes or shirts) and without adequate food (some were forced to eat a soup of burnt leaves and dirt), the army suffered acutely at Valley Forge. Notwithstanding, Washington and some of his officers saw something divine in this situation. It was the reason the Lord had

A THANKSGIVING PROCLAMATION

On November 1, 1777, Congress once again officially invoked the covenant in its Thanksgiving Proclamation. In the proclamation, Congress called on Americans to perform acts to "please God through merits of Jesus Christ" and to support "the Means of Religion, for the promotion and enlargement of that Kingdom, which consisteth 'in Righteousness, Peace and Joy in the Holy Ghost.'" The proclamation further instructed Americans to "join the penitent Confession of their manifold Sins, whereby they had forfeited every Favor; and their humble and earnest Supplication that it may please God, through the merits of Jesus Christ, mercifully to forgive and blot them out of Remembrance."[24]

General Thanksgiving.

BY THE PRESIDENT
OF THE UNITED STATES of AMERICA,
A PROCLAMATION.

WHEREAS it is the duty of all nations to acknowledge the Providence of Almighty God---to obey his will---to be grateful for his benefits---and humbly to implore his protection and favour: And whereas both Houses have, by their joint committee, requested me "to recommend to the people of the United States, a DAY of PUBLICK THANKSGIVING and PRAYER, to be observed by acknowledging with grateful hearts the many and signal favours of Almighty God, especially by affording them an opportunity peaceably to establish a form of government for their safety and happiness:"

NOW THEREFORE, I do recommend and assign THURSDAY, the TWENTY-SIXTH DAY of NOVEMBER next, to be devoted by the people of these States, to the service of that great and glorious Being, who is the beneficent Author of all the good that was, that is, or that will be: That we may then all unite in rendering unto him our sincere and humble thanks for his kind care and protection of the people of this country previous to their becoming a nation; for the signal and manifold mercies, and the favourable interpositions of his Providence in the course and conclusion of the late war;---for the great degree of tranquility, union and plenty, which we have since enjoyed;---for the peaceable and rational manner in which we have been enabled to establish Constitutions of Government for our safety and happiness, and particularly the national one now lately instituted;---for the civil and religious Liberty with which we are blessed, and the means we have, of acquiring and diffusing useful knowledge;---and in general, for all the great and various favours which he hath been pleased to confer upon us.

AND ALSO, That we may then unite in most humbly offering our prayers and supplications to the great Lord and Ruler of Nations, and beseech him to pardon our national and other transgressions;---to enable us all, whether in publick or private stations, to perform our several and relative duties properly and punctually; to render our national government a blessing to all the people, by constantly being a government of wise, just, and constitutional laws, discreetly and faithfully executed and obeyed; to protect and guide all sovereigns and nations (especially such as have shewn kindness unto us); and to bless them with good government, peace and concord; to promote the knowledge and practice of true religion and virtue, and the increase of science among them and us; and generally, to grant unto all mankind such a degree of temporal prosperity as he alone knows to be best.

GIVEN under my hand, at the city of New-York, the third day of October, in the year of our Lord, one thousand seven hundred and eighty-nine.

George Washington.

allowed the British to take Philadelphia and push the Americans into this rather hellish existence. For the British grew fat, happy, undisciplined, and ineffective in Philadelphia. Benjamin Franklin quipped that the British had not taken Philadelphia so much as Philadelphia had taken the British.[25]

In contrast, Washington's men were forced to learn humility, resilience, and other lessons that would be needful for eventual victory. Wrote Washington, "To see Men without Cloathes to cover their nakedness, without Blankets to lay on, without Shoes, by which their Marches might be traced by the Blood from their feet, is a mark of Patience and obedience which in my opinion can scarce be paralel'd."[26] Nathanael Greene concurred, adding that "we bear beatings very well . . . the more we are beat, the better we grow."[27]

Such lessons would be taught again in the not-too-distant future to a different generation of the Lord's faithful. When the Prophet Joseph Smith, as an inmate in Liberty Jail, pleaded with the Lord for an understanding of the unbearable burdens he and the Saints were required to suffer, the Lord calmed his anxiety, saying, "Know thou, my son, that all these things shall give thee experience, and shall be for thy good" (D&C 122:7). These words would also find application to Abraham Lincoln during his presidency. In my book *The Lincoln Hypothesis,* I describe in detail the darkness Lincoln had to pass through in 1862 in order to understand God's will for the Civil War and for the future of America. These scriptural words could just as easily have been spoken to Washington and his men at Valley Forge. In each case, the Lord needed to strengthen His faithful servants through the refiner's fire, that His ultimate purposes might come to pass.

Washington, as commander, could easily have justified moving himself to more comfortable personal quarters outside the dreary camp. However, he promised his men, "I will share in your hardship and partake of every inconvenience."[28] He made good on his word. He stayed close to his men and took an active role to ensure that the experience became one of learning and spiritual growth for them. A clergyman named Henry Muhlenberg visited the soldiers in Valley Forge and was pleasantly surprised at what he saw. In his memoirs he described how General Washington "rode around among his army" and "admonished each and every one to fear God, to put away wickedness that has set in and become so general, and to practice Christian virtues." I can't help but see an earlier version of such a commander. Is this not what Captain Moroni would have been doing in the camps of the Nephite warriors? Clergyman Muhlenberg concluded that "Washington does not belong to the so-called world of society, for he respects God's word, believes in the atonement through Christ, and bears himself in humility and gentleness."[29]

Two legendary stories of Washington at Valley Forge shine a light on what Muhlenberg was trying to express. First is the well-known account of the general's mighty prayer. According to the story, a local resident and Quaker named Isaac Potts, whose religion had initially compelled him to stand against the Revolution, happened upon the spiritually powerful scene. The fullest account of what he saw was written by the Reverend Nathanial Snowden (1770–1851) in his "Diary of Remembrances." Reverend Snowden, an ordained minister and graduate of Princeton, related the following experience:

> I was riding with him [Mr. Potts] in Montgomery County, Penn'a near to the Valley Forge, where the army lay during the war of ye Revolution. Mr. Potts was a Senator in our State & a Whig. I told him I was agreeably surprised to find him a friend to his country, as the

MIRACLE OF THE FISH

While in Valley Forge, American soldiers suffered greatly, many even died, for lack of food. Congress heard the pleas but was helpless to provide. Washington warned Congress that if food did not arrive soon, his army faced three choices: "Starve—dissolve—or disperse."[30] With no mortal on earth able to come to their aid, prayer was the only option. Perhaps the soldiers remembered that the Lord had once before provided His hungry disciples with fish in a miraculous way. It was about to happen again.

Suddenly, in the midst of the winter famine, there was an unexpected warming of the weather, too early to accredit to springtime. The "false spring" tricked the shad fish into beginning their run up the Delaware River early. Thousands of shad—some described them as "prodigious in number," others said they came in "Biblical proportions"—swam up the Delaware. The overabundance caused thousands more to make a turn up smaller streams and rivers, seeking any space to spawn. One of those rivers was the Schuylkill. At a certain bend in that river, the water rose only knee-deep—perfect for catching fish. And that very bend in the Schuylkill just happened to run right by Washington's camp at Valley Forge.[31]

The famine ended instantly, as thousands upon thousands of pounds of fish were caught and eaten. Hundreds of barrels were filled and salted down for future consumption. Even today, the United States Fish and Wildlife Service gives credence to the claim that the shad were responsible for "saving George Washington's troops from starvation as they camped along the Schuylkill River at Valley Forge."[32]

Shortly after the miracle of the fish, Washington wrote the following from Valley Forge:

"Providence has a just claim to my humble and grateful thanks for its protection and direction of me through the many difficult and intricate scenes which this contest has produced, and for its constant interposition in our behalf when the clouds were heaviest and seemed ready to burst upon us. . . . Since our prospects have miraculously brightened, shall I attempt the description of the condition of the army, or even bear it in re-membrance, further than as a memento of what is due to the great Author of all, the care and good that have been extended in relieving us in difficul-ties and distresses?"[33]

Quakers were mostly Tories. He said, "It was so and I was a rank Tory once, for I never believed that America c'd proceed against Great Britain whose fleets and armies covered the land and ocean, but something very extraordinary converted me to the Good Faith!"

"What was that?," I inquired. "Do you see that woods, & that plain?" It was about a quarter of a mile off from the place we were riding, as it happened. "There," said he, "laid the army of Washington. It was a most distressing time of ye war, and all were for giving up the ship except for that great and good man. In that woods (pointing to a point in view), I heard a plaintive sound as, of a man at prayer. I tied my horse to a sapling & went quietly into the woods & to my astonishment I saw the great George Washington on his knees alone, with his sword on one side and his cocked hat on the other. He was at Prayer to the God of the Armies, beseeching to interpose with his divine aid, as it was ye Crises, & the cause of the country, of humanity & of the world.

"Such a prayer I never heard from the lips of man. I left him alone praying. I went home & told my wife. I saw a sight and heard today what I never saw or heard before, and just related to her what I had seen & heard & observed. We never thought a man could be a soldier and a Christian, but if there is one in the world, it is Washington. She also was astonished. We thought it was the cause of God, & America could prevail."[34]

Critics—mostly secularists—have attempted to discredit this story due to another account of a praying Washington at Valley Forge. In this second account, as printed in the *Aldine Press,* Washington was seen by one of his soldiers praying in a barn, which critics claim is a discrepancy from the original story, and thereby they discredit any claim that Washington was ever seen praying at all in Valley Forge. Of course, the more reasonable explanation, perhaps beyond the reach of such secularists, is that a God-fearing man like Washington prayed many times at Valley Forge, and therefore many accounts were witnessed and recorded.

One of Washington's generals at Valley Forge, Robert Porterfield, told of how he once entered Washington's private quarters to report an emergency. Porterfield found Washington on his knees in prayer. He reported the incident to Washington's aide, Alexander Hamilton, who replied that "such was his constant habit."[35]

Furthermore, in light of the claims by close friends and family members that Washington consistently "maintained daily intercourse with Heaven by prayer," that he "observed stated seasons of retirement for secret devotion,"[36] and that he was constantly encouraging/ordering his men to pray often (he was, after all, never known to be a hypocrite), Potts's story becomes all the more believable.

Such prayers certainly created a shield of protection around the humble camp. At one point, Howe, uncomfortable with how close Valley Forge was to his headquarters in Philadelphia, decided to pursue a sneak attack on Washington. Considering the lowly physical state of the American army, in contrast to the well stocked and supplied British army, the attack would likely have ended the Revolution. When Howe came upon the humble camp, he withdrew and returned to Philadelphia. His justification for not attacking defies all logic and denies the reality of Washington's winter quarters. Howe explained to Lord Germain that Valley Forge had been strongly fortified.[37] Only with the help of God and His angels could Howe have perceived the condition as he described it.

The second Valley Forge story—also secondhand and anecdotal in nature—has to do with the account of Anthony Sherman, one of Washington's soldiers at Valley Forge. On July 4, 1859, Sherman, who was then ninety-nine years old, recollected the purported miracle from years earlier. He was feeble and knew he had little time remaining on earth. He also knew he was one of the last remaining veteran soldiers of the Revolution. Before he died, he wanted to tell someone of an event he had witnessed at Valley Forge. So he asked his friend and journalist Wesley Bradshaw to meet him at Independence Hall—the place where the Declaration of Independence had been signed. When Bradshaw arrived, Sherman, with shaking hands and with a rekindled brightness in his otherwise dimming eyes, stated, "I want to tell you an incident of Washington's life, one which no one alive knows of except myself. Mark me, I am not superstitious; but you will see it verified."

Sherman then invited the journalist into the iconic building, explaining that he wanted to meet there so as to gaze upon the building one more time before being gathered home to God. They sat down on a bench inside the hall, and the old man recounted a vision and prophecy Washington reportedly had received at Valley Forge. The prophecy spoke of a series of conflicts America had faced and would face, including wars and rumors of wars, whose descriptions sounded a lot like the war for independence, the American Civil War, and other future conflicts. The point of the vision was to tell Washington that America was God's creation and would endure and be victorious over all these conflicts.

The vision as reported by Sherman in 1859 was first published in the *Philadelphia Inquirer* on June 24, 1861, and in the

Pittsfield Gazette in December 1861, as the Civil War was just beginning. (It's worth noting that the vision prophesied that the Union would win that war, which perhaps explains the timing of the publication.) It was later published in the *National Tribune,* Vol. 4, No. 12, in December 1880.[38]

Below is an excerpt from the report entitled "Washington's Vision," as told directly from the memory of Sherman while sitting in Independence Hall.

> The darkest period we had I think, was when Washington, after several reverses, retreated to Valley Forge, where he resolved to pass the winter of 1777. Ah! I have often seen the tears coursing down our dear commander's careworn cheeks, as he would be conversing with a confidential officer about the condition of his poor soldiers. You have doubtless heard the story of Washington's going to the thicket to pray. Well, it was not only true, but he used often to pray in secret for aid and comfort from God, the interposition of whose Divine Providence brought us safely through the darkest days of tribulation.
>
> One day, I remember it well [in Valley Forge], the chilly winds whistled through the leafless trees, though the sky was cloudless and the sun shone brightly, [Washington] remained in his quarters nearly all afternoon alone. When he came out I noticed that his face was a shade paler than usual, and there seemed to be something on his mind of more than ordinary importance. Returning just after dusk, he dispatched an orderly to the quarters of the officer I mentioned who was presently in attendance. After a preliminary conversation of about half

Washington praying.

an hour, Washington, gazing upon his companion with that strange look of dignity which he alone could command, said to the latter:

"I do not know whether it is owing to the anxiety of my mind, or what, but this afternoon, as I was sitting at this table engaged in preparing a dispatch, something seemed to disturb me. Looking up, I beheld standing opposite me a singularly beautiful female. So astonished was I, for I had given strict orders not to be disturbed, that it was some moments before I found language to inquire the cause of her presence. A second, a third, and even a fourth time did I repeat my question, but received no answer from my mysterious visitor. . . . By this time I felt strange sensations spreading through me. I would have risen but the riveted gaze of the being before me rendered volition impossible.

"Presently I heard a voice saying 'Son of the Republic, look and learn' while at the same time my visitor extended her arm eastwardly. I now beheld a heavy white vapor at some distance rising fold upon fold. This gradually dissipated, and I looked upon a strange scene. Before me lay spread out in one vast plain all the countries of the world—Europe, Asia, Africa and America. . . . 'Son of the Republic,' said the same mysterious voice as before, 'look and learn.' At that moment I beheld . . . [another] angel, standing or rather floating in mid-air, between Europe and America. Dipping water out of the ocean in the hollow of each hand he sprinkled some upon America. . . . A second time the angel dipped water from the ocean, and sprinkled it out as before . . ."[39]

> "The angel spake unto me, saying: Look! And I looked. . . ."
> —1 Nephi 11:19–20

Before continuing with the report of this vision, I want to pause and take you to Salt Lake City. It was July 4, 1854, five years to the day before the old man Sherman recounted his witness of what happened to Washington at Valley Forge. Orson Hyde, an ordained Apostle of God, stood at the pulpit in the Tabernacle and boldly declared that the angel Moroni, even that "Prince of America" who "presides over the destinies of America . . . was in the camp of Washington."[40] Could this corroborate Sherman's account? The principal angel in Valley Forge was, of course, described as a woman. But it was a male angel (or male angels) who anointed the land.

As the vision continues, the Moroni hypothesis becomes ever more interesting. After the principal angel described to Washington what sounds like yet another conflict to hit the land—"thundering of the cannon, clashing of swords, and the shouts and cries of millions in mortal combat"—the male angel performed a familiar act, familiar to the LDS student, at least. "Son of the Republic," said the female angel, "look and learn." Washington then beheld a male angel and, according to Sherman, told of how he watched as the angel "placed his trumpet once more to his mouth, and blew a long, fearful blast." Washington continued:

> Instantly a light, as of a thousand suns, shone down from above me, and pierced and broke into fragments the dark cloud which enveloped America. At the same moment the angel . . . who bore our national flag in one hand and a sword in the other, descended from the heavens attended by legions of bright spirits. These immediately joined the inhabitants of America, who I perceived were well nigh overcome, but who immediately taking courage again, closed up their broken ranks, and renewed the battle.
>
> Again, amid the fearful noise of the conflict, I heard the mysterious voice, saying: "Son of the Republic, look and learn." As the voice ceased, the shadowy angel for the last time dipped water from the ocean and sprinkled it upon America. Instantly the dark cloud rolled back, together with the armies it had brought, leaving the inhabitants of the land victorious.
>
> Then once more I beheld the villages, towns, and cities springing up where I had seen them before, while the bright angel, planting the azure standard he had brought in the midst of them, cried with a loud voice: "While the stars remain, and the heavens send down dew upon the

earth, so long shall the Union last!" . . . while the people, kneeling down, said "Amen."[41]

I cannot read this account without thinking of the biblical prophecy of the angel Moroni found in Revelation 14:6–7: "And I saw another angel fly in the midst of heaven, having the ever-lasting gospel to preach unto them that dwell on the earth, and to every nation, and kindred, and tongue, and people, Saying with a loud voice, Fear God, and give glory to him; for the hour of his judgment is come: and worship him that made heaven, and earth, and the sea, and the fountains of waters."[42]

The Restoration of the gospel did not simply begin in 1820. The foundation was being laid years earlier in the battlefields of America—in Boston, Long Island, Saratoga, and Valley Forge. George Washington was a power player in the story of the Restoration, as he was building the nation, the foundation, for Christ to return, that He might bring His priesthood and truths of salvation. Washington had read the words of Thomas Paine: "Every spot of the old world is overrun with oppression. Freedom has been hunted round the Globe. Asia and Africa have long ex-pelled her. Europe regards her like a stranger, and England has given her warning to depart. O! receive the fugitive, and pre-pare in time an asylum for mankind."[43] Indeed, the forthcoming Restoration had nowhere safe to land. God needed to create the asylum, and Washington knew that he was helping God do just that. Writing from Valley Forge, he declared: "Even if the rest of the world continues to ignore us, we will fight on. For we are fighting not only for ourselves, but for all mankind. We are fighting for freedom and human dignity and the right to worship the God of our choice."[44]

As Sherman concluded his account, he turned to Bradshaw, and declared: "Such, my friend, were the words I heard from

On December 18, 1777, Washington again asked his men "to observe a day of prayer and fasting, to give thanks to God for blessings already received, and to implore the continuing favor of Providence upon the American cause." After Washington read a sermon by one of his chaplains, which had been given to accompany and support the general's day of fasting and prayer at Valley Forge, Washington wrote to thank him for "the force of the reasoning which you have displayed." He then added that "it will ever be the first wish of my heart to aid your pious endeavours to inculcate a due sense of the dependence we ought to place in that all wise and powerful Being on whom alone our success depends."[46]

Washington's own lips, and America will do well to profit by them." According to the account, the angel was showing Washington this vision that it might be a warning to him and the nation. At one point during the vision, the angel told Washington: "Let every child of the Republic learn to live for his God, his land, and the Union."[45] Washington, no doubt, was doing his part to get this message out.

Like Joseph at Liberty Jail, and like Lincoln in 1862, Washington was compelled to his knees while in the darkness of Valley Forge. And he was blessed for it. He had received an assurance from the Lord about the fate of America. As he led the nation in righteousness, he would be victorious. He needed to know this. Now he did.

To illustrate the assurance Washington felt about his mission, I take you to the next significant battle scene after Valley Forge. It was summer 1778 in New Jersey. Washington was taking on the British at the Battle of Monmouth. In the middle of the battle, he dashed away on his horse to get a better view, even though the ground he chose to park himself on left him dangerously exposed. He met one of his colonels on the spot and began strategizing with him. In his memoirs, George Washington Parke

Custis (adopted son of George Washington) explains what happened next:

> A cannon ball struck just at his horse's feet throwing dirt into his face, and over his clothes, [but] the general continued giving orders, without noticing the derangement of his toilette [attire]. The officers present . . . looked at each other with anxiety. The chief of the medical staff [who happened to be close friends with Washington] . . . pointed toward heaven, which was noticed by the others, with a gratifying smile of acknowledgment.[47]

This is what it means to have the assurance of the Lord. Washington had it. He knew the plan for America; he knew he would live to fulfill his mission; and he knew it in no small part due to his experiences, visions, and revelations at Valley Forge.

◆　◆　◆

As I stood in Valley Forge, an uninformed eleven-year-old boy, I looked at the statue of the praying Washington. I had no idea then why I felt what I did. But now I do. I finally understand what the true meaning was behind the statue and the sacred ground I shared with it in that moment. But only recently did I learn. In fact, as I began writing this chapter, several incidents occurred in my personal life that allowed me to see, that forced me back to my 1987 experience at Valley Forge and opened my understanding to who George Washington really was.

In December 2013, as I was researching for this book, I had my own "Valley Forge" experience. I was about to quit my twelve-year, very secure, career as a special agent for the U.S. government in order to enter perhaps the most insecure business imaginable.

I was leaving to start a nonprofit organization called Operation Underground Railroad whose mission was to rescue enslaved, kidnapped, and trafficked children. It was that December that I turned in my gun and badge with tears in my eyes. *What was I thinking?* I had a wife and six kids—and little financial security. I spent much of that month in the fetal position. In anxiety. And that forced me to my knees.

When the answers came, they came largely through the research that I had continued to conduct for this chapter. As I studied and pondered the much more serious and tragic events surrounding Washington in 1777 (which made my small issue seem of little import), I sought for inspiration. I remember sitting in my home library, glancing up on the bookshelf, and seeing a depiction of a praying Washington. It was engraved into a small award I had recently been given by the Freedoms Foundation at Valley Forge. At the time I had received the award, I had not made all the connections, except of course that I had visited the campus of the foundation as a child. But as I pondered it in my library, my aching and humbled condition allowed the Lord to teach me. For the first time, I recalled my boyhood experience at the statue. I remembered how I had felt because I was feeling it again.

From there, the important pages from the books I was studying seemed to fall open, as I pieced the story together. I saw George Washington, and his relationship with God, in a new and inspiring light. Then it happened. Just as Washington received his assurance of his calling at Valley Forge, I received the same in my "Valley Forge." I knew all would be well with my new professional enterprise, for the Lord told me it would. My mind went to the Book of Mormon, where I could read about others who had experienced similar witnesses. Helaman led his young, underdog warriors in a fierce battle that should have claimed many of their lives. Yet Helaman knew they would live, for he had received an assurance. "Yea, and it came to pass that the Lord our God did visit us with assurances that he would deliver us; yea, insomuch that he did speak peace to our souls . . . that we should hope for our deliverance in him" (Alma 58:11).

Several months later, I would have to endure my "Battle of Monmouth" experience—my faith would be tested. I found myself at the head of a special Operation Underground Railroad team, made up of former Navy SEALS and other military and law enforcement professionals. Also with us were authorities from the host country, excited to work with us on this mission. We had spent several days infiltrating what I can only call a slave village. We had gone undercover as medical charity workers in one of the most God-forsaken, underdeveloped, and primitive regions in the world. On a tip that children were being trafficked there, we entered (along with real medical professionals) and put on a legitimate medical clinic. Hundreds were treated, and our primary goal of gaining intelligence was attained. Many kids in the village were parentless, probably kidnapped, and were being forced to work as slaves.

With the clinic complete and the intelligence gained, we were prepared to report our information to the proper authorities, then return with legal orders to extract the child victims. But the traffickers decided to detain us. Though they had no idea what we were really up to, they figured they could do with us what they wanted. After all, we had already treated most of the village, and we certainly had valuables that appealed to them. The road out of town was immediately blocked to us by men armed with shotguns and machetes. Soon the crowd around us turned into an angry mob of hundreds. Threats of death and destruction were hurled at us. There was nothing my small team could do should the traffickers decide to make good on their threats. We sat there in our vehicles, surrounded at every corner by the armed mob. One of my Navy SEALS told me that, though he had seen major combat in his day, this was the closest he had ever come to death.

As I sat in the vehicle, looking over the scene, I bowed my head. I thought of my wife and children. I had to make it back to them. Then scenes of Helaman flashed through my mind. I saw George Washington. I saw myself as a child in Valley Forge. Then I felt it. Again. The assurance of the Lord. We would escape. I *knew* we would escape. He had not given me my witness only to let us die here. After an hour of deep prayer and faith that angels were working to soften the crowd, I looked up and saw that the armed men guarding the road had almost all dispersed. Many members of the mob had also dispersed—their hearts apparently softened. I called for the vehicles to move out. If a gunman were to open fire, I instructed my drivers to plow over him.

As we moved, the remaining traffickers hoisted their guns in the air and shouted threats, but we passed without incident. Our cause would move forward. We would live to fight on those grounds another day.

I learned so many lessons from this experience. I learned that it may not be wise to merely have faith in just anything we desire. First, we must seek the *assurance* from the Lord. Then we can move forward in faith, no matter the odds that may be stacked against us. The key is to get the assurance, even if it means we have to travel to our own Valley Forge to get it. I have received many assurances, for example, of the truthfulness of the restored gospel. And so, I can move forward and apply true faith (paying my tithing, going to the temple, and so on) in that God-given as-surance. I have received an assurance in my current employment and calling, and so I can move forward in true faith there as well. If for some reason I don't receive an assurance for something I am praying over, I know I can *always* put my faith in the Savior, trusting He will take care of it one way or another. I will be eternally grateful for these lessons.

For the purpose of this book, it was this lesson that allowed me to know Washington and tell his story, for I had passed through something similar (albeit much less important) to what he had passed through. And the lesson applies to all of us in the here and now. We have (or should have) the assurance (from the scriptures, from history, and from personal revelation) that Washington's mission was given to him by, and executed under the direction of, God. If so, we can have true faith in what he did, and we can apply that faith by doing to-

> From the desk of George Washington, August 20, 1778:
>
> "The Hand of providence has been so conspicuous in all this [Revolutionary War], that he must be worse than an infidel that lacks faith, and more than wicked, that has not gratitude enough to acknowledge his obligations."[48]

day what he did in the fight for liberty in this promised land. He turned the people to the covenant. He turned them to God, then worked *hard* to bring about liberty. Today we face challenges from every direction—economic threats, political threats, international threats. But none are as difficult as the challenges Washington faced. So, we will be victorious if we follow his example.

If we do this, we will be able to stare down any problem we face as individuals, families, or as a nation, and declare, as the Continental Congress did in 1779, that America, "without arms, ammunition, discipline, revenue, government or ally . . . with a 'staff and sling' only, dared, 'in the name of the Lord of Hosts,' to engage a gigantic adversary."[49]

CHAPTER 6

Miracle at Yorktown

We have all heard the name Alexander Hamilton. And if we know a few facts about him, those usually include that he was the first U.S. secretary of the treasury under President George Washington and that he was the mastermind behind the financial system of the United States. We may also recognize his face as that printed on our ten-dollar bill. But there are other interesting facts we may want to know about Hamilton. I like to think of the poor boy, the underdog, born out of wedlock, raised on a Caribbean island, and orphaned as a child. I think of the teenager who stowed away to America in search of a better life and volunteered to fight in the Revolution. But above all, I think of what he did at the Battle of Yorktown—the last major battle of the Revolution. The one that secured American independence.

Recently, I traveled to Yorktown, Virginia, with Alexander Hamilton on my mind. Yorktown is a small town, beautifully situated on the York River, with easy access to the Chesapeake Bay and the Atlantic coast. During the Revolution, Yorktown served as a tobacco port. But it never modernized. Today it looks almost exactly as it did during the Revolution. And that was good for me. It allowed me to easily trace Hamilton's steps across the great battlefield.

Not long after arriving just outside the town, I found the very place on the battlefield where I had, for some time, longed to stand. I looked up from the spot and saw, several hundred yards in front of me, the famed Redoubt No. 10. It had been a British stronghold, a solid mound of earth built up into a miniature fortress, with sharp wooden poles (creating what is called a palisade) sticking out all around to form an obstructive barrier against would-be assailants.

Hamilton, who once stood where I was standing, and who once looked upon Redoubt No. 10, as I was at that moment, would be that feared assailant. Redoubt No. 10 was one of the very last remaining British defense posts at the battle. If America could grab it, the battle would be theirs. Hamilton volunteered to lead the charge, and General Washington approved. Using the cover of night, Hamilton sprinted, stealthily, with his team and violently entered the fortress.

As I stood at the place where he began his assault, I traced his steps toward the small fortress. It looked very much like it had when Hamilton approached. As I walked, I found myself

Alexander Hamilton consults George Washington.

caught up in the moment. I'm a bit embarrassed to admit that I couldn't contain myself and, thinking of Hamilton and wanting to feel something of what he did that night, I found myself in a full sprint toward Redoubt No. 10. (Luckily nobody was on or near the battlefield, except a friend of mine who accompanied me and understood my strange ability to revert back to my childlike spirit.) As I approached the redoubt, my imagination allowed me to hear a British guard call out in a thick, obnoxious accent, "Who goes there?" I arrived at the base of the redoubt, the palisade shooting out over me, and I began my ascent. I was still sprinting.

But I'm getting way ahead of myself. To help you see how a thirty-nine-year-old man can act like an eleven-year-old school boy, let me defend my passion with the facts of this battle, which led to Hamilton's charge. Perhaps you will see why I was so taken by the battle site.

The story of the battle takes us to January 1781. By this time, the war had entered a stalemate of sorts, with the exception of the skirmishes in the South, brought on in large part by American guerilla-style attacks. General Lord Charles Cornwallis (the same officer who got tricked at Trenton and allowed Washington to best him and take Princeton) commanded the British troops in the South, and he was fed up with the American advances in his territory. He sent Colonel Banastre Tarleton to attack the Americans under General Daniel Morgan at Cowpens, South Carolina. The American commander of the southern division, Nathanael Greene, had his army in the Carolinas and had recently sent Morgan westward toward Cowpens to gather provisions and poke around at the British. Though Tarleton's British forces attacked confidently, Morgan unexpectedly defeated them. The victorious Americans, knowing they had just kicked the hornets' nest, began fleeing back to Greene and the rest of the

General Lord Charles Cornwallis.

American southern division. Greene and Morgan then began fleeing northward with their troops. They wanted to get over the
Dan River and into friendly Virginia territory before Cornwallis
hunted them down.[1]

The Americans were right to be afraid. Word of the British defeat at Cowpens enraged Cornwallis. He was determined to catch
and destroy the fleeing American troops—using all of his army, if
necessary. Cornwallis ordered his soldiers to shed their heavy baggage so they could move rapidly. The chase was on. Cornwallis
reached the Catawba River just hours after the Americans had
crossed. Confident that victory would be his in the morning,
Cornwallis decided to cross the river at dawn the following day.
But during the night a storm flooded the river, making a morning crossing impossible and allowing the Americans a head start.
Had the river flooded a few hours sooner, the Americans would
have been trapped on the British side of the river, and Cornwallis
would have annihilated them.[2]

Cornwallis would again come close to catching the Americans, first at the Yadkin River in North Carolina on February 3 and then at the Dan River, at the Virginia border, on February 13. In both cases, the Americans would safely cross just in time before storms flooded the rivers, thus blocking British attacks. The British commander, Sir Henry Clinton, to whom Cornwallis answered, had to admit that God seemed to have intervened on America's behalf. Wrote Clinton, " . . . here the royal army was again stopped by a sudden rise of the waters, which had only just fallen (almost miraculously) to let the enemy over, who could not else have eluded Lord Cornwallis' grasp, so close was he upon their rear."[3]

When Washington received word of the providential rises in the river, he responded, "We have, as you very justly observe, abundant reasons to thank Providence for its many favorable interpositions in our behalf. It has at times been my only dependence, for all other resources seemed to have failed us."[4]

Once Greene and his troops were able to regroup in Virginia, they crossed back over the Dan to confront the British again. Cornwallis was only too happy to comply. On March 15, the British attacked fiercely near Guilford Courthouse. After a back-and-forth engagement during which the Americans fought ferociously, Greene ultimately pulled his American troops out of the fight and into safe territory, allowing Cornwallis to claim victory. However, as the dust settled it became clear that, though the Americans had retreated, the British had actually suffered twice as many casualties as their foe.[5] British statesman Charles Fox warned: "Another such victory would ruin the British Army."[6] Washington and Greene had by now understood the road to victory. They did not have to win. They just had to *not lose*. As Greene declared, "We fight, get beat, rise and fight again."[7] So long as they persevered, doing all they could do, the Lord would intervene and do the rest. God's handiwork would indeed tip the scale in favor of America until the British finally gave up.

After his failed chase, followed by the crippling effects of the most recent battle, Cornwallis and his disheartened British army were now left with little to do. Clinton directed him to move his army, consisting of some 7,500 redcoats, to secure the tobacco port town of Yorktown, Virginia. From there, reasoned Clinton, Cornwallis's troops could be easily mobilized via the Chesapeake Bay by the superior British navy. As Cornwallis waited, Washington considered his options. Both sides immediately began plotting and scheming, believing that—as both armies were on the verge of collapse—whoever laid the next blow would secure ultimate victory. Times were tense.

Washington, who at the time was directing the northern campaign, thought to launch an attack on the British in the north, believing an attack on Yorktown would be fruitless—for who could stop a Cornwallis retreat by sea? Perhaps he remembered that the Lord surely could. So he changed his plans and went forward with faith, ordering his soldiers to begin congregating around the Yorktown peninsula in an attempt to box in Cornwallis. As best-selling author and historian Thomas Fleming put it, "Instead, Washington marched south [to Yorktown] and a series of miracles occurred."[8]

The first of these miracles was witnessed as the British fleet out of New York set sail for Yorktown in order to rescue Cornwallis and his troops. However, the British fleet did not expect to run into a French fleet, which had arrived just in time at the Chesapeake Bay, off the coast of Yorktown, in support of the American effort. On September 5, 1781, the French ships turned on the incoming British and defeated them in what became known as the Battle of the Capes. The British fleet was forced to return to New York to repair and refit its ships, all the while leaving Cornwallis trapped and in an even more precarious situation.

As William Bennett explained in his book *America: The Last Best Hope,* between the years 1588 and 1941, the British "with one important local exception [the waters off Yorktown, Virginia, in 1781] . . . 'ruled the waves.'"[9] This one exception in over 350 years of British naval warfare history would directly contribute to the final battlefield victory that sealed American independence. This was no coincidence.

With Cornwallis stuck, the Americans, along with their French allies, continued pouring onto the Yorktown peninsula. They had built, and continued to build, a series of trenches—called parallels—all around Yorktown to provide themselves cover as they laid siege upon the British-held town.

As my friend and I drove our rental car to the outskirts of Yorktown, I easily identified the outer, or first, parallel built by American and French forces in early October 1781. George Washington himself was the first to take a pickax and break ground on the war trenches on October 6.[10] I had earlier purchased a CD for the car stereo system, which provided the history of the battle and led drivers on a tour of the entire battlefield. I intended to cover every square inch of this place. Upon seeing the first parallel, I hopped out of the car and walked along the earthworks, imagining what it would have been like to be part of Washington's army.

Having received word that the British fleet out of New York was preparing to return to rescue the redcoats in Yorktown, Cornwallis grew confident. He even abandoned his three outlying redoubts in order to pull his troops in closer around the town to get ready to embark once the soon-to-arrive British ships landed at the port. Washington saw this and immediately took the redoubts and moved in closer to his target, building a second parallel closer to the town. American and French forces began bombarding the town, while the British returned the gesture.[11]

Tracking the movements of the allied forces, I drove my car in closer to the town, until I saw the second parallel Washington's men had built. I thought of how Washington loved being in the trenches with his men, even though he didn't need to be. At one point, Washington wanted intelligence for himself regarding British movements in the town. So he grabbed his telescope, climbed to the highest and most exposed point of the American fortifications, and watched. Witnesses remembered that, as the general stood there, British balls were "flying almost as thick as hail and were instantly demolishing portions of the embankment around him." Yet Washington stayed put for ten or fifteen minutes. His aides were going nuts and forced him from his perch a couple of times, only to watch him move back up with his telescope. He "severely reprimanded" his aides for getting in his way.[12]

As I slowly drove through the battlefield, my mind also turned to Yorktown resident Thomas Nelson Jr. Serving as governor of Virginia at the time of the battle, Nelson had had his estate in town seized by the British, and it was likely the place from which Cornwallis did much of his commanding. Nelson was a true patriot, having served in the Continental Congress and signed the Declaration of Independence. When he noticed that Congress was out of cash, Nelson borrowed almost two million dollars, using his own property as collateral, and handed it over to the American war machine. In the end, he was unable to make good on his debt and lost all he possessed. During the siege of Yorktown, Nelson commanded the Virginia militia. He was in the trenches with Washington and directed the cannons

House of Governor Thomas Nelson Jr.

to destroy his Yorktown home.[13] To this day, you can visit the Nelson home, now a museum, and see the Continental army's cannonballs still lodged firmly in its old outer wall.

As we drove closer to the town, I was happy to see that one of the main roads that circles around and into the town is called Ballard Street. I felt very welcome. I later learned that it was named for local merchant John Ballard, who lived in Yorktown during the mid-1700s. I would have to research my genealogy further. In the meantime, I would use his road to get me to the next scene in the battle—I was heading to Redoubt No. 10!

As we pulled up within eyesight of the redoubt, I turned off the CD and jumped out of the car. My friend immediately turned the CD back on and asked, "Don't you want to hear the whole story about the redoubt before getting out?"

"We can listen later," I told him. "Come on!"

He turned off the car and exited, but I was already in full sprint towards the redoubt before he could say another word.

And this, of course, leads us to me running up the side of Redoubt No. 10. Up and around the reconstructed palisade I flew. At last, I landed atop the fortress. My thoughts turned wholly to Hamilton.

"Unload your weapons!"[14] commanded Hamilton to his strike force. It was the night of October 14. Washington had decided that if he were to take the town, he had to eliminate two remaining British strongholds, which were obstructing the buildout of his second and inner parallel. Once he got rid of British Redoubts 9 and 10, it would be checkmate on the British. Hamilton would lead the sneak attack on 10, while French forces would take 9. They would use the cover of darkness to execute the stealthy advance. To eliminate the possibility of an accidental discharge, which would have given up his position, Hamilton had his men empty their muskets of any ammunition. It would be a bayonet charge only.

The British never saw it coming.

The French got hung up at the palisade that surrounded Redoubt No. 9, and they took heavy casualties as they waited for ax-wielding operators to chop down the obstructions. But they managed to take the fortress in the end. The Americans led by Hamilton simply tore down the palisade with their bare hands as they ran up No.10. After a brief but fierce episode of hand-to-hand combat, the British surrendered. Hamilton was completely unscathed, though he lost nine of his men (about a third of what the French lost).[15]

With the allied siege now in full swing, Cornwallis was in serious trouble. It is reported that he ran and hid in a cave at the bottom of a small bluff dividing the town and the river's edge. The cave is still there today.

Whether he was in the cave or holed up somewhere in Nelson's house, as he watched his men fall by the hundreds, a humiliated and panic-ridden Cornwallis was asking the same perplexing question that Washington (and every other man on the battlefield) was asking—*Where is that promised, superior British navy to rescue its soldiers?* The answer, as perplexing as the question, is the result of yet another divine intervention.

Having regrouped after their unlikely naval defeat at the hands of the French, the British at last prepared once again to move out of New York to rescue the ailing Cornwallis. With plenty of time still to save Cornwallis's troops at Yorktown, the British fleet confidently made their preparation. Then the Lord stepped in once again. As Fleming explains:

> In New York, a frantic Sir Henry Clinton proposed . . . a rescue plan that called for putting most of the army on navy ships and fighting their way into the Chesapeake to join Cornwallis. . . . On October 13, the fleet was supposed to sail—when a tremendous thunderstorm swept over New York harbor. Terrific gusts of wind snapped the anchor cable on one of the ships of the line, smashing her into another ship and damaging both of them. . . . [The British] could not leave until the damage was repaired.[16]

With the American bombardment heating up, and with a tragic recognition that the British navy would not be coming to his rescue after all, Cornwallis immediately resorted to his desperate contingency plan—evacuate the Yorktown peninsula by ferrying his men northward over the York River and then march northward toward the British-friendly New York. In a plan that resembled that of Washington's at Long Island years earlier, Cornwallis would attempt the crossing on October 16, by the cover of night. The only discrepancy, of course, was that when Washington attempted such an escape, he had been acting under a covenant with God. Unfortunately for Cornwallis, it was this single factor that would make all the difference. Fleming explains:

> About ten minutes [after midnight] . . . a tremendous storm broke over the river. Within five minutes, there was a full gale blowing, as violent, from the descriptions in various diaries, as the storm that had damaged the British fleet in New York. Shivering in the bitter wind, soaked to the skin, the exhausted soldiers and sailors returned to the Yorktown shore. Not until two a.m. did the wind moderate. It was much too late to get the rest of the army across the river. Glumly, Cornwallis ordered the guards and the light infantry to return.[17]

Cornwallis was dumbfounded. He later wrote that when he embarked on his nighttime crossing, the weather was "moderate and calm." Then suddenly, he explained, the weather "changed to a most violent storm of wind and rain."[18] Another officer observed that it was "almost as severe a storm as I ever remember to have seen."[19]

With no other option available, Cornwallis was forced to surrender to Washington on October 19, 1781. This final blow was enough to convince the British to terminate their war efforts (though the peace treaty signed at Paris—which officially ended the war—would not be realized until 1783). America was at last free.

As British soldiers approached the Americans to surrender Cornwallis's sword, the depressed British band began to play, very fittingly, a popular tune, "The World Turned Upside Down."[20] Indeed, the world was turning upside down, just as the Lord had planned it in preparation for His latter-day work.

In emphasizing the significance of the details of the Battle at Yorktown, as outlined above, Fleming offers the following insight:

The British surrender to Washington.

A Cornwallis getaway would have left the French and Americans frustrated and hopeless, facing a stalemated war they no longer had the money or will to fight. American independence—or a large chunk of it—might have been traded away in the peace conference. A Clinton invasion . . . would have triggered a stupendous naval and land battle that might well have ended in a British victory—enabling them to impose the harshest imaginable peace on the exhausted Americans and shattered French. Instead the Allies had landed the knockout blow.[21]

Though Fleming's above analysis is no doubt a sound one, Washington might take issue with one point from his conclusion. The "knockout blow" was first and foremost landed, not by the Allies, but by the Lord. "I take particular pleasure," Washington would explain in reference to his Yorktown victory, "in acknowledging that the interposing hand of Heaven, in various instances of our preparations for this operation, has been most conspicuous and remarkable."[22]

◆　◆　◆

As I stood atop Redoubt No. 10, I got lost in the scene. I looked out into the York River, exactly where Cornwallis attempted his crossing. I tried to imagine the Lord's storm crashing down upon the British there. My thoughts turned to the many instances throughout the war when the Lord entered violently, as He does so well, through His control of the weather. Boston. Long Island. Trenton. And the others. Every major and significant battle. Again and again. I felt the Spirit.

Standing upon the fortification, I thought of other instances when the Lord had done the same with another group of righteous followers—a group who, frankly, lived to continue the story of the Revolution. In 1834, Joseph Smith led the Zion's Camp march. The LDS group departed Ohio in an effort to assist the persecuted Saints in Missouri. At one point during the march, they had camped down for the night on a small piece of land nestled in between two branches of the Fishing River. Unbeknownst to the camp, some four hundred enemies of the Church waited on the opposite side of the river to raise havoc with the Saints. With a plan to "utterly destroy the Mormons," the mob had promised that Zion's Camp would "see hell by morning."

Then suddenly, a dark cloud dropped over the scene, after which Joseph exclaimed, "Boys, there is meaning to this. God is in this storm."[23] What followed was a torrent so ferocious that it forced the schemers to scatter for shelter. Whereas the evening before, the river had been ankle deep, within an hour of the storm, it was flowing up to forty feet deep. Trees and vegetation were torn to shreds. One of the mobbers was struck by lightning and killed. Another had his hand torn off. The storm formed a protective circle around Zion's Camp but left the camp itself largely unaffected. The Mormons were not harmed and felt little of the storm's devastating power.[24]

As the storm "soaked and made the mobbers' ammunition useless . . . and raised the level of the Fishing River," an attack would be impossible.[25] Joseph later commented that "the wind, rain, hail and thunder met [the enemy] in great wrath . . . and frustrated all their design to 'kill Jo Smith and his Army.' . . . When Jehovah fights, they would rather be absent."[26] Like Washington before him, Joseph received protective blessings by a covenant, which his camp and army were required to live (see D&C 105).

A similar miracle occurred in 1857 when U.S. General A.S. Johnston led a 2,500-man march on Salt Lake City, under the false assumption that Brigham Young was stirring up a rebellion against the Union. An unusually early snowstorm over western Wyoming stopped the advancing army in its tracks, giving the Church time to clear its name with the truth and thus resolve the issue peacefully.[27]

With my eyes still fixed on the York River, I thought about heavenly patterns and how these patterns, especially when seen in the aggregate, corroborate the individual instances. God's works are so easily identifiable, if only we will open our eyes and see. Whether national covenant makers, like Washington's faithful, or priesthood covenant makers, like Joseph's faithful, they were preserved in their crucial hour of need, that His work and glory might go forth.

As I walked down the redoubt, I noticed I had cut my hand, probably on the palisade. It was bleeding pretty heavily. I was so lost in thought, I didn't even remember it happening. I do remember chuckling a bit, thinking, *Cool, I've been wounded on the battlefield.* But silly thoughts were very soon replaced by a Book of Mormon prophecy that filled my mind—a prophecy about the American Revolution:

> And it came to pass that I, Nephi, beheld that the Gentiles who had gone forth out of captivity did humble themselves before the Lord; and the power of the Lord was with them. And I beheld that their mother Gentiles were gathered together upon the waters, and upon the land also, to battle against them. And I beheld that the power of God was with them, and also that the wrath of God was upon all those that were gathered together against them to battle. (1 Nephi 13:16–18)

The Book of Mormon is true! The restored gospel is real! I remember thinking and feeling these thoughts as I walked away from Redoubt No. 10. Who knew that a visit to a battle site of the American Revolution would so readily testify of these great truths?

"There is something very special about this place." Those were the first words my friend said to me as I approached him near where we had left the car. I had had no communication with him since sprinting away for the redoubt.

With a very sober look on his face, he continued, "I feel like the spirits who worked upon this ground are still here or something. Am I crazy?"

I smiled. "I don't think so."

DIVINE PROVIDENCE

Shortly after the war, Charles Thompson, secretary of the Continental Congress, proposed to Washington that the two of them collaborate on writing their memoirs of the entire war experience. After all, Thompson had been present during all the congressional actions, while Washington could account for the battles; between the two of them they could tell the entire story. However, upon outlining the project, they realized how the results simply did not add up. For no mixture of America's congressional or military maneuverings could explain the American victory. By all accounts, the British should have won. Because of this, they decided against the memoir. One renowned historian of the American Revolution, Thomas Fleming, explains the decision: "It would be too disillusioning if the American people discovered how often the Glorious Cause came close to disaster." Fleming concludes his brief narrative, explaining that Washington and Thompson "jointly agreed that the real secret of America's final victory in the eight-year struggle could be summed up in two words: Divine Providence."[28]

I explained to him that I get the same impression whenever I visit these sacred spots. "I think they are here," I concluded.

As we opened the car doors, we had fun guessing what revolutionary heroes might have spent time in or around Redoubt No. 10, and who may still show up here from time to time. (My friend clearly wanted to know whose spirits he might have been feeling around him.) With the exception of Hamilton, I really did not know who else had spent any significant time in the redoubt during the battle.

We got in the car and I pulled out my laptop to make notes about what I had just experienced. As my friend started the engine, the CD automatically picked up where we had left off. The very first words the narrator spoke as the CD began again left us both shocked and stilled: *After Hamilton took the redoubt, Washington moved in. It was from Redoubt 10 that Washington penned the Articles of Capitulation in preparation for Cornwallis's surrender.* I sat there in reverence, hardly noticing the small drops of blood falling from my hand and dripping on my keyboard.

◆　◆　◆

On October 20, 1781, only one day after Cornwallis surrendered, Washington directed yet another General Order to "[recommend] that the troops not on duty should universally attend with that seriousness of Deportment and gratitude of Heart which the recognition of such reiterated and astonishing interpositions of Providence demand of us."[29] Though the war was over, Washington would waste no time at all—not even one day—in encouraging compliance to that American covenant which he had learned so convincingly to trust in and love.

Congress followed suit shortly thereafter with its own official proclamation—yet another invocation to God and covenant:

Whereas, it hath pleased Almighty God, the supreme Disposer of all Events, father of mercies, remarkably to assist and support the United States of America in their important struggle for liberty, against the long continued efforts of a powerful nation: it is the duty of all ranks to observe and thankfully acknowledge the interpositions of his Providence in their behalf. . . .

It is therefore recommended to the several states to set apart the 13th day of December next, to be religiously observed as a Day of Thanksgiving and Prayer; that all the people may assemble on that day, with grateful hearts, to celebrate the praises of our gracious Benefactor; to confess our manifold sins; to offer up our most fervent supplications to the God of all grace, that it may please Him to pardon our offenses, and incline our hearts for the future to keep all his laws . . . and cause the knowledge of God to cover the earth, as the waters cover the seas.[30]

CHAPTER 7

American Moses

President Ezra Taft Benson declared, "Our Father in Heaven planned the coming forth of the Founding Fathers and their form of government as the necessary great prologue to the restoration of the gospel."[1] Because of this gospel prologue, temples now dot the earth. Do we take this fact for granted? Never before in the history of mankind has the fulness of the gospel, and therefore the fulness of salvation, been so readily available. This happened because God made America. He made a nation that had not existed before—one with the liberty necessary to host the Restoration.

But we are tricking ourselves if we believe that this liberty came when the British walked off the battlefield in defeat. Winning the war was not going to be enough. The Constitution, along with the God-given liberties it protected, was no foregone conclusion after the colonists had secured their independence from Britain. In fact, historical trends forecasted a gloomy immediate future in the aftermath of the war. Sadly, throughout the history of the world there has been an unfortunate pattern that seems to dictate how national revolutions are supposed to end. The hero of the revolution, utilizing his victorious armed forces, along with his national popularity, propels himself into power and makes himself dictator over his people.

Not only have we seen this pattern in ancient governments—like ancient Rome—but also in more modern ones. In the mid-seventeenth century, for example, Oliver Cromwell led a popular revolution over the British monarchy, only to then purge parliament and rule himself as king. In the late eighteenth century the French Revolution would also oust the king, only to replace him by other dictators such as Napoleon. The nineteenth century would see Mexico win its popular independence from Spain, only to see the military dictator Santa Ana throw out the constitution and rule according to his personal dictates. In the early twentieth century, the Russian Revolution would result in a series of communist dictators worse than any of the earlier Russian monarchs who had been overthrown. On through the balance of the twentieth century, the world would see a series of the most brutal dictators emerge out of popular, national revolutions: Hitler in Germany, Mao in China, Castro in Cuba, and so on.

How would the American story end? Would it be different from all the others? If so, it would be perhaps the greatest miracle of all the miracles in the American Revolution. There *was* one ancient figure with whom Americans were very familiar who had defied historical trends and did the right thing for the right reason. His name was Moses. He had followed God's command and, against all odds, freed his people from tyranny and preserved them in liberty. Americans needed a Moses now to ensure that the American story would follow the same ancient pattern. After George Washington had led the nation through many battlefield miracles, it was easy to frame him as the American Moses they sought. "He who had commanded Moses at the Red Sea," one orator of the Revolution declared, "also inspired Washington on the banks of the Delaware."[2]

But could Washington, like Moses, defy historical trends and go the distance? Americans knew what Moses had done. He was a hero-figure to America because he had brought *liberty* and *law*. It was one thing to liberate the children of Israel from the tyrannical choke hold of the Egyptians, but it was an entirely different thing to bring them a government that would protect that liberty, that would allow them to build their tabernacle (their temple), to worship freely and find their salvation. Instead of making himself a tyrant over his people, which he easily could have done, Moses built a government to God. In addition to bringing the Ten Commandments down from Sinai, which established the foundation of the law, Moses created a republic. The government was based in liberty (see Leviticus 25:10) and sustained by a division of local and national, even layered, government functions (see Exodus 18:13–26), wherein Moses dispersed power to other political figures besides himself. This created a natural system of checks and balances that protected liberty. Moses also allowed for new laws to be created by the consent of the people (see Exodus 19:7–8).[3]

Underlying all of this, of course, was a belief in a covenant relationship with the Almighty. "Keep therefore the words of this covenant," declared Moses to his nation, "and do them, that ye may prosper in all that ye do" (Deuteronomy 29:9). Israel would remember these words and try to live by them. Declared the Lord to His ancient nation: "If my people . . . shall humble themselves, and pray, and seek my face, and turn from their wicked ways; then will I hear from heaven" (2 Chronicles 7:14). Moses and ancient Israel had shown the example of how to build a nation under God. Moses turned the people to heaven and asked them to obey God and believe in miracles. Then, upon that foundation he brought *liberty* and *law,* and thus the opportunity for salvation.

Since the first settlers arrived upon American shores, they sought to use this very formula for nation building. They sought an American Moses. These founding generations of Americans even referred to their land as the "New Israel." They named their towns and cities after biblical locales—Bethel, Bethlehem, New Canaan. More than one thousand of their towns were thus named. They also regularly named their children after prominent Hebrews mentioned in the first five books of the Bible. They saw themselves as God's chosen people, fleeing the pharaohs and tyrants of Europe.[4]

A 1973 study directed by political scientist Donald Lutz demonstrated this. Dr. Lutz and his team set out to evaluate everything published in America during the time of nation building (between 1760 and 1805). They sought to settle the long-standing debate about which of the Enlightenment writers most influenced the creation of America. Was it Montesquieu? Locke? Hume? Hobbes? Or perhaps it was the more ancient writers, such as Plutarch or Cicero. The answer stunned them all. It was, overwhelmingly, the writers of the biblical covenant. More particularly, the Founders' most quoted book was Deuteronomy, which arguably does more than any book to define the covenant relationship between God and a nation.[5] Americans of the Revolution sought to build a nation under God, and so they emulated ancient Israel. They sought an American Moses.

Benjamin Franklin had even proposed that the new American nation should use as its official seal a depiction of Moses freeing Israel from its Egyptian oppressors through the power of God, represented by "Rays from the Pillar of Fire in the Clouds." Thomas Jefferson proposed that the seal depict the children of Israel being led in the wilderness "by a cloud by day and a pillar of fire by night."[6]

By the end of the War for Independence, America had indeed seen miracles. The Americans had laid a proper foundation upon a covenant relationship with God. But they had neither

Proposal for the official seal of the nation.

liberty nor law, at least not at the level required for the incoming Restoration. They had bested the British, certainly, but then what? They needed the fulness of their promised land. They needed their Constitution. They needed their Moses. Without this, the hope for sufficient liberty in the land (the kind of liberty required to sustain the building of God's temples) would remain but a hope.

Would Washington be the new Moses to save America and build the foundation for God's gospel Restoration?

◆　◆　◆

As historical trends would predict, the dark offer came to General Washington at war's end. It was the same offer Satan tempted the Christ with: "Again, the devil taketh him up . . . and sheweth him all the kingdoms of the world, and the glory of them; And saith unto him, All these things will I give thee" (Matthew 4:8–9). The same was offered to Moses (see Moses 1:12). But both Christ and Moses were two very rare men in history who turned it down flatly. *Get thee hence, Satan,* was their answer.

"There are many called, but few are chosen," states the Lord. "And why are they not chosen? Because their hearts are set so much upon the things of this world, and aspire to the honors of men. . . . It is the nature and disposition of almost all men, as soon as they get a little authority, as they suppose, they will immediately begin to exercise unrighteous dominion" (D&C 121:34–35, 39). Almost every leader of every revolution failed this test, Christ and Moses being the exceptions.

It was now Washington's turn to be tested.

I can only imagine his face as he read the offer in the letter from American Colonel Lewis Nicola. *Take your rightful place as King George I of America,* the letter encouraged. Many of Washington's leading officers were tired of having to listen to Congress. They were weary from having to deal with the inefficiencies of a republic, where the people's will slowly and sluggishly worked its way through its representatives. A king would get things done much quicker. Washington would only be doing that which had been done for thousands of years. And nobody could possibly stop him. By the end of the war, as McCullough points out, his men would "follow [him] through hell."[7] Taking over Congress, therefore, would have been easy. Indeed, the only person who could have stopped Washington was Washington. And that is exactly what happened. *Get thee hence, Satan,* was Washington's immediate reply. "By God," he would later declare, "I had rather be on my farm than be made emperor of the world!"[8]

To Colonel Nicola, Washington shot back this stinging reply:

> With a mixture of great surprise and astonishment I have read with attention the Sentiments you have submitted to my perusal. Be assured Sir, no occurrence in the course of War, has given me more painful sensations

than your information of there being such ideas existing in the Army as you have expressed, and I must view with abhorrence, and reprehend the severity. For the present, the communicatn. of them will rest in my own bosom, unless some further agitation of the matter, shall make a disclosure necessary.

I am much at loss to conceive what part of my conduct could have given encouragement to an address which to me seems big with the greatest mischiefs that can befall my Country. If I am not deceived in the knowledge of myself, you could not have found a person to whom your schemes are more disagreeable.[9]

So sure was Washington on the matter that he would express years later that God had intentionally barred him from having any children of his own (it is believed he was impotent) so as to prevent any future temptations from them or his countrymen to create a monarchy of his name. "Divine Providence," he would write, "has not seen fit that my blood should be transmitted . . . by the sometimes seducing channel of immediate offspring." He would state thankfully that there was "no family to build in greatness upon my country's ruins."[10]

Though not as flashy and apparent as the miracles that occurred on America's battlefields, it was this single decision by Washington that saved the Revolution. He himself had become the greatest miracle of them all. He had become the American Moses. He had brought and now preserved God's liberty.

When at first given his commission to lead the armies, George Washington was only forty-three years old. At war's end, and with America's fate still undetermined, he was well into his fifties. He had aged physically, emotionally, and spiritually. A comparison can be made here to the New Testament Apostles—Peter, James,

John, and the others. When they walked with the mortal Savior, they were clearly so new at this, so young and innocent in their faith. After the Savior ascended into heaven, these Apostles had already grown so much that they seemed like new men in the way they spoke, acted, and commanded their situations. True prophets of the Almighty.

Washington followed a similar pattern. During the war, the Lord was not about to let him fail. He held his hand throughout the conflict. When Washington would be on the verge of making some enormous battlefield error that was certain to lead to his death—or worse, the death of the Revolution—the Lord would intervene and save the day. By scriptural decree, the war was taken care of. God just needed a humble, brave, and smart tool who would follow heaven's program and lead the armies. Washington was that tool. The war represented his baptism, his conversion to the cause.

But now, he had become much more. He was prophet-like. That meant America was really becoming the New Israel, and people began to sense it. During this post-war era, there was a heightened sense that America was the chosen land. Public calls and announcements began to fill the air. Washington was the new Moses. The ancient covenants of the Bible found application in America like never before.

But Satan knows how to take down a nation. And he wasn't about to give up on taking down America. This new country was a severe threat to him. Within a year of Nicola's scheme being foiled, and with things still unresolved with Congress, American officers again began conspiring to turn the sword on Congress and take the country by force, even if Washington would not join them. This plot, which was being organized in early 1783 at

THE GATHERING OF ISRAEL
TO THE AMERICAN ZION

"God determined that a remnant should be saved . . . recovered and gathered . . . from the nations whither the Lord had scattered them in his fierce anger . . . and multiply them over their fathers—and rejoice over them for good, as he rejoiced over their fathers.

"Then the words of Moses . . . will be literally fulfilled; when this branch of the posterity of Abraham shall be nationally collected, and become a very distinguished and glorious people under the Great Messiah, the Prince of Peace.

"He will then make them 'high above all nations which he hath made in praise, and in name, and in honor,' and they shall become 'a holy people unto the Lord' their God."

—Ezra Styles, President of Yale University[11]

the army camp in Newburgh, would go down in history as the Newburgh Conspiracy.

When Washington received word of the movement, he at once condemned it and traveled directly to the camp. On March 13, 1783, Washington called a meeting in a large building in the camp known (perhaps fittingly) as the Temple. Washington, in a passionate speech, pled with the men not to reverse all the good they had done. The soldiers were still visibly upset and apparently unmoved. Washington then prepared to read a letter from one congressman who expressed his desire to work out a peaceful negotiation with the army. Before reading the letter, Washington took out a pair of glasses, which he had only recently needed and acquired, then stated, "Gentlemen, you will permit me to put on my spectacles, for I have not only grown gray but almost blind in your service."[12] Indeed, the old man Washington, who had begun the conflict as a relatively young man, had literally aged and transformed before his soldiers' eyes. The reminder of his own personal sacrifice not only melted the anger in the room but caused a complete change of heart. Many of those present wept openly.

Washington finished his comments and left the officers to make their decision. They called off the coup. Word of the de-escalation arrived just in time to Congress, as it was preparing to declare a preemptive war on the military factions responsible. But thankfully, all would soon be forgiven as a peaceful settlement was at last agreed upon.[13] Washington had once again proven to be the indispensable man.

Thomas Jefferson would appropriately observe that "the moderation and virtue of [Washington] probably prevented the Revolution from being closed, as most others have been, by a subversion of that liberty it was intended to establish."[14] Even King George III, Washington's nemesis (and one who knew a thing or two about political power grabs) declared, upon hearing of Washington's intention to give back all power to Congress, that he must be "the greatest man in the world."[15] And so he was.

By December 23, 1783, the country seemed stable enough. Washington was about to do the incomprehensible. Though he possessed more political and military power in one finger than the whole body of the Continental Congress did, he stood before that congressional body now. He took out his sword and laid it before them. He did not predict he would be coming back a few years later to serve as the nation's first president. In his mind, this was it. His public life was over. He would turn all power over to the people, then quietly return to his farm. But before he did, he felt he should make one final statement: "I consider it an indispensable duty to close this last solemn act of my Official life, by commending the Interests of our dearest Country to the protection of Almighty God, and those who have the superintendence of them, to his holy keeping."[16]

Thus ended the greatest revolutionary war the world has ever known. For it ended with the national leader farming his land. In the end, Washington had indeed proven to be the exception to the rule of world history's revolutionary leaders. At least one revolution and its leader needed to set the example that other nations could follow. Someone needed to show how to usher in an inspired government in preparation for the arrival of God's gospel Restoration. That this standard-bearer was Washington, a principal covenant maker in the land divinely ordained from its conception, should be of no surprise. Washington was, after all, fulfilling prophetic utterances pertaining to this chosen land, as issued by the Book of Mormon: "And this land shall be a land of liberty unto the Gentiles, and there shall be no kings upon the land, who shall raise up unto the Gentiles" (2 Nephi 10:11).

George Washington resigning his commission.

◆　◆　◆

The miracle of Washington's resignation is largely lost on America today. There is little remaining to memorialize it. There is no major monument to the event, no battlefield we can walk over as we ponder what Washington did in this instant. But several years ago, I found something when I was wandering through the Smithsonian's National Museum of American History. The sight of it immediately took me back to Washington's day of resignation. It is a thirty-ton sculpture of the general completed in 1840, entitled, simply enough, *George Washington.* It depicts the general cradling a sheathed sword upon his left forearm and open palm, extending it forward as if to be returning it. It is a symbol of the general's inspired decision to return all power to the people after the war.

That this act was part of a greater covenant is, most astonishingly, represented. First, the statue is full of imagery representing

THE AMERICAN ZION

The Protestant minister George Duffield referred to the newly independent America as the "American Zion" and connected the ancient covenants to the modern ones, likening Washington of America's national covenant to the prophet Joshua of the ancient covenant, and likening the foreigner king of France, who came to the rescue of the American Israelites, to Cyrus, the foreigner who did the same for the ancient Israelites.[17] Declared Duffield:

"With Israel of old, we take up our song: 'Blessed be the Lord, who gave us not as prey to their teeth. Blessed be the Lord, the snare is broken and we are escaped.' . . . Here also shall our Jesus go forth conquering and to conquer, and the heathen be given Him for an inheritance, and these uttermost parts for a possession. The pure and undefiled religion of our blessed Redeemer—here shall it reign in triumph over all opposition."[18]

George Washington statue in 1899, before it was installed in the Smithsonian.

ancient Greece (the first seat of democracy), which reflects the covenant blessing of freedom. Second, Washington is flanked on both sides by small statues that are attached to and part of the sculpture of the general. One depicts a Native American, reminiscent of the fulfillment of Joseph's prophesied blessings in Genesis 49 and of the Nephite prophets who foresaw the American Revolution. The other is of Christopher Columbus, reminiscent of another Nephite prophecy of the man who would be led by "the Spirit of God" to find that New World, which would eventually lead those inspired Gentiles to come forth "out of captivity, upon the many waters" and then "obtain the land for their inheritance" (1 Nephi 13:12–13, 15). They would come, and, through one of their greatest sons, George Washington, they would build one nation under God.

Finally, in a memorable symbol of the covenant, Washington is depicted sitting upon a grand throne with a robe draped over his right shoulder. While his left arm and hand are returning the sword, his right arm and hand are depicted being raised to the square, his index finger pointing to heaven.

◆ ◆ ◆

Liberty was secured. For now. But if Washington really was the American Moses, he could not forget about the law. The law needed to follow. He wanted so badly to remain on his farm and with his family. But the call came from his countrymen. He was needed once again. Through no effort of his own, he was elected to help create and administer this law. He left his home, reluctantly, to serve as the first president of the United States. With his oversight and leadership, the Constitution of the United States had recently been created. During the convention that created the document, Washington reminded the stalemated and bickering delegates why they were there and for whom they were working. "The event is in the hand of God!" he declared to them. Historian John Fiske commented that "from that moment the mood in which [the delegates] worked caught something from the glorious spirit of Washington."[19] The Constitution came forth in that spirit.

Just as God had written the Ten Commandments for Moses to deliver, so He did something similar with Washington and the Constitution. The Lord declared that the document contained "just and holy principles," after which He Himself placed His stamp of approval upon it, confirming that He had "established" it (D&C 101:77, 80). Washington seemed to agree. He stated that "The establishment of Civil and *Religious Liberty* was the motive that induced me to the field of battle."[20] "Every one shall sit

THE PROPHET AND
THE PRESIDENT TESTIFY

"The Constitution of the United States is a glorious standard; it is founded in the wisdom of God. It is a heavenly banner; it is to all those who are privileged with the sweets of liberty, like the cooling shades and refreshing waters of a great rock in a thirsty and weary land. It is like a great tree under whose branches men from every clime can be shielded by from the burning rays of the sun. . . . We say that God is true; *that the constitution of the United States is true;* that the Bible is true; that the Book of Mormon is true."

—*Joseph Smith, Jr.*[21]

"That we may then all unite in rendering unto him [God] our sincere and humble thanks . . . for the peaceable and rational manner in which we have been enabled to establish constitutions of government for our safety and happiness, and particularly for the national One now lately instituted, for the civil and religious liberty with which we are blessed. . . . And also that we may then unite in most humbly offering our prayers and supplications to the great Lord and Ruler of Nations and beseech Him to pardon our national and other transgressions . . . [and] to promote the knowledge and practice of true religion."

—*George Washington*[22]

in safety under his own vine and figtree, and there shall be none to make him afraid," declared Washington. "May the father of all mercies scatter light and not darkness in our paths, and make us all in our several vocations useful here, and in his own due time and way everlastingly happy."[23] He was proud that he had, under God's direction, helped create a Constitution with religious freedom, which he said was "unrivalled by any civilized nation of earth." Washington declared that the "bosom of America is open to receive, the oppressed and persecuted of all Nations and Religions, whom we shall welcome to a participation of all our rights and privileges."[24] The constitutional foundation had been laid so that temples might dot the earth in the very near future.

With God's fingerprints upon the new American law, Washington would need to deliver it. Like Moses, Washington too would descend his "Mount Sinai" with the law in his hand. He would descend Mount Vernon for the last time. He would abandon his desired retirement to become the president and deliver the law to the people on April 30, 1789, at his inauguration ceremony. The ceremony took place before an enormous crowd gathered at the new nation's first capitol: Federal Hall in the heart of New York City. It was the day Washington took his oath of office—the day the brand-new Constitution was activated and applied. He took his oath standing on the balcony of Federal Hall so the people standing below could witness the event. Like Moses,

> Washington was seen by his countrymen as another Moses brought to liberate America. Upon his death, hundreds of eulogies throughout the land made comparisons, such as the following: "Kind Heaven, pitying the abject and servile condition of our American Israel, gave us a second Moses, who should (under God) be our future deliverer from the bondage and tyranny of haughty Britain."[25]

he had secured his nation's liberty and would now secure the law. And the way he did this confirmed his divine role as the American Moses like nothing he had ever done before. Let me explain what I mean by that.

A while back, I stumbled upon a profound secret that connects this inaugural event to God, His covenants, and the Restoration of the gospel in a most astonishing way. When I first began learning about George Washington's inaugural ceremony, I was struck by the fact that he had felt inclined to call for a Bible to place his left hand upon, while his right arm was raised, forming a square, as he took his oath and made his covenant. Upon pondering the event, I remember thinking, with a tongue-in-cheek smile on my face, that he most certainly would have used a Book of Mormon if only he had known where to find one. After all, his story so incredibly paralleled those in the Book of Mormon.

But I was satisfied with his choice of the Bible. It was exciting to me that inside the Bible he used was a powerful biblical prophecy about the promised land of America. As detailed in the first chapter of this book, Genesis 49 is that prophecy, which speaks of Joseph's posterity. "Joseph is a fruitful bough," it proclaims, "whose branches run over the wall" to a new land of "everlasting hills," ringing with *liberty, protection, and prosperity.*[26] As Lehi made his journey over the wall of water, declaring that his family was from Joseph, he almost certainly had the Genesis 49 prophecy in the brass plates he possessed. As explained in chapter 1, he was well aware of who he was, and we might suppose he knew what ancient prophecy he was fulfilling. He was headed to the land of Joseph—the New World, the promised land, America.

Throughout the Book of Mormon record we are reminded again and again that the covenant on this land was to be projected upon the Gentiles who would one day inherit it. Nephi saw this and declared it (1 Nephi 13:16–19), and the Savior Himself saw this and declared it (3 Nephi 21:4). Other references confirm the accepted view in LDS theology that the United States of America is the latter-day promised land foreseen by the ancients.[27] U.S. history also confirms it. How else can we explain the unprecedented explosion of liberty, protection, and prosperity in a land that is still an infant among nations? Only through God and His covenant blessings can such a thing be comprehended. The Genesis 49 prophecy indeed applied to George Washington and the nation he was building. The fact that Washington's story seems like one right out of the Book of Mormon begins to make sense. Same land. Same covenant. And so, like I said, I was satisfied that Washington had his hand upon a book that contained the ancient prophecy.

I thought I was done researching, discovering, and writing about Washington's inauguration when I walked the streets of Alexandria, Virginia, some time ago. The headquarters for the National Center for Missing and Exploited Children is in Alexandria, and I had been attending a training there. It just so happens that Alexandria, located a short distance from Mount Vernon, was also Washington's town. It was where he went to church. It was where he met with business colleagues and dined with friends.

We had just finished the weeklong training, and I had an hour or so before I had to leave for the airport. I decided to walk around the town, much of which still looks like it did in Washington's day. Of course, my mind was not far from our first president as I strolled about. I entered a local bookstore, hoping to find something to read on my long flight back home to California. The most prominent building in Alexandria is the enormous, towering George Washington Masonic National

Memorial, which sits upon a hill overlooking the town. It is dedicated to and named after America's most prominent Freemason—Washington himself. And so, when I saw a little book by H. Paul Jeffers called *The Freemasons of America,* I was naturally intrigued. I bought the book.

I was flying somewhere over the middle of the country when I got to page 28 of that book. When I read the seemingly unimportant and trivial fact documented on the page, I felt that my heart was going to burst. I immediately felt faint. I remember thinking that I could not breathe. *It can't be true,* I thought to myself. *There is no way.*

A stewardess passed by in my moment of shock. She asked me something about whether I wanted a snack, a drink, headphones, or something. I can't remember. All I remember is looking at her, unable to respond. I was dizzy. I looked around the plane, and the whole place was spinning. And it wasn't due to any kind of turbulence.

I looked back at the page. "When Washington recited the presidential oath of office as required by the Constitution, the Bible was opened to Genesis, chapters 49 and 50, consisting of the prophecies of Jacob. . . ."[28] *Joseph is a fruitful bough . . . whose branches run over the wall. . . .*

I took a deep breath. Astonished.

The reference in the book really had nothing to do with the prophecy, nor did it explain why Washington had chosen that page to place his hand upon. It was simply an incidental fact to the author. He was really just interested in the history of the particular copy of the Bible Washington had used that day, as it had been brought from a local Masonic lodge. I was lucky the fact was brought to light at all. Without the further light of the gospel—without the Book of Mormon to confirm the importance and

Washington's inauguration.

meaning of Genesis 49—the scripture Washington chose seemed of little import. And so, his use of the biblical passage has gone severely underreported. In fact, upon further investigation, the few commentators and historians who brought it up at all generally wondered out loud why Washington chose such a meaningless passage. It seemed like Old Testament gibberish to them. Most concluded that he must have just opened the book at random.

That it was a random choice is highly unlikely. Washington was a man more deliberate in action than any I have ever heard of or read about. And this was the first inauguration of its kind in American history. He knew that every move he made would be documented. Everything he wore remembered. Every word he uttered memorialized. The whole event would be analyzed a hundred times over. Knowing all this, it would be a strange move indeed to throw in such a random act.

Furthermore, in the giant Mason's Bible Washington used (which includes the Apocrypha), Genesis 49 begins approximately one-twentieth of the way through the enormous text. If he had allowed the book to just open randomly, isn't it far more likely that it would have opened somewhere in the center, as opposed to somewhere so near the beginning?

And then, of course, there is the test of probabilities. There is arguably only *one* really solid reference in the entire Bible to the promised land of America. One prophecy, according to official publications of The Church of Jesus Christ of Latter-day Saints, points directly to America and its spiritual destiny. *It is Genesis 49.*[29] I have never seen any other publication outside of the Church make such a bold claim about the prophecy. That the first leader of the latter-day American nation, which Nephi and others saw in vision, would take his oath while pressing his hand upon Genesis 49 is beyond astonishing. And I believe it is no coincidence.

> "The whole of America is Zion itself from north to south, and is described by the Prophets, who declare that it is the Zion where the mountain of the Lord should be, and that it should be in the center of the land. When Elders shall take up and examine the old prophecies in the Bible, they will see it."
>
> —Joseph Smith, Jr.[30]

When I wrote my very first draft for publication about Washington's inauguration (before I knew where he had placed his hand), I included the satisfying fact that his hand was upon the Bible. I also mentioned in my first draft how important it was to recognize that within what I thought was his closed Bible was the Genesis 49 prophecy. That was enough for me, so potent was that prophecy. The reason I mention this again is to refute any claim that I learned about where Washington's hand was, then backed into my conclusions regarding Genesis 49 from there. Quite the opposite had occurred. The discovery was, needless to say, more than a shock to my system. Perhaps you see why I got so dizzy in the airplane.

As I landed home in San Diego, I remember thinking how badly I wanted to jump back on a plane and return to the East Coast. I needed verification of what I had just read. I needed something. Anything. It was all so unbelievable to me. Luckily, I knew I would be back in Alexandria in the very near future.

When I returned to the city, I didn't know where exactly to go for confirmation. I figured George Washington's house was a good place to start. When I got to Mount Vernon, I began in the museum that sits on the grand estate. It was full of artifacts, writings, and stories about Washington's life. *There has to be something here about the inauguration,* I thought.

Then I saw it. Halfway through the museum stood a large display with props and life-size, very realistic looking wax figures depicting Washington and others standing on the balcony at Federal Hall. Washington was depicted taking his oath. And there was the Bible, opened at a point toward the beginning where the book of Genesis would be. I could see text in the Bible near to where Washington's hand lay, but I could not read it from where I stood. *Was that a real Bible they used? Would the page where the wax hand rested contain the amazing reference to confirm what I had read?* I was tempted to jump over the restrictive railings and onto the raised platform, then peek over the shoulder of the wax-work Washington. But I quickly realized that such an act would have earned me the boot right out of the place. Way too many people were around.

My eyes lowered, and I saw a better option. At ground level, just below the platform, I spotted another depiction—the opened

Bible Washington used. It was an exact replica, with text and all. There was a handprint upon the opened page, showing where Washington's hand had been. It was meant to encourage patrons to place their hands in the book over the handprint, in the very spot the president had placed his during his inauguration. When I stepped up, I did just that. I looked at the text around my hand: "Joseph is a fruitful bough," it read, "even a fruitful bough by a well; whose branches run over the wall. . . ."

I felt dizzy again.

After learning this secret, I became restless. I needed to know everything I could about what had happened on April 30, 1789, at Federal Hall—the day Washington pointed us to the ancient prophecy concerning America and the house of Israel. I learned that when Washington requested a Bible for the ceremony, it fell upon Jacob Morton, a leader at the nearby St. John's Masonic Lodge, to go and retrieve one from his lodge. As custodian of the Bible, Morton stayed close to it that day and, after the ceremony, marked the page in Genesis 49 where Washington had placed his hand.[31]

I still needed more. I knew from experience that my knowledge of the event would be limited unless I went to that sacred ground myself. I had to go to the very place Washington delivered the law. I needed to stand where he stood as he took his oath and addressed the nation. I needed to walk upon the ground he walked upon that day.

I booked a flight to New York City.

◆   ◆   ◆

It was past midnight in New York City when I looked upon Federal Hall for the first time. I had arrived in the city late that night, but, after checking into my hotel, I could not sleep. All

I could think about was Federal Hall. Instead of waiting for morning, as was the plan, I took a walk that ended with me in the public square directly in front of the building, standing on the very ground where throngs of people had looked upon Washington and heralded in the Constitution on April 30, 1789. They had come to witness Washington's inauguration at this place. I had brought several history books along with me so I could study and ponder while standing on location.

> "Biblical Israel and God's New Israel were formed on the twin shoulders of liberation and law. In both cases, one man was present at both moments. Both men had the unusual combination of skills—leadership and humility, fortitude and diplomacy—that could serve them well in dramatic moments of confrontation as well as years of slowly building a people. Beloved founders, both could have clung to power but resisted the temptation to turn their nations into monarchies. Reticent speakers, both left behind some of the most quoted words ever spoken."
> —*Bruce Feiler*, America's Prophet[32]

One observer who had witnessed the inauguration noted that, while standing upon the balcony of Federal Hall looking down upon the crowd below, Washington appeared quite nervous and agitated, "more than ever he was by the leveled cannon or pointed musket."[33] I tried to imagine the ever-humble Washington standing before me. I tried to imagine that I was one among the enormous crowd looking back at him.

I tried to imagine the hundreds of colonial Americans gathered at this place. I pictured newspapers in their hands—specifically, the *New York Daily Advisor,* which had been delivered to the New Yorkers days earlier and had invited them to come to Federal Hall to witness "our illustrious President [be] invested with his office." I thought of the words that accompanied that printed invitation: "the bells will ring at nine o'clock," the paper continued, "when the people may go up to the house of God and in a solemn manner commit the new government . . . to the holy protection and blessing of the Most High."[34] This was colonial America's version of the *New York Times.* Can you imagine such an invitation appearing in the *New York Times* today?

After I had envisioned all the people in long dresses and knickerbockers standing where I was in that moment, my attention shifted to the building itself. From the street below, my eyes followed the enormous and majestic cement stairway leading to the doors of Federal Hall (now a museum), until they met with the most prominent element of the building: the statue of George Washington. As I gazed upon Washington standing tall and prophet-like, with his palm placed downward as if he were placing it upon or inside of something, the Bible and its Genesis 49 prophecy filled my mind. I saw Jacob blessing Joseph's

> "May the Children of the Stock of Abraham, who dwell in this land, continue to merit and enjoy the good will of the other Inhabitants, while every one shall sit in safety under his own vine and figtree, and there shall be none to make him afraid."
> —George Washington, 1790[35]

people with the covenant land of America. My mind flashed back to the La Cañada window with its depiction of the scroll marked with the words "Stick of Joseph."

I pictured Washington taking his oath—left hand in Bible, right hand raised. Upon completing his recital of the oath, Washington spontaneously declared: "So help me God," then "bowed down reverently" and kissed the Bible.[36] An outward expression to demonstrate with whom the covenant was made.

Fittingly, this first oath of office ushered in a new form of constitutional government, which many referred to (and still do) as the *federal* government; and the root word for *federal*—the Latin *foedus*—directly translates into the English word *covenant*. In that the oath was taken in Federal Hall, we may most fittingly say that it was taken in *Covenant Hall*.[37]

After taking his oath, Washington would give his first inaugural address. What would he say? What message would he need his countrymen to understand? Considering the eight-year war we have just finished analyzing, we assume he would fall back on the national covenant. He would not forget who or what had brought him to this point. "It would be peculiarly improper," the new president declared, "to omit in this first official Act, my fervent supplications to that Almighty Being who rules over the Universe, who presides in the Councils of Nations, and whose providential aids can supply every human defect, that his benediction may consecrate to the liberties and happiness of the people of the United States."

He then got to the core of his message, invoking the covenant relationship with God in no uncertain terms: "We ought to be no less persuaded that the propitious smiles of Heaven, can never be expected on a nation that disregards the eternal rules of order and right, which Heaven itself has ordained."[38]

It had been almost eight years since Yorktown. The people had not seen their leader in public for some time. It must have been comforting to see that the covenant theology was still strong—if not stronger than ever—with the father of their country.

He continued: "No People can be bound to acknowledge and adore the invisible hand, which conducts the Affairs of men more than the People of the United States. Every step, by which they have advanced to the character of an independent nation, seems to have been distinguished by some token of providential agency."[39]

As I stood that night looking upon the statue representing the oath-taking, covenant-making Washington, I lost myself in these powerful words—words he had spoken here on these very grounds more than two hundred years earlier. At that moment, I was awakened from my trance by a distinct and startling noise that shot out from behind me. The sound of whipping fabric. I looked and beheld a series of Israeli flags lined up along the building that stood directly behind me and directly in front of Federal Hall. The building was the New York Stock Exchange, and the flags had been recently placed there to commemorate some sort of Jewish appreciation week. For me, the timing of my visit seemed providential. Those flags represented the country called Israel. Israel had been named after Jacob-Israel, the very man whose last act in mortality was to bless his sons and to prophesy over America—the New Israel.

And there was the statue of Washington, looking *directly* at those flags, with his hand mimicking what the real Washington had done that day, resting upon the promise God had decreed. Hearkening back to that ancient moment, to that ancient prophecy regarding Israel and the future promised land he now presided over. The experience, as I stood in the street at midnight pondering all these wonders, left me quite overwhelmed.

In front of Federal Hall that night, I wondered if perhaps Washington had been concerned about whether he had made his point clear enough. For he would continue teaching these same principles on that day, this time through action. After his speech, he descended into the crowd and led the people in a procession through the city and right into a beautiful house of worship— St. Paul's Chapel. He gathered the newly elected senators and

Statue of Washington at Federal Hall.

representatives of the new nation. In essence, the first joint session of Congress in the United States then commenced. It consisted of a prayer in a church.[40]

After my midnight musings at Federal Hall, I couldn't wait for morning. As soon as the doors opened, I was inside the building, gazing in awe upon Washington's Bible on display. Shortly thereafter, I traced the steps of Washington's procession and entered St. Paul's Chapel, which still looks like it did in Washington's day. Upon arriving, I began to learn what a special place the chapel is. Special to the Lord.

I was surprised to see how close the chapel was to Ground Zero, the place where the Twin Towers once stood before September 11, 2001. The chapel is literally right across the street.

St. Paul's Chapel, where George Washington led the members of Congress to pray.

On that devastating day, while buildings all around the church caught fire and were destroyed, somehow the church, built in 1766, remained unscathed, not even a window broken. Inside the church are several photos and memorials of the miraculous preservation of this holy site. In the immediate aftermath of the attack, firefighters, police, victims, and family members of the deceased used the church as a shelter and sanctuary.

It wasn't the first time the church was miraculously spared. Remember the fire we discussed earlier that burned New York City right after Washington had crossed the East River and escaped the British? One-fourth of the city right around the chapel was destroyed in that fire, including two prominent churches. Yet St. Paul's remained, gaining the nickname "the little chapel that stood."[41]

But more amazing still was what I found inside the chapel. In 1788, one year before Washington brought the inaugural

Altar at St. Paul's Chapel.

participants through its doors, Charles L'Enfant (who designed much of Washington, D.C.) built and placed something very special front and center in the chapel, right above the altar. The piece of art is called "Glory." It depicts "Mt. Sinai in clouds and lightning, and the Hebrew name for God—'YHWH'—is found at the top of the display. The Ten Commandments on two large tablets are at its base."[42] Today, as in Washington's day, "Glory" makes the place look as much like a Jewish synagogue as a Christian chapel.

I couldn't help but think this was part of the plan. I looked at those tablets in St. Paul's Chapel representing God's law to Israel and thought of the Constitution of the United States. Again, the parallels struck me. Washington at Federal Hall acting as Moses at Sinai. The Constitution, brought down from Federal Hall, acting as God's law on the tablets brought down from Sinai. All this to bless Israel, the old and the new, respectively.

The original copy of the Constitution currently resides in the National Archives at Washington, D.C. Visitors are welcome to come view the document. When they do, they must walk over powerful words engraved in bronze upon the floor of the National Archive's entrance. The words are the Ten Commandments. God's ancient law symbolically welcomes patrons to His modern one.[43]

All of this connects back to that sacred inaugural day—April 30, 1789. It is further testimony that the day revolved around hearkening back to the biblical covenants responsible for building nations unto the Almighty. This should not be lost on any of us. The covenant Washington made on behalf of the nation was born in ancient Israel, it was brought to America by Joseph's Lehite descendants, then was extended to the Gentiles (the settlers and revolutionaries in America) upon the same land. And the covenant is with us still today, should we seek its power for good.

The Founding Fathers' example of hearkening back and finding strength in the covenants of old made me think of other men and women of God who did the same. There is no lack of examples of this in the scriptures. Nephi, for example, was commanded to build a ship in which his family might travel to the promised land. As his brothers murmured, complained, and threatened him, Nephi brought them back to the story of Israel. "Now ye know that Moses was commanded of the Lord to do that great work," explained Nephi, "and ye know that by his word the waters of the Red Sea were divided hither and thither, and they passed through on dry ground." After recounting the other miracles that brought the children of Israel into their promised land, Nephi made the application: "And now, if the Lord has such great power, and has wrought so many miracles among the children of men, how is it that he cannot instruct me, that I should build a ship?" (1 Nephi 17:26, 51).

The American revolutionaries used the same approach as Nephi. They tapped into the covenant by hearkening back. And the Lord blessed them with miracles no less powerful than those that accompanied the children of Israel under Moses seeking their promised land, or the children of Israel under Lehi seeking theirs. Benjamin Rush, a signer of the Declaration of Independence, exemplified the Founders' belief in their connection to ancient Israel when he said of America and its Constitution that "the hand of God was employed in this work, as that God had divided the Red Sea to give a passage to the children of Israel" or had delivered "the ten commandments on Mount Sinai!"[44]

By building a foundation upon God's covenants of old, the Nephites were prepared to establish the gospel of Christ in the New World. They were able to build temples and thus open the portals to eternity and salvation. The American founders led by Washington did the same. "In the providences of the Almighty, the Constitution of the United States was established," declared Elder Bruce R. McConkie. "[It] came forth to prepare the way for the restoration of the gospel, the fulfilling of the covenants God made with ancient Israel, and the organization of the Church and Kingdom of God on earth in the last days."[45] If Washington was the American Moses, it makes sense that, like the actual Moses, and like righteous Nephite leaders before him, he might have known or sensed something about this crowning blessing of America. Indeed, one wonders how much Washington comprehended about temple worship and eternal life. We will explore these possibilities in the next two chapters of this book. But what we have confirmed so far is that, like our national heroes of the scriptures, he laid the spiritual and political foundation for God to bring about His ultimate purposes.

◆ ◆ ◆

In comparing Washington to Moses of the Bible, I could not help but seek his counterpart in the Book of Mormon. The person I found there could not have stood out any brighter. Captain Moroni had the arduous task, similar to that of Washington, of rallying his people against an enemy bent on stealing mankind's God-given liberties. Also like Washington, he was a national leader trying to build and defend a nation dedicated to God and His purposes. And, like Washington, he found his strength in hearkening back to the ancient covenants and remembering from whence he and his Nephite nation had sprung.

One morning, as I pondered over these righteous leaders, I reread an account about Captain Moroni found in Alma, chapter 46.

"And it came to pass that he rent his coat; and he took a piece thereof, and wrote upon it—In memory of our God, our religion, and freedom, and our peace, our wives, and our children—and he fastened it upon the end of a pole" (Alma 46:12). Thus was created the Title of Liberty.

Moroni then did *five* very specific things. *First,* he "girded on his armor about his loins" (Alma 46:13). *Second,* he "bowed himself to the earth, and he prayed mightily unto his God for the blessings of liberty to rest upon his brethren" (Alma 46:13). *Third,* "he went forth among the people, waving [the Title of Liberty] in the air, that all might see the writing." *Fourth,* he then declared to the people: "Behold, whosoever will maintain this title upon the land, let them come forth in the strength of the Lord, and enter into a covenant that they will maintain their rights, and their religion, that the Lord God may bless them" (Alma 46:19–20). Declared Moroni: "Surely God shall not suffer that we . . . shall be trodden down and destroyed, until we bring it upon us by our own transgressions" (Alma 46:18). In response, "the people came running . . . rending their garments in token, or as a covenant, that they would not forsake the Lord their God." And as they came, they declared, "We covenant with our God" (Alma 46:21–22). And *fifth,* Moroni reminded them who they were, whose family name they bore. "Behold, we are a remnant of the seed of Jacob; yea, we are a remnant of the seed of Joseph. . . . Yea, let us preserve our liberty as a remnant of Joseph; yea, let us remember the words of Jacob, before his death" (Alma 46:23–24).

Moroni explained that Jacob had blessed Joseph that a remnant of his people would be preserved, just as a remnant of Joseph's coat (most of which had been destroyed and decayed) was preserved (see Alma 46:24). The prophecy of where that remnant would go, of course, is contained in those very "words of Jacob, before his death" (Alma 46:24). *Genesis 49.* They would be liberated, delivered, and preserved in America.

As I finished reading the fascinating account of Captain Moroni, something happened. A realization hit me like a ton of bricks. The realization was accompanied by peace and light, as images of George Washington flashed through my mind. Instantly I saw him on the battlefield. I saw him rowing over the fog-filled East River, charging the enemy on horseback at Princeton, weeping and praying with his men at Valley Forge, and standing fearlessly in the trenches at Yorktown. At last, I saw him at Federal Hall on the day he sealed the covenant on the land and brought us the United States of America. *Could it be true?* I thought. *Did history really repeat itself so perfectly?* Though stunned, I realized it had. And it was absolutely remarkable. At Federal Hall, on April 30, 1789, as if reading from some script, Washington had followed Captain Moroni's exact steps, as described in Alma 46. *All five of them.*

1. Just as Moroni had girded on his armor before presenting the covenant to the nation on that day, Washington had done something similar. Before taking to the balcony at Federal Hall, a witness observed how he had dressed "in a full suit of dark-brown cloth of American manufacture, with a steel-hilted dress sword" tied about his waist.[46]

2. Just as Moroni had prayed on that day, Washington had led the people to pray at St. Paul's Chapel, not to mention the other prayer associated with the inauguration that was called for by the *New York Daily Advisor* to commence at nine o'clock that morning.[47]

3. Just as Moroni had brought forth the Title of Liberty on that day, that the people might see it, so did Washington. The promises of the Title of Liberty are the promises of the Constitution. Both are written forms of God's governmental mandate to preserve moral agency. Washington's inauguration set the U.S. government in motion—it was the day the Constitution was activated. If there was any specific point in time where we might say Washington raised up *his* Title of Liberty, it was this day.

4. Just as Moroni had called the people to the covenant while raising the famous standard, explaining to them that righteous living was the only way to secure God's blessings, so Washington did the same. The blessings, Washington said, would only come to the United States as its people obeyed the "eternal rules of order and right, which Heaven itself has ordained."[48] And as the ancient

people responded enthusiastically to Moroni, so the modern ones responded similarly to Washington. "Huzzah!, Huzzah!, Huzzah!," cheered the Americans;[49] then they followed their beloved leader to the chapel to let God know they had accepted His covenant.

5. And finally, just as Moroni confirmed his ability to call his people to the covenant by referencing Jacob's grand blessing to Joseph, so Washington appears to have done the same. While standing on the balcony of Federal Hall, he too called out the *very same* ancient prophecy of America while raising our Title of Liberty.

My heart raced as the dots connected. It occurred to me that it would take less faith to believe this all came from God than to believe this is just one more coincidence in a long chain of coincidences that have no other explanation. I had received yet one more assurance that the Book of Mormon is true—that American history from Washington through Lincoln testifies that it is true—and it was marvelous in my eyes.

As I sat there, my focus fixed on Alma, chapter 46, I became dizzy once again.

CHAPTER 8

Clasped Hands—Eternal Lives

Y ou are now standing over the crypt built for the body of George Washington."

I was pretty surprised by these words spoken matter-of-factly by the tour guide. Surprised because of where I stood. I was inside what is probably the most famous building in America. But I had never known it was intended to be Washington's tomb. According to the guide, Washington's family rejected the proposal that his body be laid to rest at this popular location. They knew better than that. The humble servant would much prefer to be buried at home, the one place he always wanted to be but rarely could be.

This startling fact immediately caused me to see the familiar building in a whole new light. I looked around, slowly spinning so as to see the grand symbology artistically memorialized in 360 degrees all around me. I sought for the whole picture. I know by now you may be tired of me telling you about the "ah-ha" moments I have had along my trail of discovery that make me breathless and dizzy. But it is what it is, and I was having another one—and, again, not because I was spinning around.

I had no reason to believe that what I was looking at in that moment was coordinated or orchestrated by some architect or artist. The various symbolic pieces had, after all, been created by very different people and placed in the building at very different times. Only the Lord Himself could have inspired hundreds of artisans and workers to make sure this story was being told within the walls of the famous structure, even the place where millions would come to visit and learn. And by what I was perceiving in that moment, a story most certainly was being told. It was one of the most important stories that has ever been told—a story deeply connected to the national covenant, Book of Mormon principles and prophecies, temples, and one of the greatest doctrines of the Restoration.

How can this all be here? I thought to myself as I continued rotating and noting all the imagery I saw around and above me. *It's not as though I'm standing in some LDS temple or an exhibition in an LDS visitors' center.*

But I surely felt like I was.

◆ ◆ ◆

Before giving more details about the tomb built for Washington, I need to provide some context. We find this context in the final days of George Washington's life. His ending has much to teach us about eternity.

December 1799. Only two years had passed since Washington had at last been able to retire to his family and farm. A happy and healthy Washington was fulfilling his quiet dream of farming his beloved Mount Vernon. After riding his horse about the estate (checking on the operations) in the cold and blowing snow, he came in for dinner and noted his throat was a bit hoarse. Shortly after, he caught what appeared to be a common cold. Unconcerned, he refused cold medicines that his assistant offered him. Infection grew rapidly. Then, to the shock of his family and the entire nation, within twenty-four hours of becoming ill, he was dead. Perhaps due to a premonition of sorts, shortly before

Mount Vernon.

becoming ill, Washington had given specific instructions on the construction of his Mount Vernon tomb.[1]

While on his deathbed, with his sweet companion, Martha, at his side, and with a Bible very near him, he politely told the doctors, "I feel myself going. I thank you for your attentions; but I pray you take no more trouble about me, let me go off quietly." He knew it was his time. "I die hard," he whispered. "But I am not afraid to go."[2] And why should he fear? This was, after all, the man who seemed to walk with God throughout his life, even stating himself that "No Man has a more perfect Reliance on the alwise, and powerful dispensations of the Supreme Being than I."[3] Furthermore, it was Washington who stated years before his death that when the "curtain of separation shall be drawing, my last breath will, I trust, expire in a prayer for the temporal and eternal felicity of those who . . . extended their desires to my happiness hereafter, in a *brighter world.*"[4]

Upon his death, his beloved Martha would submit, saying "'Tis well! All is now over. I shall soon follow him! I have no more trials to pass through."[5] She too was a woman of great faith, a converted Christian well versed in the scriptures.[6] She was always willing to suffer with the suffering and pray for their well-being.[7] In the wake of the funeral, she tried to be strong. But when a letter of condolence arrived from Abigail Adams, full of love, warmth, and hope, her heart melted and she let down her guard. A flood of cleansing tears followed. Shortly thereafter, she found a renewal of strength and faith in the Lord's plan. "I have only to go with humble submission," she wrote, one month after her husband's death, "to the will of that God who giveth, and who taketh away, looking forward with faith and hope to the moment when I shall be again united with the partner of my life."[8]

Within two years the waiting would be over. She would join him in death. And what a reunion it would be! Though they were a private couple (Martha destroyed most of their correspondence to keep their love story from becoming a public affair), they could not hide the fact that they were soul mates. George would often write to her during the war of his longing to be near her, even inviting her, when he could, to stay with him at his ever-changing military headquarters. And she would come. Furthermore, he loved her children (from a previous marriage) and adopted them as his own, which certainly endeared him to her all the more.[9]

The "brighter world," which Washington said he looked forward to beyond the veil, certainly grew brighter with the addition of his Martha. Then, years later, it appears to have grown brighter still. In August 1877, the Founding Fathers appeared in the St. George Utah Temple to Elder Wilford Woodruff. He recorded that the spirits declared to him, "You have had the use of the Endowment House for a number of years, and yet nothing

Washington's tomb at Mount Vernon.

has ever been done for us. We laid the foundation of the government you now enjoy, and we never apostatized from it, but we remained true to it and were faithful to God."[10]

James Bleak, a temple clerk, was also there. He stated: "I was also present in the St. George Temple and witnessed the appearance of the Spirits of the Signers . . . the spirits of the Presidents. . . . And also others . . . who came to Wilford Woodruff and demanded that their baptism and endowment be done."[11] Elder Woodruff immediately had their work done and at the same time assigned Sister Lucy Bigelow Young to perform baptisms for seventy women connected to this event.[12]

In an effort to express that the above event was not some invention of mind, or a formalistic rite of passage, Elder Woodruff recorded that he spoke with these individuals (he uses the word "argued"), and that they "pled" to him that their ordinances be done "as a man pleading for his life." Later, upon performing the baptisms, Elder Woodruff noted that it seemed as if "the room was filled as with flaming fire."[13]

Whenever Wilford Woodruff spoke of his St. George temple experience, he would mention that among the group of spirits who appeared to him were the signers of the Declaration of Independence. Besides that, he did not regularly mention specific names in public, with the exception of one name: George Washington.[14] More than ten years after the temple vision, and now standing as President of the Church, Wilford Woodruff declared the following in an April 1898 general conference address:

> I am going to bear my testimony to this assembly, if I never do it again in my life, that those men who laid the foundation of this American government and signed the Declaration of Independence were the best spirits the God of heaven could find on the face of the earth. They were choice spirits. . . . General Washington and all the men that labored for the purpose were inspired of the Lord.
>
> Another thing I am going to say here, because I have the right to say it. Every one of those men that signed the Declaration of Independence, with General Washington, called upon me, as an Apostle of the Lord Jesus Christ, in the temple at Saint George, two consecutive nights, and demanded at my hands that I should go forth and attend to the ordinances of the House of God for them. . . . Would those spirits have called upon me, as an Elder of Israel, to perform that work if they had not been noble spirits before God? They would not.[15]

Washington indeed appeared to be a prominent figure in the temple experience at St. George. The prominence of

George and Martha Washington with their grandchildren.

Washington's place there is further confirmed in the fact that the Apostle ordered that, in addition to Washington, the work be done for many of Washington's family members, including his father, Augustine; his mother, Mary Ball; his grandfather Lawrence; his great-grandfather John; his brother Lawrence; his brother's wife, Anne Fairfax; several members of Martha's family; and Washington's beloved stepchildren and step-grandchildren.[16]

The men who appeared at St. George were mostly ordained to the office of elder, but five of them, for reasons unexplained, were ordained high priests: Christopher Columbus, Horatio Nelson, John Wesley, Benjamin Franklin, and George Washington.[17]

And what happened to Martha? Of course, her temple ordinances were also performed. On August 22, 1877, George and Martha were vicariously sealed for time and all eternity.[18]

◆ ◆ ◆

As I stood over the empty crypt built for Washington, I looked all around me and was overwhelmed by the thought of what had happened in the St. George temple. All that I saw seemed to testify of that experience and what had led to that experience. The place I was standing inside was the rotunda of the United States Capitol Building.

The piece inside the rotunda that most touched me is called *The Apotheosis of Washington.* It is a 4,664-square-foot fresco that consumes the entirety of the rotunda's massive canopy. The outlying areas of the fresco are adorned with several scenes reminiscent of the national covenant. For example, one scene depicts a mythological-type figure that, with raised sword, is destroying other figures representing "tyranny and kingly power." Watching over the victorious freedom fighter is a fierce bald eagle carrying thunderbolts and arrows. The covenant blessings of liberty and protection are easily seen within this scene. Other scenes show heavenly messengers (represented by goddesses) providing wisdom to great Americans such as Benjamin Franklin, teaching and showing them how to progress in science, commerce, and agriculture. The covenant blessings of prosperity are clearly depicted.[19]

Reaffirming the covenant-based symbolism of this work are the oil-on-canvas paintings also displayed within the grand rotunda. As I observed these masterpieces, I was overcome by the idea that I was standing in the middle of a 1 Nephi 13 wonderland. Nephi's entire vision of America was laid out before me: the discovery (from verse 12), the settlement (from verses 13–14), the war (from verses 17–19), even elements of the gospel. The paintings include *The Landing of Columbus, The Embarkation of the Pilgrims,* and *The Baptism of Pocahontas.* Other murals in this chain of art include depictions of subsequent moments—some

The Apotheosis of Washington.

of the most powerful moments—of America's national covenant history. There is *Discovery of the Mississippi,* reminding us of the prominent role this river would play in the Restoration, as a principal mode of transportation for the gathering of the Saints at Nauvoo. Also present are paintings depicting two of the greatest victories of the Revolutionary War, which, as detailed previously, were won by the hand of God: *Surrender of General Burgoyne* (at the Battle of Saratoga) and *Surrender of Lord Cornwallis* (at the Battle of Yorktown). We see depicted other powerful signs of the covenant in *General Washington Resigning His Commission* and in *Declaration of Independence.*

These giant works seem to support the symbolic power presented by *The Apotheosis of Washington,* not only due to the related and powerful themes carried in all the artistic wonders, but also due to the paintings' position relative to the larger and more prominent work emblazoned upon the canopy. Indeed, the murals sit upon the base of the rotunda walls, seemingly in support of the canopy on which we see *The Apotheosis of Washington.*

But these symbolisms do not even scratch the surface of the power behind *The Apotheosis of Washington.* For the real power of this work is portrayed in a scene placed climactically at the middle of the masterpiece: a depiction of George Washington himself, dressed in white robes, ascending on a cloud to heaven with the covenant symbol of a rainbow arch at his feet. Flanking Washington are the goddess Victory and the goddess Liberty, and surrounding him are thirteen maidens, representing the colonies.[20] The principal word in the artwork's title, *apotheosis,* literally means "elevation to the status of a god."[21] It comes from the ancient Greek: *apo*—"to become," and *theos*—"God." To be sure, the scene is nothing less than a depiction of Washington receiving his exaltation—becoming like his Heavenly Father.

The symbolism of it all is almost overwhelming to those with a testimony of the restored gospel. Throughout this book we have documented how Washington was responsible for laying a foundation that would allow for the existence of temples on the earth. And we know that these temples exist so that mankind might access what is needed to gain exaltation with the Father—even to become like God. And so to stand in the most prominent place of the U.S. Capitol Building and take in what clearly depicts Washington—even he who helped make possible our access to exaltation—attaining his own exaltation is simply breathtaking. Then we see that imagery in the oil-on-canvas works that depict so many Book of Mormon prophecies fulfilled, prophecies recorded in 1 Nephi 13. That vision, of course, ends in a prophecy of the Restoration of the fulness of the gospel. The national covenant moments in Nephi's vision seem to support and lead us to that prophecy at the end of the chapter. Similarly, the oil-on-canvas depictions of these same national covenant moments seem to support and lead us to the same—to the doctrines of the fulness of the gospel found in *The Apotheosis*. We see a full depiction of how America and her covenant truly serve to elevate men and women to their highest potential, even to eternal life and exaltation.

The Capitol Building emanates a feeling that reminds me of what I feel when I look upon the La Cañada window. They seem to be teaching the same principles. After the symbolic depictions of the dove (the national covenant) and the keys (heavenly authority to open that covenant), the next window image in sequential order is that of clasped hands—a man's and a woman's. I can't look upon that image without thinking about what happened at St. George in August 1877. As those spirits told Elder Woodruff, they had built the foundation. Many of the original Founders and signers of the Declaration of Independence were still alive when Joseph Smith was born—some were still living even as he had his First Vision and was preparing to translate the Book of Mormon. In other words, God sent Joseph right on their heels, and He placed him upon the foundation they had built. When temples came, they came largely because of these American Founders. Because of what they did, they could stand in that temple. Because of what they did, we can stand there, too. The handclasp—eternal marriage and eternal lives—represents the fruit of that labor that can now bless all God's children, both the living and the dead.

When gazing upon the La Cañada window, I can't help but imagine in my own mind that the joined hands are those of George and Martha Washington. As leaders of a nation, they made a covenant to bring about liberty, protection, and prosperity. As leaders of a family, and with the support of this national covenant, they apparently (possibly) made another, more powerful, covenant to bring about exaltation. George and Martha's life is emblematic of the full story of America and her gospel purposes under the Almighty.

CHAPTER 9

The Pyramid

As we explore connections between the Revolution and the Restoration, there is one prominent symbol that cannot be ignored. It is an American symbol that connects both these scriptural movements and ties George Washington to temples in an astonishing way. The symbol is a pyramid, and it serves as a prominent icon within the Great Seal of the United States.

On that spiritual and historic day of July 4, 1776, Congress commissioned the creation of the United States seal, a powerful symbol of America and her purposes.[1] As Latter-day Saints, we understand how important symbols are to the Lord as a means of teaching His children. When we are considering heaven's role in bringing about American independence for the purposes of restoring the gospel, we should not take lightly the symbols born during that sacred founding era, especially symbols within the official seal of the United States. The pyramid is part of this seal. Though admittedly all we can really do is speculate about its full meaning, it is too important to not at least try to understand.

The seal contains both a front and

Reverse side of seal.

Pyramid on the back of the $1 bill.

reverse side. Both sides of the seal are displayed today on the back of the one-dollar bill. The prominent figure on the reverse side is an Egyptian-style pyramid with thirteen steps to the top, presumably representing the thirteen colonies. The triangular capstone, or the apex, of the pyramid depicted in the seal contains a human eye and is surrounded by rays of glory. This precise image—with the triangle, the eye, and the rays of glory—is curiously found in the La Cañada chapel window, directly following the image of the handclasp. The eye, called the all-seeing eye, represents God the Father watching over the world.[2]

The secretary of Congress during the Revolution, Charles Thompson, was commissioned to finalize the seal project. Not insignificantly, Thompson was a biblical scholar who had translated the Greek Bible into Latin. A moral man, he was known as the "Soul of Congress."[3] Naturally, Thompson commented on the seal's symbolism in terms that clearly reflect the national covenant.

> The pyramid signifies strength and duration: The eye over it and the motto, Annuit Coeptus [translation: "God Has Favored Our Undertakings"], allude to the many interventions of Providence in favour of the American

cause. The date underneath is that of the Declaration of Independence, and the words under it, Novus Ordo Seclorum [translation: "A New Order of the Ages"], signify the beginning of the new American era in 1776.[4]

We don't get much more in terms of an official explanation. Yet, there is more to be explained. As renowned symbologist David Ovason has observed, "the pyramid [on the U.S. seal] has remained something of an enigma" and has been largely "unknown because it has not been understood."[5] As we have seen throughout this book, often the gospel fills in some of the mysteries of life, particularly mysteries dealing with the promised land of America. It seems to in this case. For the symbol here seems to tell the rest of America's gospel story, which ends with temples in the land. Our first clue is the fact that the all-seeing eye, surrounded by rays of glory, shows up on the outer walls of the Salt Lake Temple.[6] Our second clue is the notion that the symbol of the pyramid is, in and of itself, uniquely connected to temples.

LDS scholar Hugh Nibley researched and wrote extensively on the meaning of Egyptian pyramids and Egyptian temple worship. The pyramids are burial monuments, but the ancient symbols and texts make it clear they were more than that. Pyramid burials revolved around the hope that the deceased would resurrect and return to God. Like temples today, pyramids represented the portals to heaven. One interesting Egyptian pyramid ritual that prepares the deceased for eternity is known as the "Opening of the Mouth" rite. Essential body parts and organs are washed with water, then anointed with oil. According to renowned Egyptologist Alexandre Moret, "one was anointed on the mouth, eyes, ears, and different parts of the reconstituted body. . . . Thus the mouth, eyes, and ears can breathe, speak, and eat; see; and hear; the arms can act, and the legs can walk."[7]

Egyptologists agree that the participants in the ordinance sought "to insure the physical integrity of the deceased" and believed it would produce "a miracle . . . which restored to each [organ] its proper functions."[8]

Another of the fascinating rituals connected to the pyramid texts is that of the "embrace." As represented in ancient Egyptian texts and art, God the Father, according to Nibley, embraces the candidate to represent "the fusion of the heaven-bound deceased with [God]."[9] In explaining the relationship between God and the deceased, Nibley observes that "in the pyramid rite, the dead had to be crowned . . . before he could begin his final journey to heaven." But in this coronation rite, "the dead is not presuming to rival or supplant the god, but rather to be as much like the 'divine prototype' as possible." The ceremony was, according to Egyptologist Hans Bonnet, to produce the standard "seal of divine recognition and the promise of divine blessings."[10]

Utilizing references in Abraham 1:26–27, Professor Nibley points out that the Egyptians indeed imitated true temple ordinances. "The ordinances of the Egyptian temple," concluded Nibley, as recorded in his book *Temple and Cosmos,* "were essentially the same as those performed in ours."[11] Brigham Young University professor of ancient scripture Michael D. Rhodes explains:

> Studies of Egyptian temple ritual . . . have revealed parallels with Latter-day Saint temple celebrations and doctrine, including a portrayal of the creation and the fall of mankind, washings and anointings, and the ultimate return of individuals to God's presence. Moreover, husband, wife and children are sealed together for eternity, genealogy is taken seriously; people will be judged according to their deeds in this life, and the reward for a just life

is to live in the presence of God forever with one's family. It seems unreasonable to suggest that all such parallels occurred by mere chance.[12]

Professor Nibley further corroborates the idea that gospel truths existed in ancient Egypt by pointing out its religious doctrines of a pre-earth life, a council in heaven, the great dispute between two brothers (only one of which was the chosen one), the existence of a Heavenly Father *and* a Heavenly Mother, and their offspring known as the Great One.[13]

Considering the scriptural history of Egypt, I suppose it makes sense that such truths would remain there for our discovery. Think of the greats who spent time there: Abraham, Joseph, Moses, and the children of Israel. We are taught in the Book of Abraham that the Egyptian Pharaoh, "being a righteous man," sought to "imitate that order established by the fathers in the first generations, in the days of the first patriarchal reign, even in the reign of Adam" (Abraham 1:26). Egyptian archeology, some of which we have just discussed, corroborates this truth.

We could explore volumes written on this subject, but that would fall outside the scope of this book. For the purpose of this hypothesis, the important connection is that Egyptian pyramids can reasonably symbolize true temples. With that understanding, America's usage of the same symbol on its official seal, commissioned on July 4, 1776, seems too powerful to be a coincidence. Think about it. The gospel teaches us that the promised land of America was designed to host the restoration of temples. July 4, 1776 represents a key day in that movement. On that day, Congress commissioned the design for a seal, which ended up utilizing a symbol that seems to evoke true temple worship. And just in case we are still not convinced of a temple connection here, inside the American seal's pyramid is the all-seeing eye, surrounded by rays of glory—a symbol exactly depicted on the outer walls of the most recognized LDS temple today.

In addition, the seal's pyramid is truncated. In other words, the apex of it (the part with the eye and rays of glory) is not attached. Instead, the apex, or capstone, is hovering above the rest of the pyramid's body. According to the U.S. Treasury Department, this unfinished pyramid was the designers' way to portray the message "that there was still work to be done" in America.[14] In that America and its national covenant were but a foundation for greater things to come under God, particularly those things related to the temple, the symbolism of an unfinished pyramid being watched over by the all-seeing eye becomes even more powerful. The fact that the all-seeing eye is actually depicted inside the part that is yet to be placed onto the pyramid itself is meaningful. Whatever finishes the pyramid (what I propose to be true temple worship) will be something holy and fully consummated by God the Father. The temple is the capstone of the American experience.

George Washington seemed to seek this capstone. Or at least he expected it was coming. He never pretended to know exactly why the Lord had done what He did with America, though he readily admitted often that he could easily "trace the finger of Providence"[15] throughout the Revolution. He seemed to believe God was up to something—that some great plan was to unfold from all of this. Like Nephi, who declared that God's works were for "a wise purpose in him, which purpose I know not" (1 Nephi 9:5), Washington similarly explained that what God had done, He had done "for wise purposes not discoverable by finite minds."[16]

Washington would only speculate. "Can it be imagined," he declared, " . . . that this continent was not created and reserved so long undiscovered as a Theatre, for those glorious displays of divine Munificence, the salutary consequences of which will flow to another Hemisphere & extend through the interminable series of the ages?"

> Should not our souls exult in the prospect? Though I shall not survive to perceive with these bodily senses, but a small portion of the blessed effects which our Revolution will occasion in the rest of the world; yet I enjoy the progress of human society & happiness in anticipation. I rejoice in the belief that *intellectual light will spring up in the dark corners of the earth.*[17]

The Lord would be revealing more. Ovason records that "at the completion of this Temple [the seal's pyramid], the present era will come to an end, and be succeeded by a more splendid spiritual era."[18]

This symbol of the pyramid within the Great Seal of the United States leaves us wondering how much these American revolutionaries understood about what they were doing. Did Washington and his colleagues have any idea what the symbol they put forth seems to connect to? Was this done intentionally on their part? Or was this God inspiring them to do something that only He knew had meaning, something He hoped His American children could identify and learn from? Or is it all just one big crazy coincidence? We can't know the answers to these questions definitively. But we do know the Lord teaches us through symbols. What if He is trying to teach us through these great American symbols?

Consider the many parables in scripture and the symbolism of the temple. He provides symbols, even if their full meanings are not obvious, in the hope that we will figure them out and learn

PREDICTING A RESTORATION?

Revolutionary leaders presaged that something of a restoration or renewal of Christ's gospel was sure to follow the Revolution. Massachusetts minister David Tappan told his congregants that God had brought victory to America for one purpose—"that [God's] own name might be exalted, that His own great designs . . . extending the Kingdom of His Son, may be carried into effect."[19] Timothy Dwight, who would serve as the president of Yale College, declared that: "God brought His little flock hither and placed it in the wilderness, for the great purpose of establishing permanently the Church of Christ in these vast regions of idolatry and sin, and commencing here the glorious work of salvation. This great continent is soon to be filled with the praise and piety of the Millennium. But here is the seed, from which this last harvest is to spring."[20] Samuel Adams, whose revolutionary acts in New England caused many to refer to him as "the Father of the Revolution," concurred. Adams declared that it was now time for America to bring in "the holy and happy period when the kingdom of our Lord and Savior Jesus Christ may be everywhere established, and the people willingly bow to the scepter of Him who is the Prince of Peace."[21]

Samuel Adams.

something to help us along our mortal journey. I can see that the Great Seal of the United States, reflected in the La Cañada chapel window that I have looked upon hundreds of times, teaches me. I can't look upon it without hearing one message loud and clear: *God made this nation for the restoration of temple ordinances, that all mankind might have the opportunity to obtain eternal life. Now go out and do your part to make sure this nation and this gospel fulfill this grand purpose.* That's what I hear. Whether by design or not, the symbols are working for me.

I could end this chapter on that note. It would likely be meaningful enough. But what if there is more to discover? There appear to be more connections that support this hypothesis. I acknowledge this is speculation. But it's speculation that can add meaning to these symbols.

I begin with a simple question: What did Washington think of the pyramid and the all-seeing eye? Did they have any significant association for him? Did he look upon these symbols in his day as Latter-day Saints might look upon them (whether in the La Cañada chapel or upon the wall of the Salt Lake Temple) in our day? There is evidence that he might have.

George Washington would have been very familiar with these symbols, as they were both prominently presented within the fraternal order of Masonry (or Freemasonry), of which he was a member. Because of mysteries surrounding Masonry, and its many unique and "secret" signs and symbols, some people get nervous and connect its origins to the occult. Such conclusions are founded in ignorance. Would George Washington attach himself to something dark? I don't believe he would have.

In order to understand what Washington might have thought of these symbols, it's important to understand what Masonry meant to him. Masonry is not a religion (any more than the

Boy Scouts of America is a religion). One must believe in God to join, though membership in any specific religious denomination is not a requirement. One must also desire to progress and become a better man. Washington testified that his participation in Masonry was largely due to the "private virtue" it promoted.[22] One of the greatest Masonic philosophers was the devout Christian scholar Walter Wilmshurst. He taught that Masonry would allow men to "perfect their own nature and transform it into a more godlike quality." Referring to certain Masonic rites and ceremonies that depict an eternal resurrection, he concluded, "by utter surrender of his old life and losing his soul to save it, he rises from the dead a master, a just man made perfect, with larger consciousness and faculties, an efficient instrument for use by the Great architect [God] in His plan of rebuilding the Temple of fallen humanity, and capable of initiating and advancing other men to a participation in the same great work."[23] Washington would agree. The purpose of Masonry, he said, was "to promote the happiness of the human race."[24]

Washington, of course, lived in a time void of the fulness of the gospel. But a chosen spirit such as his, it seems, would be searching for light and truth. Did he recognize in Masonry a remnant of truth—ancient truth, perhaps tarnished by years of apostasy and lack of priesthood, but still emanating a light that attracted the father of our nation? Perhaps George Washington was on to something. Perhaps his Masonic associations give us insight to his searching soul.

LDS Church Educational System scholar Kenneth W. Godfrey wrote that the "Prophet Joseph Smith suggested that the Endowment and freemasonry in part emanated from the same ancient spring. . . . The philosophy and major tenets of freemasonry are not fundamentally incompatible with the teaching, theology, and doctrines of the Latter-day Saints. Both emphasize morality, sacrifice, consecration, and service, and both condemn selfishness, sin, and greed. Furthermore, the aim of Masonic ritual is to instruct—to make truth available so that man can follow it."[25] There are those who are uncomfortable at the suggestion that remnants of ancient priesthood and temple worship may exist today in certain organizations like Masonry. As I've considered it, I find myself wondering, why shouldn't these remnants exist? If they were revealed to ancient prophets throughout the history of the world, shouldn't we expect to find remnants?

Is it not significant, then, that when Washington came across what may have been a remnant of ancient priesthood and truth, he seized upon it? Does Washington's attraction to an organization that promotes such ideals not warrant attention from Latter-day Saints? Should it not make us wonder about how much he truly understood? Remember, Washington was the one who brought the national covenant, as defined in the Book of Mormon, back to the promised land so that temples might return to the earth. Miracles followed him. His mission was prophesied of by ancient prophets (see 1 Nephi 13:16–19) and recognized by God through a modern prophet (see D&C 101:80). These facts alone should compel us to really take a hard look at this man. So when he belonged to a purportedly ancient order that shares unique commonalities with sacred principles and symbols of the LDS temple, how can we not explore it and try to learn something from it?

Masons admit that while they believe their symbols and ceremonies have sacred significance, the precise meaning is largely unknown, even to them.[26] Masonic historians tend to agree that many members hold only "the vaguest notions . . . about the origin and history of the Craft."[27] Freemasons admit that many of

Masonry's secrets "could unfold a message deeper than they at present realize," and that when teaching the secrets "the most one can do is to offer a few hints or clues, which those who so desire may develop for themselves in the privacy of their own thought."[28] They knew this was not the end-all. Something else was coming.

In their ceremonies, Masons symbolically emphasize the building of a spiritual temple, that temple of their own spiritual growth referred to by Paul in the New Testament.[29] In their rituals they reenact the building of King Solomon's temple. Although the allusions were probably not intentional, some of the Masonic degree ceremonies can also remind us of future temples prophesied by Ezekiel that would come. One ceremony in particular requires the initiate to enter the temple and ascend seven steps on a journey that eventually culminates in the east, where they are taught about the importance of worshipping God.[30] These requirements—namely, the "east gate" and the "seven steps"—fully reflect what Ezekiel saw in vision relative to the latter-day temple (see Ezekiel 40: 6, 26; 43:1–4).

Ezekiel clearly saw the last days, and because of this has been deemed by Latter-day Saint authorities as a true "prophet of the Restoration."[31] In chapter 1, we discussed his vision of the Book of Mormon, even that vision of the "Stick of Joseph." But his vision of the great latter-day Restoration was extended beyond that, in that he also saw the future of the temple at Jerusalem. Specifically, he saw that it would be restored and rebuilt in the last days (Ezekiel 37:26–28). Latter-day prophets have confirmed that Ezekiel's temple will indeed come to pass, that it will be of God, and that true ordinances will be received therein.[32] This temple, patterned after Solomon's, is clearly connected to the Restoration; for it is the Restoration, and the building of temples to accompany it, that will eventually lead to the reconstitution of the Jerusalem temple. Furthermore, LDS scholars have linked Ezekiel's proclamation that "the glory of the Lord filled the house" to all temples given by God (Ezekiel 43:5).[33] It is easy to see how Washington and his brethren might have looked forward to greater things to come in the land and nation they were building.

Perhaps there is a reason that these thoughts and hopes of Masonry took root most predominantly in the one land set apart to be the host nation of the Restoration. More than that, it is likely no coincidence that the very American generation that accepted and proliferated the fraternal order was the same generation Nephi saw in vision, even that generation of American revolutionaries. Indeed, Masonry did not just casually appear in the chosen land—it was an explosive import! The first Masonic lodges in America were established by 1730. In fact, one of the first records we have of Freemasonry in America was printed by none other than Benjamin Franklin in December 1730.[34] Franklin joined the Masonic order in 1731 and eventually became the Masonic grand master of Pennsylvania.[35] Franklin testified that "Masonic labor is purely a labor of love."[36] Once that chosen American generation came in contact with the order, it grew exponentially. According to one Masonic historian, "the fraternity spread throughout the colonies as one of the few social institutions that transcended colonial boundaries. . . . It soon attracted well-established and respectable colonists and, later, leading revolutionaries."[37] In little time, there would be "more Freemasons in the United States than anywhere in the world."[38]

Not surprisingly, Washington filled his leading councils of war with his brethren of the fraternal order; half of his generals were Freemasons, and almost every single one of his highest ranking and most trusted commanders was a member. Furthermore,

Freemasons filled the rank and file of America's revolutionary fighters. A significant portion of these adherents were active participants in famed events such as the Boston Tea Party and the signing of the Declaration of Independence.[39] An astonishing twenty-eight percent of the signers of the Declaration of Independence were most likely members of the order.[40]

Though many tend to exaggerate the influence of Freemasonry in the building of the United States, few doubt that Masonic ideals, including freedom, liberty, and equality—which were, in and of themselves, revolutionary ideals at the time—helped shape the nation.[41] In the end, with its members consisting of revolutionary heroes like George Washington, Benjamin Franklin, John Hancock, James Madison (the father of the Constitution), James Monroe, Paul Revere, John Jay, John Paul Jones, La Fayette, and many others, the Masonic influence can hardly be ignored.[42]

Why is any of this significant to us today? Because it seems to open up our understanding of who the Founders of America really were. It helps us comprehend what they were building. They were building a land of God, where temples could come at last and bless God's children. If their hearts were in fact turned to these ideals in their day, should this not make us turn our hearts toward the same ideals in our day? Should we not seek the greater light God has prepared for us in this land?

There is reason to believe that the Founders or God (or both) meant to leave us symbols in the land to encourage us to make these connections—to make us remember that America was built for the restoration of temple worship. Again, I point out how important symbols are to God. According to President Boyd K. Packer, the Lord has proven time and again that He loves to utilize symbols in teaching His children. When it comes to teaching "spiritual ideals," according to President Packer, "it can be done most effectively by using symbols." He further adds that "the most conclusive certification of man's intelligence is his ability to re-create in symbolic form the world in which he lives."[43] Let us consider what is trying to be taught. Again, whether by design of man or God or both, it is hard to see the following and not be touched by a deeper meaning.

Two symbols that George Washington seemed to have a particular affinity for were the compass and the square. These symbols, both of which were depicted upon ceremonial regalia that Washington wore during special Masonic occasions, have special significance. Masonic historians define the compass and the square, tools they symbolically use in building Solomon's temple, as reminding the initiate to "square our actions" and "circumscribe the desires of Masons wherever dispersed."[44] Apparently, Washington wanted future generations of Americans to see these symbols engraved into their capital. After selecting the land (taken from surrounding states) that would be the new capital, which he did in 1790, George Washington drew up its exact perimeters by connecting two right angles, or symbols of the Masonic square. The four points of the connected squares face directly to the north, south, east, and west, forming a perfectly squared diamond. Though in 1848 part of the federal land was given back to Virginia, any map of the D.C. area will reveal the symbolic power of the two tilted Masonic squares. On April 15, 1791, a Masonic ceremony, which included a prayer to the Almighty, was conducted to lay the symbolic cornerstone of this federal land. Cement markers (small cement columns) were then laid out at every mile around the sacred diamond.[45]

Not long ago, I took a trip around the border of Washington, D.C. I was pleasantly surprised to see that most of these markers

*Map of the Washington, D.C., area, showing the outline as
a diamond and the compass patterns of its design.*

placed by Washington are still there—though they appear in
funny places, like modern parks, people's private residences, and
half buried in a muddy riverbank. When I got to the diamond's
origin point—the southernmost tip of the diamond—I found an
interesting placard near the marker. Upon the placard were the
words of the man commissioned to design Washington, D.C. His
name was Charles L'Enfant, the same architect discussed earlier
who built the Hebrew-like artwork "Glory" for St. Paul's Chapel.
The words on the placard included his intended plan for the origin point of the diamond. At this southern tip of Washington,
D.C., he was to build a "column or a grand pyramid" directly

"where a corner stone of the Federal District is to be placed." This pyramid, according to L'Enfant, "would produce the happiest effect and completely finish the landscape." For reasons left unexplained, the pyramid has yet to be built.

But L'Enfant did appear to get other sacred symbolism permanently memorialized into the design of the capital. Indeed, the compass and the square are seen throughout his design, particularly in the layout of streets and monuments. Any good map of the D.C. area, for example, reveals the compass patterns of its original design. With the Capitol Building serving as the point of the compass, one easily sees its two legs running down Pennsylvania Avenue and Maryland Avenue, respectively. Of particular interest is the layout of three of the first and most important landmarks: the White House, the Washington Monument, and the Capitol Building. An aerial view of these powerful fixtures shows that together they form the symbol of the square. According to architecture and symbolism expert David Ovason, "It is almost as though L'Enfant laid upon his virgin parchment the Masonic square as symbol of the spirit of George Washington, and dedicated its three points to the founder of the nation."[46] The many artistic renditions of George Washington, along with other Founders, wearing ceremonial clothing with symbolic signs of the compass and square reflect this same spirit. Such art can be found, among other places, displayed inside the Capitol Building.[47]

Indeed, Washington was not shy about sharing these symbols with the nation. In fact, he seemed to want to share them. Apart from commissioning the design of the capital city like he did, Washington also brought forth sacred symbolism to the cornerstone ceremony of the Capitol Building in 1793. Led by Washington dressed in his Masonic regalia, complete with his ceremonial apron depicting compass and square, it was written up

WASHINGTON'S PRAYERS

Washington once wrote to a Masonic brother, wishing for him that "the Great Architect of the Universe may bless you and receive you hereafter into his immortal Temple."[48] For himself, he also prayed. Among the papers of Washington, preserved for over two hundred years, is a handwritten prayer, attributed to him, which he reportedly recited on Sunday mornings. In the prayer, he asked that the Father would forgive him his sins "and accept of me for the merits of Thy son Jesus Christ, that when I come into Thy temple, and compass Thy altar, my prayers may come before Thee."[49]

as "one of the grandest Masonic processions" ever seen. In the full symbolic and ritualistic character of Freemasonry, the cornerstone was laid, after which a prayer to the Almighty was offered.[50]

In death, Washington seemed to testify one last time. One of his Masonic ceremonial aprons was placed on his coffin along with a sprig from an acacia tree—a symbol of the Resurrection.[51]

Is it too bold to suggest that these signs and symbols might be a testimony to us today about the true spiritual purposes of America? Is it possible that the Lord wants us to see these symbols, which He inspired through the hearts and minds of Founders like Washington and L'Enfant, so that we might make the connection and think about why God gave us America in the first place? If the signs of the compass and the square left by Washington and his colleagues are projections from the past calling out for the restoration of temples of the future, it seems the calls have been answered. It seems that the undiscovered parts of Washington's Masonry have at last been discovered—have at last been restored. The very first temple in this last dispensation that included the fulness of the temple endowment and the sealing ordinances of salvation was the Nauvoo Temple. This temple was capped by a weather vane depicting the angel Moroni in priestly robes and cap, carrying a book. Above him hung the signs of the compass and the square.[52] Does this answer Washington's call? Is it a symbol of the fulfillment of that mission God sent him to commence? Is it a sign that the apex of the truncated pyramid at last landed firmly upon its foundation?

Either way—whether by design or coincidence—when we see these symbols in the broad daylight of our nation's capital, perhaps we should remember what we are here for, as individuals, families, and nations. Perhaps Washington wanted us to remember. Most certainly the Lord does.

Fittingly, ancient Egyptian temple worship also utilized these same signs. The sign of the square, or what Egyptians called the "ka sign," figures prominently in ancient Egyptian pyramid/temple rites. According to Nibley, the Egyptian symbol of the ka—raising the arm to the square—signifies the act of "calling upon God, or praising him in the rising sun, of receiving his protection, and of fusion with his being."[53] This brings us back to where we began our discussion, to the first proposed symbol of America and temples that we discussed: the pyramid. And it's on this very symbol where we will conclude.

There are a few prominent structures in or near the capital that include pyramid imagery: the House of the Temple (home of Scottish Rite Masonry), the Alexandria Lodge and Memorial (Masonic lodge), and the Washington Monument. All of these structures are capped with pyramids, reflecting the image in the seal. Of these, the most prominent, of course, is the Washington Monument. As we analyze this symbol, lessons of America and its spiritual purposes overwhelm us. I already mentioned how the Washington Monument forms the center of the large symbolic "square" that seems to fill in the middle of our capital. But that's just the beginning of its temple allusions.

Though L'Enfant had chosen the site for the Washington Monument when designing the city, the cornerstone was not laid until July 4, 1848.[54] And the fact that this dedicatory service was wholly Masonic only emphasizes the above-mentioned temple symbolism and thus connects the monument to this theology. The Masonic grand master who laid the stone even used the same trowel, apron, and sash Washington used and wore in the Capitol's cornerstone ceremony in 1793. The compass and square were also included on a plaque that was affixed to the monument.[55] Interestingly, depictions of pyramid-capped obelisks, like that of the monument, are found in Masonic imagery dating back well before the construction of the monument.[56] Furthermore, the monument's original designers, which included Freemason architect Robert Mills, put forth many ideas for the monument— but the pyramid cap was included in all of them. The pyramid symbolism was clearly intentional.[57] Its symbolism should therefore be significant to us today.

Also, during the cornerstone ceremony a Bible was used and put on display. It had traveled from New York City just for the occasion. It was the Bible from St. John's Lodge that Washington had used on his inauguration day.[58] The Bible that pointed us to the singular prophecy that speaks of America's divine role as the chosen land for the New Israel, the land where temples to the Most High would one day be restored.

But the religious themes in the monument (which themes we might connect to the temple) do not stop there. For the monument also includes inscriptions of prayers for the well-being of the nation, and placed inside its cornerstone is a copy of the Bible. Upon the capstone of the monument, facing ever symbolically to the east (the same direction the statue of the angel Moroni generally faces atop our temples), in a place where perhaps only heaven can see, is the Latin inscription *Laus Deo,* which literally means "Praise be to God."[59] In that this inscription would be completely unseen to any mortal eye, we must recognize to whom the monument was directed and dedicated. I imagine Washington would have wholeheartedly approved.

◆ ◆ ◆

I have made dozens of trips to Washington, D.C., throughout the years. Rarely do I go without walking, jogging, or (if I'm feeling lazy) driving around the city, visiting the monuments. When

The Washington Monument.

I do this, I try to always do it at night, so I can better appreciate the spiritual eminence shooting out against the backdrop of darkness.

During one of my trips there, my friend and brother-in-law Todd (whom I wrote about in the prologue) happened to be in D.C. on business. We visited the Washington Monument together around midnight. We had been to visit the other monuments and were commenting on the rich spiritual lessons contained in each of them. But I was about to receive the greatest lesson at the Washington Monument on this particular night.

"Do you think God was behind the earthquake?" Todd asked suddenly.

In 2011, a rare earthquake shook the D.C. area and caused the monument to crack. For three years it was shut down to visitors, under repair. It was still shut down at the time Todd posed the question.

I had no answer for him.

"Don't you think it's interesting? Perhaps even symbolic?" he continued. "Might it be a lesson to us?"

As I looked at the monument with all its powerful imagery before me, I knew what Todd was hinting at. This great nation, built in large part by a man who understood God, covenant, and the spiritual purposes of the promised land, seems to be fading. There seems to be a crack running down the nation.

"If we get much worse," Todd declared, "we as a nation might close down, just like the monument."

As I thought of the leaders of the land and the populace in general, I wondered where our Washington was today. Where is the leader who will stand unashamed of his love and trust in God? Who will rise up and invoke the covenants of old? Who will lead the nation in shunning sin, promoting righteousness, and preserving that liberty God has granted? Where is our Captain Moroni? "Yea, verily, verily I say unto you, if all men had been, and were, and ever would be, like unto Moroni, behold, the very powers of hell would have been shaken forever; yea, the devil would never have power over the hearts of the children of men" (Alma 48:17). We the people of this covenant nation need to find men and women like this. We need to engage them, promote them, elect them. We need to *become* them. And we need to do it quickly. In so many ways, it seems, we are falling further and further away from this ideal.

> "And now, we can behold the decrees of God concerning this land, that it is a land of promise; and whatsoever nation shall possess it shall serve God, or they shall be swept off when the fulness of his wrath shall come upon them . . . it is the everlasting decree of God."
> —Ether 2:9–10

I thought of the prophet who did more than any other for my

growing testimony when I was a youth. Speaking of America and her covenant, President Gordon B. Hinckley declared:

> For a good while there has been going on in this nation a process that I have termed the secularization of America. . . . We as a nation are forsaking the Almighty, and I fear that He will begin to forsake us. We are shutting the door against the God whose sons and daughters we are. . . . Future blessings will come only as we deserve them. Can we expect peace and prosperity, harmony and goodwill, when we turn our backs on the Source of strength? If we are to continue to have the freedoms that evolved within the structure that was the inspiration of the Almighty to our Founding Fathers, we must return to the God who is their true Author. . . . God bless America, for it is His creation.[60]

As my eyes ran up the great monument that night, I noticed the obvious discoloration about 150 feet up. The stones change colors—a different shade of stone was used at some point to complete the monument. Why? Another learning opportunity. In 1861, with the nation crippled by the Civil War, construction of the monument halted immediately. According to Mark Twain, the incomplete structure looked like nothing but a "hollow, oversized chimney."[61] I thought of why that war had taken place. It was national sin. It was a consequence from heaven. Fortunately, the Lord had worked wonders through Abraham Lincoln and brought the nation out of deep sin, thus restoring its purposes under God.[62] In the aftermath, the monument (with a different shade of stone) was completed. I thought of how I was glad for the discoloration. It's a battle scar, a reminder of what sin can do to a nation.

State of Deseret stone in Washington Monument.

Was the cracked monument something similar? A battle scar? A reminder that we need to heed our prophets, turn from wickedness, and adhere to the covenant on this land?

As I stood at the base of the monument with Todd, those questions haunted me, and they still haunt me. So much is at stake.

"You know," I finally replied to Todd, "if you like symbolism, there is something inside the shaft of this monument, about 220 feet up from the base. It's a reminder of what Washington *really* built. It's a reminder of the crowning feature of the American Revolution. It's a reminder of what this monument *actually* stands for. It's a reminder of why we can't fail as a nation, why we must live the national covenant and fight to preserve the liberty God has granted."

I had his attention.

"It's a stone," I told him, "sent by Brigham Young to Washington, D.C., in 1853, and it was placed inside this monument to Washington."

Todd's eyes were wide open, his mouth was agape, his whole body in paralyzed, focused silence.

I continued: "The stone contains four words, four words that you will recognize immediately. Words that represent a place worth fighting for, a place that should make us all do what we can to prevent any more cracking in the national foundation.

"Engraved upon the stone," I said, "are the very words that are inscribed on every LDS temple in the world: *Holiness to the Lord.*"[63]

EPILOGUE

The Door

I had been finished with the manuscript for this book for some time when I called Todd.

"I can't turn it in until I visit the window one more time," I told him. "Do you have a key to the church building?"

I was in the area on business when I made the call to Todd. He met me late that night at the La Cañada church building, and we entered. We walked across the cultural hall, and I could not help but revisit the scene from my boyhood, as described in the prologue of this book. Todd had been there with me that night some thirty years earlier, bouncing balls off the great beams and hoping to make the miracle shot. We laughed as I recounted the story of my ball flying into no-man's-land. Sensing my desire to re-create that moment, Todd ran ahead and turned on the back-lights to the stained-glass window. He left the rest of the chapel as pitch-black as it had been when I entered as a frightened Scout.

I went into the chapel and sat in the back pew. I beheld the beautiful window in front of me. Like American history itself, the window could teach us. I looked upon the depictions of the scrolls of Judah and Joseph. They remind us of the covenants of old and their application to us today. They remind us who we are and where we came from. We recognize that God is the same yesterday, today, and forever. The scriptures, both the Stick of Judah and the Stick of Joseph, are real and fully applicable to us

Stained-glass window in the La Cañada chapel.

today. What happened then, as recorded in those scriptural texts, no matter how miraculous, can happen now. Just ask George Washington.

From the scroll depictions, I allowed my eyes to focus in on each image surrounding the centerpiece of the window. I saw the dove of the national covenant and the keys giving authority to the servants of God. I was reminded of the eternal importance of promised lands and of our callings as individuals, families, and nations to live and serve under the covenant. The handclasp and pyramid remind us that all God does, including His building of nations, leads us to temple ordinances, eternal marriage, and eternal life. Ultimately, that is why we are here on earth.

But most of my attention went to the center of the window, to the depiction of Him who makes the whole thing possible. The Christ stands patiently, knocking at the door. With His right hand He knocks; with His left He holds a lantern draped in signs of America—the stars and stripes. The plan of God requires that all people are free to choose their own path. This is key to eternal progression. They should be free to live the religion of their choice and worship God according to their own conscience. This is the only way we can truly progress: letting God, not man or man's government, lead us along our mortal journey. Satan hates this idea. He hates liberty because it can lead to exaltation. He stands wherever he can to stop it. But the lantern in Christ's hand will thwart him every time. The power of God's national covenant, if received and applied in righteousness, will always defeat our enemy. Again, just ask Washington.

There the Lord stands, offering this liberty. Knocking at the door. All we have to do is answer. Seems so simple. But like the children of Israel, who refused to choose the simple solution by looking upon Moses's staff for healing, so America seems unable to simply open the door.

How do we get our countrymen to open the door?

As I sat there in the chapel, I thought deeply about the experience I had had in this sacred room as an eleven-year-old Scout. As I described in the prologue, that experience ended with my father giving me a one-hundred-dollar bill. You will recall that the depiction of Benjamin Franklin on that bill, which hung for well over two decades, first in my bedroom, then my office, made me feel as though he was looking at me, taunting me, challenging me to figure out the mysteries of America and its connections to the window. My thoughts turned to Franklin as I sat there in the back pew. Perhaps Franklin has the answer to my question. Perhaps his story teaches us how to get our countrymen to open the door.

By way of introducing Franklin's story, I want to say that Franklin loved Washington, and Washington loved Franklin. Shortly after independence was won, Franklin wrote the following to British publisher William Strahan: "An American Planter, who had never seen Europe was chosen by us to command our troops and continued during the whole War. This Man sent home to you, one after another, five of your best Generals baffled, their heads bare of laurels, disgraced even in the opinion of their employer."[1]

Washington's last letter to Franklin, sent shortly before Franklin's death, summed up what he thought about their long friendship: "If to be venerated for benevolence, if to be admired for talents, if to be esteemed for patriotism . . . can gratify the human mind, you must have the pleasing consolation to know that you did not live in vain . . . so long as I retain my memory, you will be recollected with respect, veneration, and affection, by your sincere friend, George Washington."[2]

But at the beginning of the conflict with Britain, this relationship was not nearly so certain. You see, Benjamin Franklin tended to be strictly cerebral and not necessarily spiritual about the decisions he made. If there was a deist in the group, it was Franklin. This posed a problem for him because the American cause was spiritual. As pointed out earlier in this book, most Americans opposed independence initially because, on so many levels, it simply did not make sense. The Spirit was needed to convert people to the cause. Once conversion happened, the revolutionaries became relentless on the point they were fighting for. As whispers of the possibility of independence were threating to turn into screams for action, Franklin sat in the halls of Congress almost emotionless, cold, rational, scientific. He did not want to open the door.

He sat there like so many Americans sit today: unmoved, unconcerned, unconverted. But if we don't get them converted, then the cause of America will continue to fall. Similarly, Franklin—with his uncanny skills in everything from science to diplomacy—would further the cause in ways others could not. Just as the Lord needs good Americans to be converted to the cause of

His promised land in our day, so He needed to somehow prompt Franklin off the sidelines in his.

So, what did the Lord do to accomplish that? What did Franklin do in response? The answers to those questions may be the answers to our national dilemma today.

To recognize Franklin's significant conversion, consider his initial and very open opinion against American claims of overbearing British persecution, which implied to many that Franklin had taken a firm stance against the need for any talk of independence. As late as January 1775, he would comment that "the two countries really have no clashing interests," and that it was merely an issue that "reasonable people might settle in half an hour."[3] Even after the dreaded Stamp Act and the colonial outrage that followed—and though he was no proponent of the act—he would write to a friend that "A firm Loyalty to the Crown and faithful Adherence to the Government of this Nation . . . will always be the wisest Course for you and I to take, whatever may be the Madness of the [American] Populace or their blind Leaders."[4]

In addition to such comments, which clearly undermined the American cause, as a delegate to Congress in the spring of 1775, the usually opinionated Franklin remained silent and passionless, even after the British had sacked Boston in response to the colonists' Tea Party. Franklin had sided with Britain in expressing disgust at America's destruction of the tea in the first place. He called the heralded event "an act of violent injustice on our part."[5] Such behavior was alarming to his fellow delegates. One observer reported to James Madison that the delegates "beg[a]n to entertain a great suspicion that Dr. Franklin came rather as a spy than as a friend, and that he means to discover our weak side and make his peace with the ministers."[6] Even after the Battle of Bunker Hill and the burning of Charleston, both in June 1775, Franklin still supported a policy of unification with Britain by signing the Olive Branch Petition (written by delegate John Dickinson, the same delegate who would refuse to ever sign the Declaration of Independence).[7]

Furthermore, and on a personal level, why should he desire to revolt over the very system that had permitted him to become one of the wealthiest men in America, and perhaps the most famous individual in the world? Indeed, by risking an unlikely revolution, which seemed doomed to failure, he might have both his wealth and fame pulled out from under him. Or worse, his life might be taken by the hangman's noose.

In spite of all this, by the end of July (seemingly overnight) Franklin had become "one of the most ardent opponents of Britain in the Continental Congress." This he would remain even after the British accepted the basic terms from his Olive Branch Petition. "He does not hesitate at our boldest measures," wrote John Adams, "but rather seems to think us too irresolute."[8]

Almost immediately, Franklin volunteered to replace the British-run postal service and serve as America's first postmaster general. He designed and oversaw construction of a secret system of underwater obstructions to prevent enemy naval invasions. And he rushed to the scene of war—a Boston recently seized by the British. He went there that he might consult the newly appointed commander-in-chief, General Washington, on everything from warfare and troop discipline to ration allocation. At age seventy, he could have been expected to remain in Philadelphia and consult from the comforts of his home. Instead, he insisted not merely on traveling to Boston but on taking a life-threatening diplomatic journey to Canada (during which he almost died). Then he traveled to New York in a final (and unsuccessful) attempt at independence through diplomacy with the recently landed British invaders. Then, after returning to Philadelphia and acting as editor of the Declaration of Independence, he most poignantly relocated to France (in yet another death-defying voyage), where he would spend the balance of the war seeking and, through masterful diplomacy, securing France's support—an act that was largely responsible for the American victory. Finally, he would lead negotiations with Britain in the treaty officially ending the war, wherein Britain recognized the United States "to be free, sovereign and independent."[9]

But what caused the sudden and almost overwhelming change in Franklin that not only led to the dramatic chain of events mentioned above, but also cost him his relationship with his only son, the British Loyalist William (a relationship never to be recovered)? What prompted the change within that he knew would place him squarely onto the death list of the British? Upon signing the Declaration of Independence, he would declare, "We must indeed all hang together, or most assuredly we shall all hang separately."[11] While scholars theorize over his unlikely change of heart, a gospel perspective perhaps fills in the missing pieces. Knowing what we do about what American independence meant to God's purposes, and knowing the indispensable role played by this elder American, it seems likely that the Lord changed his heart and converted him with His Spirit. Such an idea is even supported by Franklin himself, who declared while serving in France: "Glorious it is for the Americans to be called by Providence to this post of honor."[12] He later said, "It is

> In an almost humorous understatement, a follow-up report to James Madison, shortly after Franklin's sudden and passionate conversion, included the reassurance that "the suspicions against Dr. Franklin have died away. . . . I believe he has now chosen his side and favors our cause."[10]

THE PATRIOTISM OF FRANKLIN

The insightful Abigail Adams, herself devoutly dedicated to the Lord, even saw or felt this spiritual conversion in Franklin. Upon meeting Franklin shortly after his public commitment to independence, she wrote to her husband, stating, "I thought I could read into his countenance the virtues of his heart; among which patriotism shone in its full luster, and with that is blended every virtue of a Christian: for a true patriot must be a religious man."[13]

a miracle in human affairs . . . the greatest revolution the world ever saw."[14]

Of course, critics will argue that his sudden change of mind came about by what was expected of him politically as an American delegate to Congress, and that God had nothing to do with it. Franklin was—so the theory goes—simply playing to the American crowd. Historian Gordon Wood, for example, suggests that Franklin's actions for independence came about as a result of his having to "overcome suspicions that many of his countrymen had of him." Wood further explains that "some thought his position in the 1760s and 1770s had been sufficiently ambiguous that he might not be a true patriot after all."[15]

However, there are problems with that interpretation. First, Franklin had just as many, if not more, friends and supporters in Britain and other European countries as he did in America. After all, he had spent over two decades enjoying celebrity status (as scientist and philosopher) in Europe. Further, he was devoid of any family ties that would sway his allegiance to America rather than Great Britain. His wife had already died, and his only son was a British Loyalist. In other words, he had just as many people to disappoint—just as much political pressure on him—whether he voted for or against independence. If the only reason he could find for supporting American independence was the pressure he felt from his American colleagues, then it would have made much more sense for him to shun what appeared to be an ill-conceived revolution and simply return to any number of European nations with the celebrity status that would be awaiting him there.

Second, if Franklin had been unconvinced of the wisdom behind revolution, but did not want to shun his country and hazard a trip back to Europe, there was a much easier solution for him. He could have simply voiced his support for independence and then floated off into retirement, even casually consulting from the comforts of his home just to keep up the act. He was already in his seventies and suffering from chronic gout and kidney stones; nobody would have batted an eye.

Yet his actions, as outlined above, reflect an unnaturally passionate, even overactive, approach to the American cause. Indeed, Franklin's conversion and subsequent actions are overwhelmingly inconsistent with the allegation that he acted on pressures stemming from colonial political correctness, especially in light of the alternatives available to him. The truth of the matter is that no other solid, secular explanation for Franklin's actions has ever been offered. Even Wood, putting his own analysis into question, ultimately concedes this fact, stating that "[Franklin] had everything to lose and seemingly nothing to gain by participating in a revolution."[16] Only when we place God and His powerful inspiration into the equation are Franklin's actions comprehensible.

Unfortunately, many scholars would rather have *no* explanation than give credit to God, and thus they attempt to secularize Franklin as much as possible. However, such scholars have to contend with the fact that Franklin himself explained on several occasions that his conversion to the cause was indeed based in divine intervention. Admittedly, critics may claim that the few quotes offered above regarding what was said by and of Franklin during the actual conflict represented nothing but quintessential politicking—even the disingenuous act of invoking God's name only to stir an audience. However, a glimpse into his postwar life confirms that when Franklin declared during the war that he had been "called by Providence,"[17] he meant it.

Consider, for example, the following statement he made near the end of his life, while reflecting upon the war for independence and his conversion to it: "If it had not been . . . for the interposition of Providence, in which we had faith, we must have been ruined. . . . If I had ever before been an atheist, I should now have been convinced of the Being and government of a Deity."[18] That he had felt this during and after the war is supported by his obvious change of focus from scientist and rational philosopher (prewar) to servant of the Almighty (postwar). Whereas before the war he tended to find limited use for God and religion, his post-war activities included the following: penning defenses against early American secularist attacks on religion,[19] proposing that the nation use as its official seal a depiction of Moses freeing Israel by the power of God,[20] proposing to the Congress that it open sessions with prayer,[21] promoting the general need for religion and virtue in order to stabilize the Republic,[22] and, as his final project in this life, publicly invoking the Almighty and exerting much energy in an effort to eradicate the evil practice of slavery.[23] Indeed, in the sunset of his life, and within the context of the miraculous revolution he had experienced, Franklin was a changed man. "Doing good to men," the old man would say, "is the only service of God in our power; and to imitate his beneficence is to glorify him."[25]

> "I believe in one God, Creator of the Universe. That he governs it by his Providence. That he ought to be worshipped. That the most acceptable service we render to him is doing good to his other children."
>
> —Benjamin Franklin[24]

But perhaps the most telling event that testifies of his conversion occurred during the Constitutional Convention. Without the Constitution, the Revolution would have been made void and purposeless. Years after gaining independence, America had still not been established with God's laws of liberty to usher in His Restoration. In the summer of 1787, as the delegates fiercely debated the formula for the new government, it seemed as though they would never come to an agreement. As Franklin observed, "all their prejudices, their passions, their errors of opinion, their local interests, and their selfish views"[26] came close to ruining the whole endeavor. Some delegates had threatened to leave; others actually did so. At the lowest point in the Convention, the eighty-one-year-old Franklin, who could barely walk, stood and delivered one of the most powerful improvised speeches ever given on American soil.

In the speech, Franklin declared:

In this situation of this Assembly, groping as it were to find political truth, and scarce able to distinguish it when presented to us, how has it happened, Sir, that we have not hitherto once thought of *humbly applying to the Father of lights to illuminate our understandings?* In the beginning of the Contest with G. Britain, when we were sensible of danger we had daily prayer in this room for the divine protection.—Our prayers, Sir, were heard, and they were graciously answered. All of us who were engaged in the struggle must have observed frequent instances of a Superintending providence in our favor. To that kind Providence we owe this happy opportunity in consulting in peace on the means of establishing our future national felicity. *And have we now forgotten that powerful friend? Or do we imagine we no longer need his assistance? I have lived, Sir, a long time, and the longer I live, the more convincing proofs I see of this truth—that God governs in the affairs of men.* And if a sparrow cannot fall to the ground without his notice, is it probable that an empire can rise without his aid? We have been assured, Sir, in the sacred writings, that "except the Lord build the House they labour in vain that build it." I firmly believe this; and I also believe that without his concurring aid we shall succeed in this political building no better than the builders of Babel: We shall be divided by our little partial local interests; our projects will be confounded, and we ourselves shall become a reproach and bye word down to future ages. And what is worse, *mankind* may hereafter from this unfortunate instance, despair of establishing Governments by Human Wisdom and leave it to chance, war and conquest.

I therefore beg leave to move—that henceforth prayers imploring the assistance of Heaven, and its blessings on our deliberations, be held in this Assembly.[27]

Consider those words of Franklin. What had happened to him? How had he come so far from where he began when the Revolution commenced? First, he allowed God to touch his heart. He experimented with the invitation to join the cause. As Alma taught, he "g[a]ve place, that a seed may be planted in [his] heart." Then he saw that the seed began to grow and determined that "it must needs be that this is a good seed . . . for it beginneth to enlarge my soul" (Alma 32:28). And how might Americans conduct such an experiment today? Again, I turn you to Franklin. In his speech at the Convention, he said it all. By reflecting over the history of the American Revolution, he had no other option but to believe George Washington. God had made it happen, and He will intervene again and again on behalf of the nation, if only we will ask—if only we will open the door upon which the Lord is knocking.

Imagine what would happen if all Americans would open that door just as Franklin did. What if they learned the true history of their land, especially when reading it with the scriptures in their hands? The Spirit would testify. They would understand the covenant. And we would, at long last, elect men and women who carry the righteous spirit of Washington. We must find ways to teach the true history of this land. We must teach our children properly. If we do, we will see the change. If Franklin, with all his scientific doubts and his singular trust in the arm of the flesh, can change, then any of us can.

John Adams understood. "But what do we mean by the American Revolution?" he asked. "Do we mean the American war? The Revolution was effected before the war commenced. The Revolution was in the minds and hearts of the people; a change in their religious sentiments of their duties and obligations."[28] This is the spiritual change we need today.

If Washington could lead America out of the darkest of days through invoking the covenant, then we can be led out of anything under similar leadership. Think about how dark those days were. The world's military superpower had landed on American beaches, after which over half of all American troops abandoned the cause. Picture that happening to our America today. How frightening! And yet, they overcame. They knew how. If we apply the same covenant theology today, which it is our right to do, then no obstacle, no matter how dark, scary, or difficult, can get in our way. The purposes of the Almighty can then move forward in ways we have not yet seen. Conversely, should we choose to continue putting our faith in the arm of the flesh, we will have no guarantee.

> "Obtain a knowledge of history, and of countries, and of kingdoms, of laws of God and man, and all this for the salvation of Zion" (D&C 93:53). "[Understand] things which are at home, things which are abroad; the wars and the perplexities of the nations, and the judgments which are on the land."
>
> —D&C 88:79

"I, the Lord, am bound when ye do what I say; but when ye do not what I say, ye have no promise" (D&C 82:10).

As a reminder of the wondrous blessings that have become available because many were willing to convert to the Lord's side, let us follow Franklin into the eternities. "If [God] loves me," he declared, "can I doubt that he will go on to take care of me, not only here but hereafter?"[29]

Franklin entered the spirit world on April 17, 1790. At his bedside was a picture of the Day of Judgment. As further expression of his hope for eternity, he had originally penned the following epitaph for his tombstone:

> The body of B. Franklin, Printer;
> (Like the cover of an old book,
> Its contents worn out,
> and stripped of its lettering and gilding)
> Lies here, food for worms.
> But the work is not lost:
> For it will (as he believed) appear once more,
> In a new and more elegant edition,
> Revised and corrected
> By the Author.[30]

Upon his entering immortality, it appears that Franklin's faith and works during his life were acceptable to the Lord. According to both temple records and the testimony of Wilford Woodruff, Benjamin Franklin was counted among the spirits who participated in the St. George temple miracle. His ordinance work was done, making it possible for him to receive those most sacred covenants.

On March 19, 1894, Woodruff recorded an experience that makes a fascinating epilogue to this story. Franklin, who had been one of the few along with Washington to be ordained a high priest pursuant to the St. George temple vision,[31] appeared once again to President Woodruff, this time in a dream. President Woodruff wrote the following concerning this event:

"I spent some time with him [Benjamin Franklin] and we talked over our Temple ordinances which had been administered for Franklin and others. He wanted more work done for him than had already been done. I promised him it should be done. I awoke and then made up my mind to receive further blessings for Benjamin Franklin and George Washington."[32]

As it ended for Franklin, so it can end with any and all of us. And so it can end with America. But we had better get moving.

◆　◆　◆

"We are running out of time," Todd said, jolting me from my thoughts of America, Washington, Franklin, and the window. I hadn't even noticed that he had taken a seat next to me on the back pew. I felt bad. I knew we had been in the chapel too long, and my sister no doubt wanted her husband back home. As I apologized for lingering, Todd chuckled.

"No, not that," he said. "Make no mistake; I will get an earful for being out so late," he smiled, "but that's not what I'm talking about. Look at the window," he said. He pointed out that the entire piece of art was bordered in each corner by green tiles. "To me, green represents this earth. This earth life." Todd continued: "The lessons of the window are confined to the here and now. To mortality. We have a limited opportunity to get it right. *And we are running out of time.*"

I understood his sense of urgency for our nation. I had felt it many times before.

As we stood to leave the chapel, Todd began walking down

the aisle to turn the window's backlights off. As I pondered the images in the window one last time, the green tiles reminding me that the clock was ticking, I felt a bit sad. I wondered if we could turn things around and bring the Lord full force back to America again. I started losing hope until my eyes wandered one last time to the depiction of Christ upon the window. I noted the red robe draped about Him. I glanced down at the stars and stripes on His lantern. Hope returned. He was in charge.

In the few seconds remaining before Todd hit the light switch, and with my eyes still fixed on the beautifully lit window, the message became overwhelmingly clear. Christ is at the door knocking now, the light of His covenants in His hands, His liberty ready to be delivered. He offers us the opportunity to use that liberty to receive Him fully, to receive His grace and Atonement and enjoy life everlasting.

Our nation is on the other side of the door. Will we answer? "And they are free to choose liberty and eternal life, through the great Mediator of all men, or to choose captivity and death, according to the captivity and power of the devil" (2 Nephi 2:27).

The choice is ours to make.

Notes

Introduction:
The Bulletproof Soldier

1. See Michael A. Shea, *In God We Trust: George Washington and the Spiritual Destiny of the United States of America* (Derry, NH: Liberty Quest, 2012), 40–41.

2. In William Thayer, *Young People's Life of George Washington: Boyhood, Youth, Manhood, Death, Honors* (New York: John R. Anderson & Co., 1883), 199.

3. In David Barton, *The Bulletproof George Washington* (Aledo, TX: Wallbuilder Press, 2013), 38–39.

4. See ibid., 64.

5. This account was taken from "The Recollections of Washington," written by Washington's own adopted grandson George Washington Parke Custis in 1827, as quoted in Robert Hieronimus, *Founding Fathers, Secret Societies: Freemasons, Illuminati, Rosicrucians, and the Decoding of the Great Seal*, revised ed. (Rochester, NY: Destiny Books, 2006), 51–52.

6. See Joseph J. Ellis, *His Excellency: George Washington* (New York: Alfred A. Knopf, 2004), 22.

7. See Barton, *Bulletproof George Washington*, 51.

8. In Steven Waldman, *Founding Faith: Providence, Politics, and the Birth of Religious Freedom in America* (New York: Random House, 2008), 57.

9. In Barton, *Bulletproof George Washington*, 49.

10. In ibid., 59.

11. In Thayer, *Young People's Life of George Washington*, 285.

12. In Hieronimus, *Founding Fathers, Secret Societies*, 52.

Chapter 1:
The Dove and the Covenant

1. Andrew C. Skinner, *Temple Worship: 20 Truths That Will Bless Your Life* (Salt Lake City: Deseret Book, 2007), 132.

2. See Chris Stewart and Ted Stewart, *The Miracle of Freedom: Seven Tipping Points that Saved the World* (Salt Lake City: Shadow Mountain, 2011), 12.

3. See Timothy Ballard, *The Lincoln Hypothesis* (Salt Lake City: Deseret Book, 2014).

4. "Abraham, covenant of," in Bible Dictionary, 602.

5. For more information on how this prophecy connects to the New World, see *Old Testament Student Manual: Genesis–2 Samuel*, 2nd ed. rev. (Salt Lake City: The Church of Jesus Christ of Latter-day Saints, 1981), 98–99; *Old Testament Seminary Student Study Guide* (Salt Lake City: The Church of Jesus Christ of Latter-day Saints, 2002), 40–41.

6. See Matthew B. Brown, *All Things Restored: Confirming the Authenticity of*

LDS Beliefs (American Fork: Covenant Communications, 2000), 187–88.

7. For a more detailed analysis of Ezekiel's usage of the word *stick,* see Keith Meservy, "Ezekiel's Sticks and the Gathering of Israel," *Ensign,* February 1987, available at www.lds.org/ensign/1987/02 /ezekiels-sticks-and-the-gathering-of -israel?lang=eng.

8. Nephi also stated his knowledge that he was a descendant of Joseph; see 2 Nephi 4:1–2.

9. L. Tom Perry, "The Tradition of Light and Testimony," devotional address given January 24, 2012, at BYU–Idaho, available at https://www.lds.org /ensign/2012/12/the-tradition-of-light -and-testimony?lang=eng.

10. See Bruce Feiler, *America's Prophet: Moses and the American Story* (New York: HarperCollins Publishing, 2009), 102–3; Robert Hay, "George Washington: American Moses," *American Quarterly,* vol. 21, no. 4 (Winter 1969): 781, 785.

Chapter 2: Miracle at Boston

1. See Charles W. Akers, *Abigail Adams: A Revolutionary American Woman,* 3rd ed. (New York: Pearson Longman, 2007), 39–40.

2. In ibid., 38–40, 46.

3. See Harlow Giles Unger, *John Quincy Adams* (Boston: Da Capo Press, 2012), 14–16.

4. Ibid., 16–17.

5. In ibid., 17.

6. In ibid. For scripture reference, see Nehemiah 4:14.

7. In Akers, *Abigail Adams,* 41.

8. In Steven Waldman, *Founding Faith: Politics, Providence, and the Birth of Religious Freedom in America* (New York: Random House, 2008), 70.

9. See John Bowman, *The History of the American Presidency,* rev. ed. (North Dighton, MA: World Publication Group, Inc., 2002), 12–13.

10. Joseph J. Ellis, *His Excellency: George*

Washington (New York: Alfred A. Knopf, 2004), 80.

11. David McCullough, *1776* (New York: Simon and Schuster, 2005), 49.

12. See David McCullough, *John Adams* (New York: Simon and Schuster, 2001), 20, 41.

13. "John Adams to Abigail Adams, 11 June 1775," Founders Online, National Archives (http://founders.archives.gov /documents/Adams/04-01-02-0146).

14. "Address to the Continental Congress, 16 June 1775," Founders Online, National Archives (http://founders .archives.gov/documents/Washington /03-01-02-0001).

15. "From George Washington to Martha Washington, 18 June 1775," Founders Online, National Archives (http:// founders.archives.gov/documents /Washington/03-01-02-0003).

16. In William M. Thayer, *George Washington: His Boyhood and Manhood* (London: Hodder and Stoughton, 1883), 175–76.

17. See William H. Wilbur, *The Making of George Washington,* 2nd ed. (Madison, WI: Patriotic Education, Inc., 1973), 42; Michael Novak and Jana Novak, *Washington's God: Religion, Liberty, and the Father of Our Country* (New York: Basic Books, 2006), 8.

18. See *Church History in the Fulness of Times,* 2nd ed. (Salt Lake City: The Church of Jesus Christ of Latter-day Saints, 2000), 15, 18.

19. See Ellis, *His Excellency,* 71.

20. In Michael Novak, *On Two Wings: Humble Faith and Common Sense at the American Founding* (San Francisco, CA: Encounter Books, 2002), 13–14.

21. Michael A. Shea, *In God We Trust: George Washington and the Spiritual Destiny of the United States of America* (Derry, NH: Liberty Quest, 2012), 58.

22. In Stephen E. Ambrose, *To America: Personal Reflections of a Historian* (New York: Simon and Schuster, 2002), 10–11.

23. "From George Washington to Lieutenant

Colonel Joseph Reed, 14 January 1776," Founders Online, National Archives (http://founders.archives.gov/documents/Washington/03-03-02-0062).

24. In Shea, *In God We Trust*, 71.

25. In McCullough, *1776*, 72.

26. In ibid.

27. Letter from Washington to his brother John Augustine Washington, March 31, 1776, as quoted in *The Writings of George Washington, Volume 4*, Electronic Text Center, University of Virginia, available from http://etext.virginia.edu/toc/modeng/public/WasFi04.html.

28. "From George Washington to Lieutenant Colonel Joseph Reed, 19 March 1776," Founders Online, National Archives (http://founders.archives.gov/documents/Washington/03-03-02-0366).

29. McCullough, *1776*, 111.

30. See Marquis de Chastellux, *Travels in North America in the Years 1780, 1781, and 1782*, Howard C. Rice, ed. (Chapel Hill: University of North Carolina Press, 1963), 112.

31. McCullough, *1776*, 82.

32. In Francis S. Drake, *Life and Correspondence of Henry Knox, Major-General in the American Revolutionary Army* (Boston, MA: Samuel G. Drake, 1873), 29.

33. Henry Knox Diary, January 8, 1776, Massachusetts Historical Society, Boston, MA. Retrieved from: http://www.masshist.org/database/viewer.php?item_id=463&img_step=25&pid=15&mode=transcript#page25.

34. William Gordon to Samuel Wilcon, April 6, 1776, *Proceedings of the Massachusetts Historical Society*, LX (October 1926–June 1927), 363. Retrieved from http://www.jstor.org/stable/25080203.

35. McCullough, *1776*, 92.

36. In ibid., 93

37. In Shea, *In God We Trust*, 67.

38. See Thomas Fleming, "Unlikely Victory," in *What If? The World's Foremost Military Historians Imagine What Might Have Been*, ed. Robert Cowley

(New York: G. P. Putnam's Sons, 1999), 163.

39. McCullough, *1776*, 96.

40. In Benjamin Hart, "Faith and Freedom," in *The Christian Roots of American History*, available at http://leaderu.com/orgs/cdf/ff/chap18.html.

41. In Shea, *In God We Trust*, 69; Henry Barton Dawson, *Battles of the United States: By Sea and Land*, vols. 1–2 (New York: Johnson, Fry & Company, 1858), 95.

42. McCullough, *1776*, 111.

43. "From George Washington to Lieutenant Colonel Joseph Reed, 26 February–9 March 1776," Founders Online, National Archives (http://founders.archives.gov/documents/Washington/03-03-02-0274).

44. Letter from Washington to his brother John Augustine Washington, March 31, 1776.

45. In "Library of Congress, Headquarters, Cambridge, July 4, 1775," found at http://www.loc.gov/teachers/classroommaterials/presentationsandactivities/presentations/timeline/amrev/contarmy/orderone.html.

46. "General Orders, 14 November 1775," Founders Online, National Archives (http://founders.archives.gov/documents/Washington/03-02-02-0340).

47. See William Jackson Johnson, *George Washington the Christian* (New York: Abingdon Press, 1919), 71, 72.

48. In Marshall Foster and Mary-Elaine Swanson, *The American Covenant: The Untold Story* (Thousand Oaks: The Mayflower Institute, 1981), 33; this congressional act was issued on July 6, 1775.

49. Proclamation of the National Day of Humiliation, Fasting, and Prayer, 1775, as quoted in Waldman, *Founding Faith*, 70.

50. Letter from John Adams to Abigail Adams, 11–17 June 1775, in *Adams Family Papers: An Electronic Archive*, available at http://masshist.org/digitaladams/.

51. General Orders from George Washington, March 6, 1776, as quoted in *The Writings of George Washington, Volume 4,* Electronic Text Center, University of Virginia, available from http://etext.virginia.edu/toc/modeng/public/WasFi04.html.

52. See McCullough, *1776,* 106.

53. See D&C 84:11–5; D&C 57:1–3; Articles of Faith 1:10.

54. See Alvan Lamson and Ezra Stiles Gannett, *The Christian Examiner and Religious Miscellany,* vol. 35, 32.

55. "Abigail Adams to John Adams, 16 March 1776," Founders Online, National Archives (http://founders.archives.gov/documents/Adams/04-01-02-0233).

Chapter 3: Miracle at New York

1. In George F. Scheer and Hugh F. Rankin, *Rebels and Redcoats: The American Revolution through the Eyes of Those Who Fought and Lived It* (New York: Da Capo Press, 1957), 148.

2. See David McCullough, *1776* (New York: Simon and Schuster, 2005), 163.

3. "From George Washington to John Adams, 15 April 1776," Founders Online, National Archives (http://founders.archives.gov/documents/Washington/03-04-02-0051).

4. In William Jackson Johnson, *George Washington the Christian* (New York: Abingdon Press, 1919), 82.

5. See McCullough, *1776,* 179–80.

6. Thomas Fleming, "Unlikely Victory," in *What If? The World's Foremost Military Historians Imagine What Might Have Been,* ed. Robert Cowley (New York: G. P. Putnam's Sons, 1999), 165.

7. In William J. Bennett, *The Spirit of America: Words of Advice from the Founders in Stories, Letters, Poems, and Speeches* (New York: Touchstone, 1997), 393.

8. In Michael Novak and Jana Novak, *Washington's God: Religion, Liberty, and the Father of Our Country* (New York: Basic Books, 2006), 71.

9. In Bennett, *Spirit of America,* 390.

10. In Novak and Novak, *Washington's God,* 89.

11. In McCullough, *1776,* 123.

12. In Peter Marshall and David Manuel, *God's Plan for America: The Light and the Glory, 1492–1793,* revised and expanded ed. (Grand Rapids, MI: Revell, 2009), 394.

13. In Frank Moore, *Diary of the American Revolution* (New York : Scribner, 1860), 172; emphasis added.

14. In Walter Isaacson, *Benjamin Franklin: An American Life* (New York: Simon and Schuster, 2003), 339.

15. From Thomas Paine's *Common Sense,* as quoted in John Ferling, *Adams vs. Jefferson: The Tumultuous Election of 1800* (New York: Oxford University Press, 2005), 25; emphasis added. The full text of Paine's *Common Sense* is available at www.earlyamerica.com/earlyamerica/milestone/commonsense/text.html.

16. In John Wingate Thornton, *The Pulpit of the American Revolution: Or, the Political Sermons of the Period of 1776* (1860), 311.

17. In ibid.

18. In ibid.

19. See William Thayer, *Young People's Life of George Washington: Boyhood, Youth, Manhood, Death, Honors* (New York: John R. Anderson & Co.,1883); Michael A. Shea, *In God We Trust: George Washington and the Spiritual Destiny of the United States of America* (Derry, NH: Liberty Quest, 2012), 82–83.

20. In ibid., 310.

21. See McCullough, *1776,* 184.

22. See David McCullough, "What the Fog Wrought," in *What If? The World's Foremost Military Historians Imagine What Might Have Been,* ed. Robert Cowley (New York: G. P. Putnam's Sons, 1999), 197.

23. McCullough, "What the Fog Wrought," 198; McCullough, *1776,* 191.

24. In Henry A. Buckingham, *Harry*

Burnham, the Young Continental: Or, Memoirs of an American Officer During the Campaigns of the Revolution and Sometime Member of Washington's Staff (New York: Burgess and Garrett, 1851), 205.

25. In McCullough, *1776*, 191–92.

26. In Michael A. Shea, *In God We Trust: George Washington and the Spiritual Destiny of the United States of America* (Derry, NH: Liberty Quest, 2012), 88–89.

27. McCullough, "What the Fog Wrought," 199–200; McCullough, *1776*, 191.

28. In Michael Novak, *On Two Wings: Humble Faith and Common Sense at the American Founding* (San Francisco, CA: Encounter Books, 2002), 15.

Chapter 4: Miracle at New Jersey

1. See David McCullough, *1776* (New York: Simon and Schuster, 2005), 249.

2. In William S. Stryker, *The Battles of Trenton and Princeton* (Boston: Houghton, Mifflin and Company, 1898), 5.

3. "From George Washington to Lund Washington, 30 September 1776," Founders Online, National Archives (http://founders.archives.gov/documents/Washington/03-06-02-0341).

4. "To George Washington from Brigadier General Thomas Mifflin, 26 November 1776," Founders Online, National Archives (http://founders.archives.gov/documents/Washington/03-07-02-0156).

5. See Joseph Ellis, *Patriots, Brotherhood of the American Revolution,* lectures (Recorded Books, Inc., and Barnes and Noble Publishing: 2004), lecture 7, 3:40 min.

6. See Ellis, *Patriots,* study guide, 10.

7. McCullough, *1776,* 158

8. Ellis, *Patriots,* lecture 7, 2:00 min.

9. Edmund Burke, *The Annual Register, or a View of History, Politics, and Literature, for the Year 1777,* 3rd ed. (London: Printed for J. Dodsley, in Pall-mall, 1783), 295.

10. Walter Isaacson, *Benjamin Franklin: An American Life* (New York: Simon and Schuster, 2003), 318–19.

11. See McCullough, *1776,* 258.

12. In William Cobbett, *The Parliamentary History of England from the Earliest Period to the Year 1803, XVIII* (London: T.C. Hansard, 1813), 696.

13. See McCullough, *1776,* 255–56.

14. See ibid., 270.

15. Francis Rawdon-Hastings, "Letter to Robert Auchmuty, November 25, 1776, about the Capture of Fort Lee"; "The Fall of Fort Lee: 'Their Army Is Broken to Pieces': Lord Francis Rawdon," in *The Spirit of Seventy Six: The Story of the American Revolution as Told by Participants,* edited by Henry Steele Commager and Richard B. Morris, 496 (New York: Da Capo Press, 1995). *American History Online.* Facts On File, Inc. http://www.fofweb.com/activelink2.asp?ItemID=WE52&iPin=EAWd0054&SingleRecord=True.

16. Stephen Ambrose, *To America, Personal Reflections of an Historian* (New York: Simon and Schuster, 2002), 12.

17. See Marshall Foster and Mary-Elaine Swanson, *The American Covenant: The Untold Story* (Thousand Oaks: The Mayflower Institute, 1981), 118–19.

18. Brigham Young, *Discourses of Brigham Young,* comp. John A. Widtsoe (Salt Lake City: Deseret Book, 1954), 359–60.

19. See Ellis, *Patriots,* lecture series; McCullough, *1776,* 213. In an effort to rally his men, Washington was seen exposing himself dangerously close to the enemy at the Battles of Kips Bay, Trenton/Princeton, and Yorktown.

20. In Robert F. Dalzell, Jr., and Lee Baldwin Dalzell, *George Washington's Mount Vernon: At Home in Revolutionary America* (New York: Oxford University Press, 1998), xiii.

21. See McCullough, *1776,* 48.
22. In William J. Bennett, *America: The Last Best Hope, vol. 1: From the Age of Discovery to a World at War, 1492–1914* (Nashville: Nelson Current, 2006), 163.
23. See Joseph J. Ellis, *His Excellency: George Washington* (New York: Alfred A. Knopf, 2004), 191.
24. In Michael A. Shea, *In God We Trust: George Washington and the Spiritual Destiny of the United States of America* (Derry, NH: Liberty Quest, 2012), 91.
25. "Fast Day Proclamation of the Continental Congress, December 11, 1776," in Michael Novak, *On Two Wings: Humble Faith and Common Sense at the American Founding* (San Francisco, CA: Encounter Books, 2002), 18.
26. See Shea, *In God We Trust,* 94.
27. In Stephen Brumwell, *George Washington: Gentleman Warrior* (New York: Quercus Publishing, 2012), 280.
28. In ibid., 279.
29. See ibid., 278.
30. Ibid., 280.
31. Henry Knox to Lucy Knox, December 28, 1776 (The Gilder Lehrman Institute of American History, n.d.), retrieved from https://www.gilderlehrman.org/sites/default/files/inline-pdfs/t-02437-00497.pdf.
32. In Peter Marshall and David Manuel, *God's Plan for America: The Light and the Glory, 1492–1793,* revised and expanded ed. (Grand Rapids, MI: Revell, 2009), 400.
33. See Brumwell, *Gentleman Warrior,* 282.
34. In Marshall and Manuel, *God's Plan for America,* 401.
35. See Bennett, *America: The Last Best Hope,* 1:89.
36. In Brumwell, *Gentleman Warrior,* 281.
37. In Shea, *In God We Trust,* 95.
38. In ibid., 92.
39. Sergeant R——, "The Battle of Princeton," *Pennsylvania Magazine of History and Biography,* vol. 20 (1896), 516.
40. Thomas Paine, *The American Crisis* (Philadelphia: Styner and Cist, 1776–77); available at http://www.indiana.edu/~liblilly/history/american-crisis.html.
41. "Nathanael Greene to Nicolas Cooke, Jan. 10, 1777," in *The Papers of General Nathanael Greene,* vol. 2, ed. Richard K. Showman and Dennis Conrad (Chapel Hill: University of North Carolina Press, 1980), 4.
42. In Brumwell, *Gentleman Warrior,* 288–89.
43. See ibid., 290.
44. Francis S. Drake, *Life and Correspondence of Henry Knox, Major-General in the American Revolutionary Army* (Boston, MA: Samuel G. Drake, 1873), 39.
45. In Richard Brookhiser, *Founding Father: Rediscovering George Washington* (New York: Free Press Paperbacks—Simon and Schuster, 1996), 31–32.
46. In George F. Scheer and Hugh F. Rankin, *Rebels and Redcoats: The American Revolution through the Eyes of Those Who Fought and Lived It* (New York: Da Capo Press, 1957), 219.
47. Mercy Otis Warren, *History of the Rise, Progress and Termination of the American Revolution, vol. 1* (Boston: Manning and Loring, 1805), 358–59.
48. McCullough, *1776,* 291.
49. "From George Washington to John Parke Custis, 22 January 1777," Founders Online, National Archives (http://founders.archives.gov/documents/Washington/03-08-02-0133).

Chapter 5:
Miracles of 1777 and 1778

1. In William Jackson Johnson, *George Washington the Christian* (New York: Abingdon Press, 1919), 36.
2. "From George Washington to John Parke Custis, 22 January 1777," Founders Online, National Archives (http://founders.archives.gov/documents/Washington/03-08-02-0133).
3. In Michael A. Shea, *In God We Trust:*

George Washington and the Spiritual Destiny of the United States of America (Derry, NH: Liberty Quest, 2012), 101–2.

4. See Robert Middlekauff, *The Glorious Cause: The American Revolution, 1763–1789,* revised and expanded ed. (New York: Oxford University Press, 2005), 380.

5. See Larkin Spivey, *Miracles of the American Revolution: Divine Intervention and the Birth of the Republic* (Fairfax, VA: Allegiance Press, 2004), 176–82.

6. See Larry Schweikart and Michael Allen, *A Patriot's History of the United States: From Columbus's Great Discovery to the War on Terror,* (New York: Sentinel, 2004), 81–83.

7. Stephen Brumwell, *George Washington: Gentleman Warrior* (New York: Quercus Publishing, 2012), 319.

8. George Washington, *The Writings of George Washington,* John C. Fitzpatrick, editor (Washington: U. S. Printing Office, 1931), Vol. VIII, 152–53; "General Orders, Head Quarters, Middle-Brook, May 31, 1777," available at http://wallbuilders.com/libissues articles.asp?id=85.

9. See Brumwell, *Gentleman Warrior,* 313.

10. In Spivey, *Miracles of the American Revolution,* 193.

11. "General Orders, 18 October 1777," Founders Online, National Archives (http://founders.archives.gov /documents/Washington/03-11-02 -0549).

12. See Brumwell, *Gentleman Warrior,* 316.

13. See "Arthur St. Clair," *Mount Vernon Digital Encyclopedia,* available at http://www.mountvernon.org/research -collections/digital-encyclopedia/article /arthur-st-clair/.

14. In Philip Schaff, *Church and State in the United States; or, The American Idea of Religious Liberty and Its Practical Effects* (New York: Charles Schribner's Sons, 1888), 125.

15. In "The Philadelphia Campaign 1777—The Battle of the Clouds:—Part 5 of 5," Independence Hall Association, available at http://www.ushistory.org/march /phila/clouds_5.htm.

16. See Brumwell, *Gentleman Warrior,* 306–7.

17. In Shea, *In God We Trust,* 104.

18. In Middlekauff, *Glorious Cause,* 401.

19. See Brumwell, *Gentleman Warrior,* 311.

20. See ibid., 312.

21. See ibid., 314.

22. In ibid., 311.

23. In Benjamin Franklin Morris, *Christian Life and Character of the Civil Institutions of the United States* (Oxford: Benediction Classics, 2010), 292.

24. Pilgrim Hall Museum, "Thanksgiving Proclamation 1777 by the Continental Congress, The First National Thanksgiving Day Proclamation" available at http://www.pilgrimhallmuseum.org /pdf/TG_First_National_Thanksgiving _Proclamation_1777.pdf.

25. See Schweikart and Allen, *Patriot's History,* 82.

26. In Joseph J. Ellis, *His Excellency: George Washington* (New York: Alfred A. Knopf, 2004), 112.

27. In Schweikart and Allen, *Patriot's History,* 86.

28. In Shea, *In God We Trust,* 124.

29. In ibid., 130.

30. In Brumwell, *Gentleman Warrior,* 323.

31. In Shea, *In God We Trust,* 112.

32. "American Shad," US Fish and Wildlife Service report, available at http://www .fws.gov/chesapeakebay/shad.htm.

33. In Shea, *In God We Trust,* 132.

34. In "A Prayer at Valley Forge," *National Review,* December 5, 2005; variation of the story recorded by William J. Bennett, *The Spirit of America: Words of Advice from the Founders in Stories, Letters, Poems, and Speeches* (New York: Touchstone, 1997), 372–73.

35. In Peter Marshall and David Manuel, *God's Plan for America: The Light and*

the Glory, 1492–1793, revised and expanded ed. (Grand Rapids, MI: Revell, 2009), 457.

36. Michael Novak and Jana Novak, *Washington's God: Religion, Liberty, and the Father of Our Country* (New York: Basic Books, 2006), 221.

37. See Benson Bobrick, *Angel in the Whirlwind: The Triumph of the American Revolution* (New York: Simon and Schuster Paperbacks, 1997), 287.

38. See "Washington's Vision as told by Anthony Sherman," available at http://www.ushistory.org/valleyforge/washington/vision.html.

39. In Robert Hieronimus, *Founding Fathers, Secret Societies: Freemasons, Illuminati, Rosicrucians, and the Decoding of the Great Seal,* revised ed. (Rochester, NY: Destiny Books, 2006), 49–50.

40. Orson Hyde, in *Journal of Discourses,* 26 vols. (Liverpool, England: F. D. and S. W. Richards, 1859), 6:368.

41. "Washington's Vision as told by Anthony Sherman."

42. See Mark E. Petersen, "The Angel Moroni Came!," *Ensign,* November 1983, 29–31.

43. Thomas Paine, "Common Sense," 1776; available at http://www.digitalhistory.uh.edu/disp_textbook.cfm?smtID=3&psid=151.

44. In Shea, *In God We Trust,* 124.

45. In ibid., 122.

46. "To Reverend Israel Evans—March 13, 1778," in *The Writings of George Washington from the Original Manuscript Sources, 1745–1799,* vol. 11—March 1, 1778–May 31, 1778, ed. John C. Fitzpatrick (Washington, DC: Government Printing Office, 1934), 78; available at http://babel.hathitrust.org/cgi/pt?id=mdp.39015074926281;view=1up;seq=27.

47. In Shea, *In God We Trust,* 135–36.

48. In Janice T. Connell, *The Spiritual Journey of George Washington* (Hobart, NY: Hatherleigh Press, 2007), 96.

49. "Letter from Congress, May 26, 1779," in *Journals of the American Congress from 1774 to 1788,* vol. 3: From August 1, 1778, to March 30, 1782, inclusive (Washington, DC: Way and Gideon, 1823), 289.

Chapter 6: Miracle at Yorktown

1. See Stephen Brumwell, *George Washington, Gentleman Warrior,* (New York: Quercus Publishing, 2012), 378–79.

2. See Marshal Foster and Mary-Elaine Swanson, *The American Covenant: The Untold Story* (Thousand Oaks: The Mayflower Institute, 1981), 161–62.

3. In William Hosmer, "Remember Our Bicentennial—1781," *Foundation for Christian Self-Government Newsletter,* June 1981, 5; see also Foster and Swanson, *American Covenant,* 162; Peter Marshall and David Manuel, *God's Plan for America: The Light and the Glory 1492–1793,* revised and expanded ed. (Grand Rapids, MI: Revell, 2009), 416–18.

4. In Benjamin Franklin Morris, *Christian Life and Character of the Civil Institutions of the United States* (Oxford: Benediction Classics, 2010), 292.

5. See Brumwell, *Gentleman Warrior,* 379.

6. In General Henry B. Carrington, *Washington the Soldier,* originally published in 1898 (Scituate, DSI Digital Reproduction: 2001), 320.

7. In Peter Marshall and David Manuel, *God's Plan for America: The Light and the Glory, 1492–1793,* revised and expanded ed. (Grand Rapids, MI: Revell, 2009), 418.

8. Thomas Fleming, "Unlikely Victory," in *What If? The World's Foremost Military Historians Imagine What Might Have Been,* ed. Robert Cowley (New York: G. P. Putnam's Sons, 1999), 179.

9. William J. Bennett, *America: The Last Best Hope, vol. 1: From the Age of*

Discovery to a World at War, 1492–1914 (Nashville: Nelson Current, 2006), 29.

10. See Brumwell, *Gentleman Warrior,* 401.

11. See ibid., 400–402.

12. Ibid., 405.

13. See Foster and Swanson, *American Covenant,* 118–19.

14. Not a direct quote. For dramatic effect only.

15. See Brumwell, *Gentleman Warrior,* 403–4.

16. Fleming, "Unlikely Victory," 180.

17. Ibid.,181.

18. Marquis Charles Cornwallis, *Correspondence of Charles, First Marquis Cornwallis* (n.p., 1859), 511.

19. In Larkin Spivey, *Miracles of the American Revolution: Divine Intervention and the Birth of the Republic* (Fairfax, VA: Allegiance Press, 2004), 212.

20. See Marshall and Manuel, *God's Plan for America,* 420; Bennett, *America: The Last Best Hope,* 102.

21. Fleming, "Unlikely Victory," 182.

22. In Foster and Swanson, *American Covenant,* 163.

23. In *Church History in the Fulness of Times,* 2nd ed. (Salt Lake City: The Church of Jesus Christ of Latter-day Saints, 2000), 148.

24. See Joseph Smith, *History of the Church of Jesus Christ of Latter-day Saints,* 7 vols. (Salt Lake City: Deseret Book, 1976), 2:104.

25. *Church History in the Fulness of Times,* 148.

26. In Richard Lyman Bushman, *Joseph Smith: Rough Stone Rolling* (New York: Alfred A. Knopf, 2005), 243–44.

27. See *Church History in the Fulness of Times,* 374–75.

28. Fleming, "Unlikely Victory," 186.

29. Washington, "General Orders—October 20, 1781," in *The Writings of George Washington from the Original Manuscript Sources, 1745–1799,* vol. 23—August 16, 1781–February 15, 1782, ed. John C. Fitzpatrick (Washington, DC:

30. Government Printing Office, 1937), 247; available at http://babel.hathitrust .org/cgi/pt?id=mdp.39015074926158 ;view=1up;seq=19.

30. United States Congress, "Thanksgiving Proclamation 1781, by the United States in Congress Assembled, a Proclamation"; available at http://www.pilgrim hallmuseum.org/pdf/TG_Continental _Congress_Proclamations_1778_1784 .pdf.

Chapter 7: American Moses

1. Ezra Taft Benson, "Our Divine Constitution," *Ensign,* November 1987, 4.

2. Bruce Feiler, *America's Prophet: Moses and the American Story* (New York: HarperCollins Publishing, 2009), 103.

3. See Kerry Muhlestein, *The Essential Old Testament Companion: Key Insights to Your Gospel Study* (American Fork: Covenant Communications, 2013), 112–13; Cleon Skousen, *The Five Thousand Year Leap* (Washington, DC: The National Center for Constitutional Studies, 1981), 15–17.

4. See Jon Entine, *Abraham's Children: Race, Identity, and the DNA of the Chosen People* (New York: Grand Central Publishing, 2007), 143.

5. Donald Lutz, "The Relative Influence of European Writers on Late Eighteenth-Century American Political Thought," *The American Political Science Review* 78, no.1 (March 1984): 189–97, retrieved from http://www .jstor.org/stable/1961257?seq=1#page _scan_tab_contents.

6. In Steven Waldman, *Founding Faith: Politics, Providence, and the Birth of Religious Freedom in America* (New York: Random House, 2008), 107.

7. David McCullough, "The Glorious Cause of America," BYU Devotional Address, September 27, 2005; available at https://speeches.byu.edu/talks /david-mccullough_glorious-cause -america/.

8. In William J. Bennett, *America: The Last Best Hope, vol. 1: From the Age of Discovery to a World at War, 1492–1914* (Nashville: Nelson Current, 2006), 163.

9. "To Colonel Lewis Nicola—May 22, 1782," in *The Writings of George Washington from the Original Manuscript Sources, 1745–1799,* vol. 24: February 18, 1782–August 10, 1782, ed. John C. Fitzpatrick (Washington, DC: Government Printing Office, 1938), 272–73; available at http://babel.hathitrust.org /cgi/pt?id=mdp.39015074926000;view =1up;seq=13.

10. In Gordon S. Wood, *Revolutionary Characters: What Made the Founders Different* (New York: Penguin Press, 2006), 51.

11. From "The United States Elevated to Glory and Honor," 1781, in Cleon Skousen, *The Majesty of God's Law* (Salt Lake City: Ensign Publishing, 1996), 16.

12. In Thomas Fleming, "Unlikely Victory," in *What If? The World's Foremost Military Historians Imagine What Might Have Been,* ed. Robert Cowley (New York: G. P. Putnam's Sons, 1999), 184–85.

13. See ibid.,185.

14. In Michael Novak and Jana Novak, *Washington's God: Religion, Liberty, and the Father of Our Country* (New York: Basic Books, 2006), 34.

15. In Joseph J. Ellis, *His Excellency: George Washington* (New York: Alfred A. Knopf, 2004), 139.

16. "Address to Congress on Resigning His Commission—December 23, 1783," in *The Writings of George Washington from the Original Manuscript Sources, 1745–1799,* vol. 27: June 11, 1783–November 28, 1784, ed. John C. Fitzpatrick (Washington, DC: Government Printing Office, 1939), 284; available at http://babel.hathitrust.org/cgi /pt?id=mdp.39015011913475;view=1u p;seq=340.

17. See Jon Meacham, *American Gospel: God, the Founding Fathers, and the Making of a Nation* (New York: Random House, 2007), 81.

18. In Peter Marshall and David Manuel, *God's Plan for America: The Light and the Glory, 1492–1793,* revised and expanded ed. (Grand Rapids, MI: Revell, 2009), 426.

19. John Fiske, *The Critical Period of American History: 1783–1789* (Boston and New York: Houghton, Mifflin & Co., 1888), Kindle edition, location 3050.

20. In Novak and Novak, *Washington's God,* 111; emphasis added.

21. Joseph Smith, *Teachings of the Prophet Joseph Smith,* comp. Joseph Fielding Smith (Salt Lake City: Deseret Book, 1976), 147–48; emphasis added.

22. "Thanksgiving Proclamation—October 3, 1789," in *The Writings of George Washington from the Original Manuscript Sources, 1745–1799,* vol. 30: June 20, 1788–January 21, 1790, ed. John C. Fitzpatrick (Washington, DC: Government Printing Office, 1939), 427–28.

23. "From George Washington to the Hebrew Congregation in Newport, Rhode Island, 18 August 1790," Founders Online, National Archives (http://founders .archives.gov/documents/Washington /05-06-02-0135).

24. In Waldman, *Founding Faith,* 63.

25. In Robert P. Hay, "George Washington: American Moses," *American Quarterly* 21, no. 4 (Winter 1969), 783.

26. See chapter 1 of this book.

27. Ibid.

28. H. Paul Jeffers, *The Freemasons in America: Inside the Secret Society* (New York: Citadel Press, 2006), 28.

29. See *Old Testament Seminary Student Study Guide* (Salt Lake City: The Church of Jesus Christ of Latter-day Saints, 2002), 40–41.

30. *Teachings of the Prophet Joseph Smith,* 362.

31. See Feiler, *America's Prophet,* 80, 83.

32. Ibid., 104.

33. Ibid., 78.
34. *The New York Daily Advisor,* April 23, 1789, in *David Barton's WallBuilder's Blog;* "The Constitutional Convention," blog entry by David Barton, July 22, 2010; available at http://davidbarton wallbuilders.typepad.com/blog/2010 /07/the-constitutional-convention-by -david-barton.html.
35. "From George Washington to the Hebrew Congregation in Newport, Rhode Island, 18 August 1790."
36. Description by Washington Irving, in William J. Bennett, *The Spirit of America: Words of Advice from the Founders in Stories, Letters, Poems, and Speeches* (New York: Touchstone, 1997), 381; "Inaugural History," PBS Online News Hour (data online); http://www .pbs.org/newshour/updates/white _house-jan-june01-inauguration_01 -20/.
37. See Feiler, *America's Prophet,* 28, 78.
38. "Washington's Inaugural Address of 1780," available at the National Archives and Records Administration, http:// www.archives.gov/exhibits/american _originals/inaugtxt.html.
39. Ibid.
40. See Ron Chernow, *Washington: A Life* (New York: Penguin, 2010), 569.
41. Judge Roy Moore, "The Little Chapel That Stood," *World Net Daily,* September 5, 2007, available at http://www .wnd.com/2007/09/43358/.
42. Ibid.
43. See Newt Gingrich, *Rediscovering God in America: Reflections on the Role of Faith in Our Nation's History and Future* (Nashville: Integrity House, 2006), 27. The U.S. Supreme Court building is prominently decorated with symbolism of the ancient national covenant. In no fewer than four locations in and around the building are depictions of Moses and the Ten Commandments (this imagery is at the center of the sculpture over the east portico of the building, on the bronze

doors of the building, inside the courtroom itself, and engraved over the chair of the Chief Justice). Similarly, perched upon the wall of Congress overlooking the interior of the House chamber is a large image of Moses. Other ancient lawmakers are depicted around the chamber as well, but all have their heads turned to Moses, who is the only full image and the only one that hangs directly in the middle of the room. See Gingrich, *Rediscovering God,* 87, and Feiler, *America's Prophet,* 283.
44. In Meacham, *American Gospel,* 91.
45. Bruce R. McConkie, *Mormon Doctrine,* 2nd ed. rev. (Salt Lake City: Bookcraft, 1966), 160.
46. Feiler, *America's Prophet,* 77–78.
47. See *The New York Daily Advisor,* April 23, 1789.
48. "Washington's Inaugural Address of 1780."
49. See Feiler, *America's Prophet,* 82.

Chapter 8:
Clasped Hands—Eternal Lives

1. See Michael Novak and Jana Novak, *Washington's God: Religion, Liberty, and the Father of Our Country* (New York: Basic Books, 2006), 204–5.
2. In ibid., 207.
3. In ibid., 61.
4. In ibid., 190; emphasis added.
5. In ibid., 208.
6. See Jon Meacham, *American Gospel: God, the Founding Fathers, and the Making of a Nation* (New York: Random House, 2007), 13.
7. See Peter Marshall and David Manuel, *God's Plan for America: The Light and the Glory, 1492–1793,* revised and expanded ed. (Grand Rapids, MI: Revell, 2009), 404.
8. In Novak and Novak, *Washington's God,* 209.
9. See ibid., 26.
10. "Discourse by Elder Wilford Woodruff," in *Journal of Discourses,* 26 vols.

(Liverpool: William Budge, 1878), 19:229.

11. Personal journal of James Godson Bleak, in Vicki Jo Anderson, *The Other Eminent Men of Wilford Woodruff*, 2nd ed. rev. (Malta, ID: Nelson Book, 2000), 420.

12. See Wilford Woodruff Journal, 7:367–69, in Anderson, *Other Eminent Men,* 420.

13. Wilford Woodruff, as quoted by Truman G. Madsen, *The Presidents of the Church,* recorded lecture series (Salt Lake City: Bookcraft), tape/track 4, "Wilford Woodruff."

14. See Jennifer Ann Mackley, *Wilford Woodruff's Witness of the Development of Temple Doctrine* (Seattle: High Desert Publishing, 2014), 186.

15. Wilford Woodruff, in Conference Report, April 1898, 89–90.

16. See Anderson, *Other Eminent Men,* preface and 411–13.

17. See Mackley, *Wilford Woodruff's Witness,* 194.

18. See ibid., 194, 349.

19. The facts, descriptions, and interpretations of *The Apotheosis of Washington,* as described in this book, can be verified at the official government website: www.aoc.gov/cc/art/rotunda/apotheosis.

20. See ibid.

21. See ibid.

Chapter 9: The Pyramid

1. See Michael Haag, *The Templars, The History and the Myth* (New York: Harper, 2009), 275–76.

2. See Giles Morgan, *Freemasonry: Its History and Myths Revealed* (New York: Fall River Press, 2009), 182; Robert Hieronimus, *Founding Fathers, Secret Societies: Freemasons, Illuminati, Rosicrucians, and the Decoding of the Great Seal,* revised ed. (Rochester, NY: Destiny Books, 2006), 122.

3. Hieronimus, *Founding Fathers, Secret Societies,* 91.

4. In Haag, *Templars,* 276.

5. David Ovason, *The Secret Architecture of Our Nation's Capital: The Masons and the Building of Washington, D.C.* (New York: Harper, 2000), 220, 225–26.

6. See Gerald Hansen Jr., *Sacred Walls: Learning from Temple Symbols* (American Fork: Covenant Communications, 2009), 75–81.

7. In Hugh Nibley, *The Message of the Joseph Smith Papyri: An Egyptian Endowment* (Salt Lake: Deseret Book, 2005), 168.

8. Ibid., 165.

9. Ibid., 428–29.

10. In ibid., 352.

11. Hugh Nibley, *Temple and Cosmos* (Salt Lake: Deseret Book, 1992), 26–27.

12. Michael D. Rhodes, "Book of Abraham: Studies About the Book of Abraham," in *Encyclopedia of Mormonism,* 4 vols., ed. Daniel H. Ludlow (New York: Macmillan, 1992), 1:37; available at http://eom.byu.edu/index.php/Book_of_Abraham. BYU Professor Andrew Skinner points out LDS temple theology reflected in panel art found in an ancient Egyptian temple; see Andrew Skinner, *Temple Worship* (Salt Lake: Deseret Book, 2007), 63–65.

13. See Nibley, *Temple and Cosmos,* 179–82.

14. H. Paul Jeffers, *The Freemasons in America: Inside the Secret Society* (New York: Citadel Press, 2006), 103.

15. In William J. Bennett, *The Spirit of America: Words of Advice from the Founders in Stories, Letters, Poems, and Speeches* (New York: Touchstone, 1997), 365.

16. In Michael Novak and Jana Novak, *Washington's God: Religion, Liberty, and the Father of Our Country* (New York: Basic Books, 2006), 130.

17. In Novak and Novak, *Washington's God,* 192–93; emphasis added.

18. Ovason, *Secret Architecture,* 235.

19. In Peter Marshall and David Manuel, *God's Plan for America: The Light and the Glory, 1492–1793,* revised and

expanded ed. (Grand Rapids, MI: Revell, 2009), 427.

20. In ibid., 427.

21. In Steven Waldman, *Founding Faith: Politics, Providence, and the Birth of Religious Freedom in America* (New York: Random House, 2008), 88.

22. Jeffers, *Freemasons in America,* 21.

23. W. L. Wilmshurst, *The Meaning of Masonry* (San Francisco: Plumbstone, 2007), 34.

24. In Hieronimus, *Founding Fathers, Secret Societies,* 42.

25. Kenneth W. Godfrey, "Freemasonry and the Temple," in *Encyclopedia of Mormonism,* 4 vols., ed. Daniel H. Ludlow (New York: Macmillan, 1992), available at http://eom.byu.edu/index .php/Freemasonry_and_the_Temple.

26. See Wilmshurst, *Meaning of Masonry,* 19–20.

27. Ibid., 20.

28. Ibid., 21–22.

29. See ibid., 33.

30. See Malcom C. Duncan, *Duncan's Masonic Ritual and Monitor* (ZuuBooks .com, 2011), 65, 75.

31. *Old Testament Student Manual: 1 Kings– Malachi,* 2nd ed. (Salt Lake City: The Church of Jesus Christ of Latter-day Saints, 1982), 279.

32. See ibid., 284–87.

33. Ibid., 285–87.

34. See S. Brent Morris, *The Complete Idiot's Guide to Freemasonry,* 2nd ed. (New York, Penguin, 2013), 36.

35. See David G. Hackett, *That Religion in Which All Men Agree: Freemasonry in American Culture* (Berkeley and Los Angeles: University of California Press, 2014), 49.

36. In Jeffers, *Freemasons in America,* 25.

37. Morris, *Complete Idiot's Guide,* 35.

38. Jeffers, *Freemasons in America,* xiii.

39. See ibid., 21.

40. See ibid., 24.

41. See Steven C. Bullock, *Revolutionary Brotherhood: Freemasonry and the Transformation of the American Social Order, 1730–1840* (University of North Carolina Press, 1996), 3–4.

42. See Jasper Ridley, *The Freemasons, A History of the World's Most Powerful Secret Society* (New York: Arcade Publishing, 2001), 108–9; Jeffers, *Freemasons in America,* 30.

43. Boyd K. Packer, *The Holy Temple* (Salt Lake City: Bookcraft, 1981), 38–41.

44. Carl H. Claudy, *Introduction to Freemasonry,* vol. II, *Fellowcraft,* 12; vol. 1; *Entered Apprentice,* 32 (Bensenville, IL: Lushena Books, 2014).

45. See David Shugarts, *Secrets of the Widow's Son* (New York: Sterling Publishing, 2005), 112–13.

46. Ovason, *Secret Architecture,* 253.

47. See ibid., 72–74.

48. Washington (January 1792), in Steven Waldman, *Founding Faith: Politics, Providence, and the Birth of Religious Freedom in America* (New York: Random House, 2008), 62.

49. In Janice T. Connell, *The Spiritual Journey of George Washington* (Hobart, NY: Hatherleigh Press, 2007), 34–35.

50. Jeffers, *Freemasons in America,* 30–33.

51. See Shugarts, *Secrets of the Widow's Son,* 194.

52. See http://www.ldschurchnews.com /articles/54236/Another-angel.html.

53. Nibley, *Message of the Joseph Smith Papyri,* 435.

54. The original location chosen for the Washington Monument would have been the axis point between the Capitol Building and the White House to form a perfect square. However, before constructing the monument, engineers determined the exact location to be too marshy and unstable. They moved the location several hundred feet east of the axis point. Though the basic square symbol is still very present, the move altered the exact mathematical square that was intended. See Ovason, *Secret Architecture,* 126.

55. See Jeffers, *Freemasons in America,* 35; Shugarts, *Secrets of the Widow's Son,* 134–36.
56. See W. Kirk MacNulty, *Freemasonry: A Journey Through Ritual and Symbol* (New York: Thames & Hudson, 1991), 67.
57. See Ovason, *Secret Architecture,* 125–29.
58. See Bruce Feiler, *America's Prophet: Moses and the American Story* (New York: HarperCollins Publishing, 2009), 81.
59. Newt Gingrich, *Rediscovering God in America* (Nashville: Integrity House, 2006), 38.
60. Gordon B. Hinckley, *Standing for Something* (New York: Times Books, 2000), xviii, xxiii, xxv.
61. In Gingrich, *Rediscovering God in America,* 11–12.
62. See Timothy Ballard, *The Lincoln Hypothesis* (Salt Lake City: Deseret Book, 2014).
63. For facts regarding the State of Deseret stone, see Thomas Burr, "The Washington Monument's Mormon Inscription," *Salt Lake Tribune,* May 19, 2014, available at http://www.sltrib.com/sltrib/politics/57938488-90/washington-utah-monument-stone.html.csp.

Epilogue: The Door

1. Benjamin Franklin, *Writings,* ed. J. A. Leo Lemay (New York: Library of American Press, 1987), 1100.
2. *Writings of George Washington, Vol XI,* ed. Worthington Chauncey Ford (New York and London: G. P. Putnam and Sons, 1890), 431.
3. In Walter Isaacson, *Benjamin Franklin: An American Life* (New York: Simon and Schuster, 2003), 285.
4. In Gordon S. Wood, *Revolutionary Characters: What Made the Founders Different* (New York: Penguin Press, 2006), 80.
5. In Isaacson, *Benjamin Franklin,* 275.
6. In ibid., 292.
7. See ibid., 296.
8. In ibid., 298.
9. In ibid., 415.
10. In ibid., 298.
11. In ibid., 313.
12. In ibid., 332.
13. In ibid., 304.
14. In ibid., 339.
15. Wood, *Revolutionary Characters,* 84.
16. Ibid., 70.
17. In Isaacson, *Benjamin Franklin,* 339.
18. In ibid., 467.
19. See ibid., 468.
20. See Derek H. Davis, *Religion and the Continental Congress, 1774–1789* (Oxford: Oxford University Press, 2000), 138.
21. See William J. Bennett, *The Spirit of America: Words of Advice from the Founders in Stories, Letters, Poems, and Speeches* (New York: Touchstone, 1997), 383–85.
22. See ibid., 468.
23. See ibid., 465.
24. In Isaacson, *Benjamin Franklin,* 468.
25. In Bennett, *Spirit of America,* 366.
26. In Dallin H. Oaks, "The Divinely Inspired Constitution," *Ensign,* February 1992, 70.
27. In Bennett, *Spirit of America,* 384–85; emphasis added.
28. "Letter to H. Niles—February 13, 1888," in Charles Francis Adams, *The Works of John Adams, Second President of the United States,* vol. 10 (Boston: Little, Brown and Co., 1856), 282.
29. In Steven Waldman, *Founding Faith: Politics, Providence, and the Birth of Religious Freedom in America* (New York: Random House, 2008), 24.
30. In Isaacson, *Benjamin Franklin,* 470.
31. See Jennifer Ann Mackley, *Wilford Woodruff's Witness of the Development of Temple Doctrine* (Seattle: High Desert Publishing, 2014), 194.
32. In Mathias F. Cowley, *Wilford Woodruff—His Life and Labors* (Salt Lake City: Bookcraft, 1964), 586.

Index

IMAGE CREDITS

Photograph of the stained glass window in the La Cañada chapel by Timothy Ballard: xiii, 9 (dove detail), and 219.

Bridgeman Images. The Colonies of North America at the Declaration of Independence Stanford, Edward (1827–1904)/Private Collection/Peter Newark Pictures/Bridgeman Images: 11. George Washington at Dorchester Heights, Massachusetts (colour litho), Leutze, Emanuel Gottlieb (1816–68) (after)/Private Collection/Peter Newark American Pictures/Bridgeman Images: 50. George Washington directing the retreat from Brooklyn Heights, 29 August 1776 (litho), American School, (19th century)/Private Collection/Peter Newark American Pictures/Bridgeman Images: 69. Dr John Witherspoon, engraved by James Barton Longacre (1794–1869) (litho), Peale, Charles Willson (1741–1827) (after)/Private Collection/Ken Welsh/Bridgeman Images: 70. Washington Crossing the Delaware River, 25th December 1776, 1851 (oil on canvas) (copy of an original painted in 1848), Leutze, Emanuel Gottlieb (1816–68)/Metropolitan Museum of Art, New York, USA/Bridgeman Images: 83. First meeting of George Washington and Alexander Hamilton, from 'Life and Times of Washington', Volume I, published 1857 (litho), Chappel, Alonzo (1828–87) (after)/Private Collection/Ken Welsh/Bridgeman Images: 125. Statue of George Washington, Washington, D.C. 1899 (photo)/Universal History Archive/UIG/Bridgeman Images: 156. Portrait of Joseph Smith (oil on canvas), American School, (19th century)/National Portrait Gallery, Smithsonian Institution, USA/Bridgeman Images: 158.

Mary Evans Picture Library/Classic Stock/H. Armstrong Roberts: 96.

Presidential Proclamation: General Thanksgiving Holiday as reported in The Massachusetts Centinel, Wednesday, October 14, 1789. Public Domain: 105.

Proposal for the official seal of the nation/Originally printed in The New Harper's Magazine, Volume 13, Issue 74, July 1856, page 180, article Great Seal of the United States by Benson J. Lossing. Public Domain: 147.

Museum of the City of New York/St Paul's Church altar/ the reredos in St. Paul's Chapel: 173.

Commemorative Stone donated by the Utah Territory, in September 1853. National Park Service/Washington Monument/Photos & Multimedia: Washington Monument Stones (nps.gov). Public Domain: 216.

Shutterstock.com Images. Shutterstock/© James E. Knopf: xv. Shutterstock/©Everett Historical: 24, 32, 33, 34, 108, 136, 140, 158, 163, 182, 186, 199, 209, 225. Shutterstock/©Daniel M. Silva: 45. Shutterstock/© Susan Law Cain: 61. Shutterstock/© Mr Doomits: 97. Shutterstock/© Subbotina Anna: 102. Shutterstock/© Camek: 109. Shutterstock/© Georgios Kollidas: 127. Shutterstock/© thatsmymop: 151. Shutterstock/© Zack Frank: 171. Shutterstock/© Mary Terriberry: 188. Shutterstock/© VDex: 193. Shutterstock/© Ambient Ideas: 213.

iStock.com/© Camek: 114.

Library of Congress Prints and Photographs Division. LC-DIG-pga-02466 Popular Graphic Arts Collection: 2. LC-DIG-ds-05283: 4. LC-USZ62-43019: 38. LC-DIG-pga-03229 Popular Graphic Arts Collection: 40. LC-DIG-det-4a26205 Detroit Publishing Company Collection: 48. LC-DIG-pga-03036: 59. LC-DIG-pga-03036 (from the same drawing): 64. LC-DIG-ppmsca-30581 Popular Graphic Arts Collection: 79. LC-USZ62-51811: 85. LC-USZC4-2542 Popular Graphic Arts Collection: 89. LC-DIG-det-4a26289: 91. LC-DIG-cwpb-01542: 132. LC-DIG-npcc-432426: 154. LC-USZ62-112964. Popular Graphic Arts Collection: 155. LC-G612- 60919 Gottscho-Schleisner Collection: 172. LC-DIG-highsm-12650 Carol M. Highsmith Archive: 184. LC-USZ62-45509 Rare Book and Special Collections Division: 192. Geography and Maps Division: 207.

Timothy Ballard graduated cum laude from Brigham Young University in Spanish and political science, then went on to receive an MA (summa cum laude) in international politics from the Monterey Institute of International Studies. Tim has worked for the Central Intelligence Agency and as a Special Agent for the Department of Homeland Security. He is the founder and CEO of Operation Underground Railroad, which rescues children from child-trafficking organizations throughout the world. The best-selling author of *The Lincoln Hypothesis,* he recently received the distinguished George Washington Honor Medal from the Freedoms Foundation at Valley Forge. Tim is a devoted husband and the father of six children.